THE HAVANT BOY RIPPER

The Murder of Percy Knight Searle

DAVID GREEN

Mango Books

Published by Mango Books
www.mangobooks.co.uk
18 Soho Square
London W1D 3QL

THE HAVANT
BOY RIPPER

Contents

Part Three

List of Illustrations

The author and publishers would like to thank the following for their kind permission to reproduce illustrations:

Plates 2, 3, The National Archives; 4, Ralph Cousins; 5, 8, The British Library Board; 6, 7, 10, 21, Hampshire Library and Information Service; 9, 11, Tom Bennett; 13, (by 'Spy' in *Vanity Fair*, 1892); 14, (by 'Spy' in *Vanity Fair*, 1885); 16, 17, 19 (outer images), Gavin Maidment Archive, Spring Arts and Heritage Centre, Havant; 18, 19 (middle image), David Oborne; 20, Lesley Marley. Plates 12, 15, and 22 are from the collection of the author.

A Note on Money

In the nineteenth century, British currency was divided into pounds, shillings and pence. One pound (£1) was made up of 20 shillings (20s.) and there were 12 pence (12d.) to the shilling. In 1888, £1 could buy goods that in 2018 cost about £102; a shilling back then is roughly equivalent to just over £5 today. An old threepence has a relative value today of about £1.33. These comparisons are explained on the website www.measuringworth.com.

PART ONE

Book of the Dead

Martha Burrows was a familiar figure in the streets and lanes around Havant, trundling her hand-cart laden with the bodies of the dead. She was a short woman, sturdy with powerful shoulders, always attired in a grey wool dress and shawl. Whenever people died in Havant, the call went out for Martha. Her job was to collect the corpses from their homes and places of work, and wheel them across town to the workhouse mortuary on West Street or to the makeshift laying-in chapel at the back of the undertaker's shop a few doors further down. She was a devout Christian woman and we can be sure she knew exactly the right words of condolence to comfort the bereaved families.

When fetching bodies from farms and homesteads farther afield, she will have driven a horse-drawn wagonette, but for regular work around town Martha will have deployed a small barrow of some description, one which tilted forwards to deposit its load. There would have been a tarpaulin sheet rigged over the back like a canopy. She employed young boys, twelve or thirteen years of age, to assist her with the collection of the corpses.

In 1888 Havant was still a small market town with a population of just over 3,000. Situated midway between Chichester and Portsmouth, it had its own little port a mile away at Langstone. The town was on the main rail line between Portsmouth and London Waterloo (in 1888 the average journey time between Havant and Waterloo, a distance of 66 miles, was just over two hours), and there were regular train services to Winchester in the north, to Chichester and Brighton to the east, and to Fareham and Southampton to the west. A now-defunct branch line wended its way southwards over

Langstone Bridge to Hayling Island.

Writing in 1905, seventeen years after the events recorded in this book, at least one newspaper correspondent was still entranced by the idyllic charm of the town on a Sunday morning:

> Havant on a Sunday morning was quite Arcadian. At least so thought one who spends his week-days and a too frequent Sabbath day at work in Portsmouth's wilderness of bricks and mortar. To such a one there is real joy in the sloping fields between Cosham and Havant, bright with sunshine, brilliant in their greenness, the corn ripening for the harvest covered with glinting undulations born of the gentle breeze. Havant itself wore an air of genteel respectability. So deserted were the streets that it might have been a city of the dead. The cyclists and motorists passing through represented, with a lazy few basking in the sun, the sum total of human activity.[1]

Martha's father, George Burrows, started a carrier's business in the town in 1830. After he died in 1847, Martha took over the business and by 1860 she was making the daily round between Havant and the King's Head tavern in Chichester. In July 1873 she began renting premises at the bottom of North Street, next to the coal yard, opening first a carrier's office and later diversifying as a stationer's and tobacconist's shop. But she never gave up transporting the dead.

It seems she started her mortuary transport service around 1849 when she was still in her early twenties. Many years later, around 1875, she possibly came to an arrangement with John Staples, who ran an undertaker's and carpenter's business at 80 West Street: in return for repairing and maintaining the wheels on her carts and wagons, Martha would bring the bodies of the dead right to his door.

We know quite a lot about Martha's business activities because she kept a diary in which she recorded the everyday mundane happenings of her working life – journeys made or cancelled, weather conditions on the road to Portsmouth, the wages paid to her boys, the health of her horses. Her diary can be viewed at the Portsmouth History Centre. It's a small black notebook speckled with orange-brown mildew. As you leaf through the pages, even

---

1   *Portsmouth Evening News*, 3 July 1905.

with the greatest of care, you can hear the spine of the notebook breaking softly like the creak of a cart wheel.

In part, her diary is a necrologue, a book of the dead. In black ink, with a fine steel nib, in her neat copperplate script, she has recorded the names of more than 1800 people who died in and around Havant between 1849 and 1896. The old and the young, the rich and the poor, the comely and the plain, Martha will have escorted all of them on their final journeys to the mortuary or to the coffin maker's workshop or to the cemetery on New Lane. Each entry is meticulously dated, often giving details of the decedent's age and place and cause of death:

> 1855.   13th January, Child of Mr. Chas Pitt. Smallpox.
> 1874.   20th April, Mr. Black. Drowned himself.
> 1874.   15th December, Mr. Joseph Till. Found dead in ditch.
> 1876.   4th October, Mr. Awick, Porter, killed with luggage train (21).
> 1895.   30th June, Mr. Shoosmith hung himself in his woodhouse; very depressed.

The year 1888 was especially busy for Martha. She was called out fifty-nine times. On seventeen occasions she attended the bodies of babies and infants. She even collected the body of Emma Staples, the undertaker's first wife, who died in the June quarter of that year.

At around twenty to seven, on the evening of 26 November, she was called to an especially tragic scene. It was a cold, wet night. It had been pelting down a little earlier, though the rain had quickly turned to drizzle. Then this too had cleared. There was the tang of sea salt in the air, coming in across the mudflats from Langstone Harbour. Wild birds cawed and screeched.

Turning her cart into the Pallant, Martha saw crowds of people gathered around the body in the road. They parted to let her through. Thoughtfully, a bystander had placed a coat over the body. Martha saw that it was a small child, no bigger than a bundle of twigs. Someone told her the dead boy was called 'Percy'. Martha lifted the body into the barrow. It weighed next to nothing. Another small lad, perhaps one of Percy's playmates, stepped forward and adjusted the position of Percy's hands and legs so that they rested in a more comfortable position.[2] Martha recognised the second boy as one of the children who laboured in the coal yard behind her house. She drew the tarpaulin sheet over the remains as carefully and tenderly as a mother might draw the bedclothes over her sleeping child. Then, without further ado, she steered the cart out of the Pallant and turned left and then right towards the Union mortuary. The crowds were slow to disperse, even after the cart had disappeared and the creak of its wheels could no longer be heard.

That evening, Martha inscribed a new entry in her diary:

1888.   26th November, Percy K. Searle. Murdered by a Strange Man (9).[3]

---

2   *Dundee Courier & Argus*, 29 November 1888.
3   For a brief biography of Martha Burrows see 'Martha Burrows (1825–1902) Carrier' in *The Making of Havant* (4) published by The Havant Local History Group, 1980, pp. 1–7. See also Michael Kennett, 'Historic Havant', *Hampshire* magazine, April 1981, pp. 49–50. Martha Burrows's diary can be viewed at Portsmouth History Centre (shelf-mark 1358a/1). Percy Searle was actually eight years and seven months old when he was murdered.

2

Thrills in the Dark

The Band of Hope was a temperance organisation for working-class children. In the 1880s they had around 10,000 branches in the UK. At a time when there was very little in the way of organised recreational activity for children outside of the home, the Band of Hope provided a community to which young people felt they could belong. Their meetings generally consisted of lectures on the evils of hard liquor and recitations promoting the benefits of healthy living and good citizenship; but they also included fun items such as sing-a-longs, sporting activities, board game tournaments, and competitions of various kinds. Achievement badges were awarded, and at the end of the meeting every child was given a bag of sweets, a bun and perhaps half an orange. But the highlight of most Band of Hope meetings was the magic lantern show.[4]

The Band of Hope met in Havant every Thursday evening in the little church hall on Market Lane. The hall had been built in 1835 originally as a schoolroom for the education of the poor before becoming a church property many years later.[5] It was usually William Stewart, the Superintendent of the Wesleyan Sabbath School in Havant and Emsworth, who chaired the meetings and manipulated the magic lantern. Upward of twenty or thirty children between the

---

4   For background information on the role of the magic lantern in Victorian society, see Steve Humphries, *Victorian Britain Through the Magic Lantern* (London: Sidgwick & Jackson, 1989). The Band of Hope is discussed in Michael J. Child, *Labour's Apprentices: Working-Class Lads in Late Victorian and Edwardian England* (McGill-Queen's University Press, 1992).

5   Lewis Lasseter, *These Fifty Years 1891 to 1941* (Havant United Reformed Church, 1991), p. 8 & 17.

ages of six and ten would crowd into the draughty hall. In the semi-darkness they'd perch on hard seats or sit cross-legged on the floor in front of a white canvas screen pinned against the wall. The room would be filled with the smoke from mineral oil lamps. Occasionally a goods train could be heard rattling along on the Guildford–Portsmouth line close-by. Then the magic lantern show would begin! Dramatic special effects could be achieved by dissolving one view into another – day into night, summer into winter, new into old. By 'slipping' two or more hand-painted slides into a sequence, rudimentary animation was possible – *skipping clowns, an erupting volcano, a parlour maid with her broom endlessly sweeping from side to side, a rat scampering into a sleeping mayor's open mouth, then popping out again, and scampering back inside.* Occasionally, one of the slides would be 'accidentally' inserted the wrong way up; the sight of a village policeman riding his bicycle upside down would elicit howls of laughter from the junior audience.

Little Percy Searle was a great fan of the magic lantern shows. He was agog at the lime light and the multi-coloured images. He couldn't contain his delight, wriggling on his seat, waving his arms about, screaming with pure glee at each new slide. It was good to see Percy enjoying himself because in all other respects he was a rather quiet, shy, sad-looking little boy who tended to keep to himself, preferring to play with his toy paint set rather than join in the rough and tumble games with the other boys.

Superintendent Stewart took a fatherly interest in all the young children. He knew Percy well, and described him as the 'merriest of the merry with delight at the pictures'.[6] He was, he said, devoid of malice and always eager to please. As an illustration of Percy's obliging nature, Stewart related the story of how one Sunday afternoon Percy had promptly volunteered to fetch a glass of water from his home, some distance away along a muddy lane, when a young woman fainted during the Sabbath service.

---

6   'Tribute from a Sunday School Superintendent', *Hampshire Telegraph*, 1 December 1888.

Percy's father, Robert, was a Sussex man. He was born in 1844 in Amberley, a picturesque village nestling at the foot of the South Downs. It has a Norman church, many thatched cottages, and an ancient castle. In Victorian times, farming was the main industry, although from the 1840s onwards chalk began to be quarried commercially from the lime works to the south of the village. Robert was only five or six when his father died; as a result, the Searle family – mother Sarah and elder sister Elizabeth, along with Robert – became paupers in the village workhouse.

In 1854 his mother remarried. She wed an agricultural labourer called Charles Withers. Shortly afterwards, the family moved to Warblington, just outside Havant.

Aged twenty-five, Robert began courting a nineteen-year-old Portsmouth girl called Elizabeth. He got her pregnant, but curiously, in March 1870, three months before the child was due, he married Sarah Couzens. This relationship was almost certainly doomed from the start; within months the newly-weds were living apart and Sarah had reverted to her maiden name. Thereafter, although unmarried, Robert and Elizabeth began living together as husband and wife in Warblington with Robert's mother and stepfather helping to bring up their first child, Charles. In fact, all the Searle children, including Percy, would be illegitimate because Robert was still legally married to his estranged wife Sarah Couzens. A second child, Ethel, came along in 1872 but she died aged two and was buried in Havant cemetery.

For a while, Robert was employed as a carman, but as the brood expanded – first Herbert in 1875, then Frederick in 1877 – the family moved to West Street in Havant, where Robert eventually found work as a labourer at the Portsmouth Water Company in Brockhampton to the south-west of town. And it was here, at 33 West Street, on 11th April 1880, that Percy was born.

A younger brother, Sydney, followed in 1884, and the family celebrated the arrival of baby sister Florence in the first quarter of 1888.

They were a very poor family. Sometime around 1882 or 1883 they moved to a terrace of eight cottages at the top of New Lane (now Fairfield Road) on the northern edge of town, close to the burial ground. The cottages had been built in the 1840s, around the same time the railway line opened between Havant and Portsmouth. The 1861 census identifies the terrace as Somerstown (a name possibly derived from the Somers Town area of London between Euston and St Pancras stations) but locals were soon referring to the place as Bug (or Bug's) Row. It was a fitting name. Somerstown was probably the largest and most populous slum in Havant. By 1871 there were fourteen properties on the site providing accommodation for around sixty-six residents. The houses were notoriously squalid and riddled with vermin. One Somerstown resident, John Allen, regularly slaughtered horses in his back yard and was threatened with legal action by the Board of Health for 'bringing horse flesh in an unfit state upon his premises'.[7]

Each property consisted of a scullery and living room on the ground floor with two bedrooms upstairs. There was a privy of sorts in the back yard – in reality little more than a plank with a hole in it placed over a pit connected to a brick-lined cesspool. It hummed with dung beetles and bluebottles. The cesspools were shared between houses and often overflowed resulting in stagnant pools of foul water flooding the yard. As a consequence, outbreaks of dysentery and other illnesses were common among the residents. It wasn't until 1876, following a damning report by Havant's Medical Officer of Health, Dr Aldersley, that plans were drawn up for the installation of a street drain linking Somerstown to the main sewer in North Street. Until then, the tenants of Bug's Row depended on the occasional services of a night soil man who collected the faeces and other waste in a tub and disposed of it underground somewhere out of town.

By the time the Searle family moved into Bug's Row several of the older dwellings had already been demolished and newer, more

---

7   See Robert West, 'The Rookery and Somerstown: Two of Havant's former Slum Areas' in *The Making of Havant* (5) published by The Havant Local History Group, 1980, pp. 42–46.

substantial properties were being erected, but even then the terrace remained a filthy place to live. A report from the 1920s describes Bug's Row as '...very poor houses, very damp, terrible... They were dreadful.'[8]

Records suggest that Percy began his schooling when he was four years old. He attended the Anglican National School on Brockhampton Lane, which catered for boys, girls and infants. In 1888 he was in the standard second class (other reports say standard fourth class). The National School attracted more scholars than its dissenting rival, the St Joseph Roman Catholic School, and was supported partly by contributions and partly by weekly penny payments from the children.[9] The school was really just one huge room divided into several 'classrooms' by temporary partitions.[10] It had recently earned an unfortunate (and perhaps undeserved) reputation for its brutal and merciless punishment regime: one of the schoolmistresses had been fined 5s. 6d. and 23s. costs at the Petty Sessions for excessively caning a twelve-year-old pauper girl from the Workhouse. The child had been left with large weals on both arms, across the small of her back, and on the back of both hands.[11]

Percy was an intelligent child and the headmaster, Mr Cornelius Davis, was pleased with his progress. But Havant was not populous enough to warrant its own secondary tier of public education, and for bright but poor children like Percy, whose parents could not afford the fees of grammar or private secondary schools, there were few opportunities to develop academically.[12] After leaving elementary

---

8   Recollection of Peter Street in Jacqui Penrose (ed), *Heavenly Days: The Borough of Havant Remembered by Its Inhabitants* (privately published 1990), p. 22.
9   In 1891 there were around 112 children at the National School compared to fewer than 40 at the Catholic School.
10   Recollection of Frederick Hart in Jacqui Penrose (ed), *Heavenly Days: The Borough of Havant Remembered by Its Inhabitants* (privately published 1990), pp. 30–1.
11   *Hampshire Telegraph*, 23 June 1888.
12   See A.J.C. Reger, 'Road to Secondary Education', *Hampshire Telegraph*, 13 August 1960. The Manor House Academy in the Pallant had a very good reputation, but it provided education for only a very small percentage of the local population who could afford the fees.

school in a couple of years' time, Percy might have expected to secure employment as a general labourer. Possibly his father could have put in a good word for him at the water works.

Percy was a rather puny, sickly-looking child. He was 4ft 1in tall. Tellingly, one newspaper described him as 'one of those weak and inoffensive little creatures that are especially subject to the ill-usage of young bullies'.[13] We have one picture of him seated in the back row of a class photograph at the National School. He is looking forlornly into the camera and seems on the brink of tears, although smiling wasn't part of the Victorian portrait convention. He has wavy fair hair which his mother has hacked into an uneven fringe. There are lumps or swellings on his forehead, possibly caused by scrofula. His left ear sticks out a bit, almost as if offering itself up to be gripped and tugged by a sadistic schoolmistress. Yet by all accounts he was a well-behaved and placid lad, always clean, neat and tidy, or at least as clean, neat and tidy as was practical for someone in Percy's circumstances. As far as we know he was well-liked among his companions at school, although it does seem he was picked on from time to time simply because he was weedy and a rather dreamy, introspective and solitary child.

On Thursday evening, 22 November, Percy went along to the Band of Hope where he enjoyed the magic lantern show as always. The following Sunday he would ordinarily have attended Sunday School service with his brothers at the small Wesleyan chapel close to the Pallant, but he was sickening for something so stayed at home with his mother. In the event this proved a blessing because after the service there was rowdiness in the stable yard behind the Bear Hotel, and fighting broke out among a few of the boys. Percy was better off at home out of harm's way.

As Percy was not feeling any better on Monday, his mother decided to keep him off school for the day. During the morning he stayed indoors. Baby Florence cried fitfully from the cradle beside the fireside. His father came home from work on his dinner break

---

13   *Hampshire Post,* 30 November 1888.

between twelve and one o'clock, and father and son sat down and ate a quick meal together. They had a good relationship: Mr Searle could honestly say he had never once raised his hand to discipline Percy.

As the day wore on, Percy seemed to perk up a little. In the afternoon Mrs Searle took the boys for a brief walk in the fields behind Bug's Row, returning around half past three. Percy had an afternoon snack, afterwards playing for a while on the living room floor with his toy paint set and marbles. Shortly before six o'clock in the evening his mother judged him well enough to go on an errand for her into town to pick up three quarters of a yard of shirting from Mrs Randall's drapery shop on North Street. The fresh air would do him good. It was already quite dark outside, spitting rain, and the wind was getting up. Percy asked his mother to help him with his coat. He put on his cap and neckerchief and set off on his way. It was the last time his mother would see him alive.

3

In the Pallant

Bug's Row was barely three hundred yards from the centre of town. It would have taken Percy only a few minutes to reach Mrs Randall's shop.

Opposite Bug's Row was Waterloo Road, which ran parallel to the railway line and connected at its far end to the top of North Street. It was still under construction; the footpath paving had been laid down but the road itself was a wasteland of mud and drainage ditches filled with dirty water.[14] Wisely, Percy didn't risk going that way in the dark; instead, he turned left and headed into town along New Lane.

Although New Lane was an unlit and rather deserted thoroughfare, Percy won't have felt alarmed at being out on his own in the early evening. After all, this was his neighbourhood; he knew everyone and everyone knew him, and this was the route he took most days to and from school and to church at the weekends.

The rain was beginning to fall a little harder now, stinging his face. He could hear the wind coursing through the fir and poplar trees on the right side of the road. Beyond were the remains of an old deer park, one of Percy's favourite places to explore in the summer. Farther along, in the distance, were the playing fields and grass tennis courts of Manor House Academy, a private school founded nearly a century earlier.[15] Paraffin lamps could be seen burning in the top floor windows of the Manor House in the Pallant.

---

14 *Hampshire Telegraph*, 8 December 1888.
15 See Madeleine Bailey, *Memories of Manor School Havant* (privately published, 2009), p. 1.

To his left was pastureland known locally as Fair Field. Once, this had been the site of the livestock fair held every year in October on St Faith's Day. Itinerant traders used to come from all over Hampshire to buy and sell cattle, sheep, pigs, and poultry. Visitors were entertained by troupes of minstrels, acrobats and jugglers. There were performing bears, too, and drinking booths for the men and the older boys. But the fair couldn't survive the coming of the railway and long before Percy had been born it was abolished by Act of Parliament. Only sheep and cattle grazed in the fields now, although the land was starting to be developed to provide housing for the expanding town population.

Percy could just remember the firework displays that used to take place on the Fair Field when he was an infant. Hundreds of local people congregated there and a gibbet would be erected to burn the Pope or Fenian terrorists in effigy. On clear autumn nights, Percy would lie on the bedroom floor in Bug's Row and listen as the sound of the bonfire celebrations carried across the darkened meadows.[16]

He continued on down the road, kicking his way through puddles and holding onto his cap whenever a sudden gust of wind threatened to dislodge it. He passed the side entrance to the Manor House with its grand driveway adorned with apple and pear trees and gooseberry bushes. Virginia creeper, russet and brilliant red in the autumn, was beginning to festoon the walls of the Academy.

At the bottom of New Lane the road veered to the left, passing what remained of the old pound where stray animals were once confined. But Percy turned right into the Pallant, a curious wedge-shaped area of land enclosed on its right side by the eight foot high boundary wall of the Manor House Academy and on the left by the large, and at that time unoccupied, dwelling known as Pallant House. There was only one gas lamp in the whole of the Pallant, located at the far end in an alleyway leading to the stable yard of the Bear Hotel, but

---

16 See Ann Buckley, *Fairfield Then and Now* (Fairfield First School Parent-Teacher Association, 1987), pp. 1–3; Robert West and John Pike, *The Havant Bonfire Boys* (Havant Borough Council, 2013); Bill Harris, *Manor Close, Havant: A Short History* (Manor Close Residents' Association, n.d.), p. 10.

its light was partially obscured by a tree and by a growth of ivy on a lean-to against Pallant House. It hardly illuminated the road at all.

The Pallant was therefore a somewhat gloomy and secluded locality at night, despite there being several cottages and other buildings scattered around. Percy will have been alert for danger here. It was a meeting-place much favoured by the rowdy youth of the town, who gathered there to smoke their pipes and plot mischief. Just the day before, fighting had spilled over into the Pallant following a quarrel among boys after evening service at the temporary Wesleyan chapel nearby. Tonight, though, the inclement weather was keeping troublemakers indoors. Even so, Percy probably sprinted through the Pallant till he reached Mrs Randall's drapery shop which stood at the junction of the Pallant and North Street.

Percy arrived at Mrs Randall's a few moments before six o'clock. He will have been glad to get inside out of the rain. Another little boy, eight-year-old William Farnden, who lived round the corner in the Pallant, was just leaving the shop when Percy entered. The two boys were friends, so it's likely they will have chatted briefly in the doorway; perhaps Percy explained to William why he had been off school that day.

Percy was served by Henry Shirley, the draper's assistant; he had to wait a few minutes while his order was made up. It would have been warm and cosy inside the shop, with fabrics and bolts of cloth lining the walls and hanging from hooks in the ceiling. The mahogany counter glinted with packets of needles and brass buttons among the lace and balls of wool. At near enough ten minutes past six Percy collected his parcel of shirting, wrapped up for him by Henry Shirley in brown paper, and left the shop.

We can imagine him dashing out of the shop with his head down, skidding in the mud and trying to dodge the worst puddles in the road. He would have been keen to get home for supper. Retracing his steps back through the Pallant, he got as far as the boundary wall of the Manor House when he was suddenly attacked from behind by someone wielding a knife. It seems he had been hiding in the shadows of the wall, waiting to pounce as Percy passed by.

There was a brief struggle, but Percy was easily overpowered. An attempt was made to cut the boy's throat by drawing the edge of the knife across the windpipe; however the bluntness of the knife only resulted in grazing of the skin, so the assailant plunged the tip of the blade into Percy's neck just below the angle of the right jaw bone. It was a vicious, cowardly attack, utterly without provocation. Percy fell and lay in the thick mud of the roadway, blood flowing freely from the savage puncture wound in his throat. In his hands he still gripped the parcel of shirting he had collected for his mum. His attacker made off under cover of darkness, leaving Percy for dead.

Captain Charles Purvis Boyd had passed through the Pallant only moments before. Captain Boyd is a colourful figure and we'll be meeting him many times during the telling of this story. He regularly commuted to Portsmouth and Fort Monckton in Gosport where he was involved in a classified experimental research project to develop submarine torpedo systems. That evening he'd caught the train from Portsmouth, and arrived punctually in Havant at precisely four minutes past six. As was his routine, he left the railway station, walked down Prince George Street, crossed the Pallant, and made his way along East Pallant to the town hall. It was extremely dark, pouring with rain, and a gusting wind made it difficult for him to keep his umbrella up. He was a naval man and could state quite fastidiously that the wind came from a S.S.W. direction. At precisely nine and a half minutes past six he passed the spot where the body of Percy would shortly be found. In fact, he actually traversed along the wall of the Manor House Academy in order to avoid the mud in the roadway. If the body had been there then he would surely have tripped over it.

William Farnden's older sister, Ellen, was at home with her family that evening. She was in the front room writing a letter to friends in Alton. At around ten minutes past six she heard a disturbance outside.

'What commotion is that, mother?'

'Oh, it's only the boys,' answered Mrs Farnden.

Ellen went to the window and looked behind the blind, but as she couldn't see what had caused the commotion, she returned to her letter writing.

Next door was Orlando Outen, the blacksmith, whose shop was at No. 12 in the Pallant. His teenage son James was working in the shop that evening with a companion called Toogood. James also heard a disturbance. It sounded like the cry of a boy. He mentioned it to Toogood but neither of them thought to investigate since boys often congregated noisily in the street outside.

Mrs Kate Spurgeon was in one of the first floor bedrooms of the Manor House. She was the wife of Tom Spurgeon, the principal's son. From the upstairs front window there was an unobstructed view across the Pallant: to the right was Bear Yard stretching almost as far as the carriage archway on East Street; to the left, visible behind the gardens of Pallant House, was the upper storey of a red brick gazebo. In winter the gazebo windows glared orange and yellow with the light from a roaring fireplace. Although Mrs Spurgeon was very sensitive to noises – on several occasions in the past she had asked her husband to 'have words' with the raucous youths hanging around outside – that evening she heard nothing unusual at all.

Yet a daring and ruthless attack had just taken place almost directly beneath her window, and the killer – for the wounds would prove fatal – had made good his escape into the night.

MAP OF THE MURDER SCENE

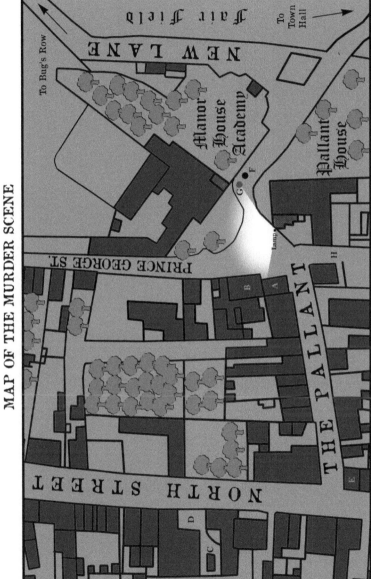

A. Smithy
B. Farnden house
C. Husband cottage
D. Coal yard

E. Randall's drapery shop
F. Murder spot
G. Location of knife
H. Bear Yard

4

A Tall Dark Man

Robert Husband was also in the Pallant that evening. His father worked in the coal depot on North Street and Robert often helped him around the yard. He was nearly twelve years old. At six o'clock closing time his father asked him to pop round to Mr Farnden's house in the Pallant to collect threepence owed for coal. He went there straight from the yard, a journey of two minutes or so. His face and hands were smudged with coal dust and soot, making him almost invisible in the evening murk.

As Robert was passing the gas lamp affixed to a wall at the end of the lane leading into the Pallant he heard a squeal, a sort of 'queer gurgling noise'. Shielding his eyes from the glare of the street lamp, he looked across the road toward the wall of Manor House school. There, he distinctly saw the form of a tall dark man; he had hold of a little boy and he was stabbing him repeatedly. Robert saw the blade of the uplifted knife flashing in the gaslight.

He was frightened out of his wits. Instinctively he shouted 'Murder!' and ran off as fast as he could back the way he had come, heart thumping. Seeing Henry Shirley in the draper's shop doorway, he went over to him, popped his head inside the door, and breathlessly exclaimed, 'There's a man killing a boy up there!' He begged Mr Shirley to investigate, but Mrs Randall appeared from the back of the shop and told Shirley to go and fetch Mr Ford, the coachbuilder, instead.

Meanwhile, John Platt was making his way down the Pallant. Some newspaper reports describe him as a milkman or dairy farmer who had been out in the Fair Field that evening herding his cows. In fact, he was a carpenter employed by a building firm in West Street. He owned a piggery in Prince George Street and was on his way home after feeding the animals. Robert ran up to him, grabbed him by the sleeve, and repeated the story he'd told Shirley.

'There's a man up there killing a boy.'

Mr Platt was incredulous. 'No such thing!'

'It's true, sir; he's murdering a little boy up under the wall.'

'Come and show me,' Platt said.

Robert was understandably a little nervous about returning to the Pallant, but Mr Platt took hold of his hand and they hastened toward the school. Robert stopped about ten yards short of the body as if afraid to go any further. 'There, it's across there,' he said, pointing to the dark shadows under the wall. It was so dark Mr Platt couldn't see a thing, not even with the lamp he carried with him. He advanced a little, then a few steps more – and suddenly there was the body, looking like a bundle of clothes discarded in the road. It was a child's body, lying on its left side, feet toward the wall. Covered in blood and mud. It was a pitiful sight. According to the *Illustrated Police News*, Percy was 'foaming at the mouth, screaming piteously, and rolling in the thick mud that covered the lane';[17] in fact, he was semi-conscious, unmoving, and on the point of death.

Platt knelt down beside the body and cradled the boy's head in his arms. He recognised Percy straightaway; he'd often seen him walking to school in the mornings. Horrific throat wounds were 'staring him in the face', and blood was gushing from Percy's nose and mouth. Both of his hands were covered with blood, suggesting he had struggled with his assailant. His coat sleeves and the wrist bands of his shirt were steeped in gore. Platt lifted up the child's head in an effort to staunch the bleeding. Amazingly, Percy was still alive – but close to death. Without speaking, he gave three deep sighs, and then he was gone.

Platt glanced back over his shoulder and told Robert to run as fast as he could and fetch the police. But Robert just stood there in the

17 *Illustrated Police News*, 8 December 1888.

darkness, watching, not saying a word. Platt felt spooked; he was dry-mouthed and his skin started to crawl. An eternity seemed to pass before Robert turned around and padded off into the night.

Alone with the body, Platt didn't know what to do. Crouched there in a dim pool of fading lantern light, in the rain and the howling wind, he must have been terrified. In panic he started yelling for help. He dashed across the road to the blacksmith's shop. James Outen quickly fetched a second lantern and together they returned to the body. James was horror-stricken at what he saw: for one dreadful moment he even thought it was his own little brother, Orlando, lying there dead in the street.

Commendably, police sergeant William Knapton was quick to arrive at the scene. Moments before he'd been chatting with the landlord of the Bear Hotel when a boy called William Richardson brought him news of the incident.[18] It took the sergeant only half a minute to race through the Bear Yard into the Pallant. It was 6.23 pm.[19]

Sergeant Knapton bent down to examine the body. Unfastening the child's necktie he noticed a puncture mark, more of a shallow cut really, on the left hand side of the neck, and a two inch abrasion across the windpipe. So far as he could tell these were only flesh wounds. The real damage had obviously been done by a large gaping laceration under the right ear, which was still bleeding heavily. A large quantity of blood had pooled around the victim's head, staining the mud.

He searched the body but all he could find was a marble in one of the trouser pockets. The boy's clothing was not disarrayed. A quick inspection of the immediate area revealed no trace of the murder weapon. Nor were there any footmarks, the mud being too soft to retain any permanent impressions. A couple of feet away he spotted

18   Richardson was employed in some capacity at the Bear Hotel. It seems he was working in the yard that evening when he must have heard Platt's cries for help. Investigating, he was told by a member of the Outen family to summon the police.

19   Sergeant Knapton's arrival time at the crime scene is taken from his statement at the magistrates' hearing on 29 November, as reported in the *Portsmouth Times,* 1 December 1888.

the boy's cap, and a brown paper parcel saturated with blood.

On being told that Robert Husband had raised the alarm, Sergeant Knapton asked Platt to go and bring the boy back to the Pallant for questioning.

By now a large crowd was gathering. Nothing like this had ever happened in Havant before, and the townsfolk were morbidly drawn to the scene. Men, women and children were milling around in an excited fashion, splashing in the puddles and churning up the muddy soil in the road. The scene was given an eerie quality by the blue smoke from several paraffin lanterns drifting across the lane. Sergeant Knapton cordoned off the body as best he could and sent James Outen to fetch Dr Bond.

The Husband family lived in a ramshackle cottage just behind the coal yard in North Street, a couple of minutes' walk from the Pallant. There was no answer when Platt rapped on the front door, so he went round the back where Robert's father let him in.

The boy Robert was in the kitchen. In fact, the entire family was in the kitchen, all nine of them – father, stepmother, and seven children including a baby. They all stared at Platt as he entered. Their heads moved in unison as if they were components of a mechanical toy joined by a single crank pin. The room was lit by a double burner oil lamp: the cranberry glass shades gave a watery blood tint to the light. There was a pan of soup warming on the fire, and bread and jam on the table. Robert had just washed his hands and was wiping them dry on a towel hanging from the back of the scullery door. Platt was annoyed: earlier he'd ordered Robert to go and fetch the police, but it seemed he'd come straight home for his tea instead.

'You must come with me,' Platt said. 'Sergeant Knapton wants to see you.'

There are conflicting reports about what happened next. According to the *West Sussex Gazette*, Platt unceremoniously dragged Robert into the street and marched him screaming back to the Pallant. Other sources suggest Robert compliantly returned to the murder scene with Platt, man and boy walking silently together down North Street, each immersed in his own dark thoughts. According to Platt's own statement at the coroner's inquest, Robert came willingly and there was no conversation between them on the way.

What does seem clear is that John Platt, the thirty-six-year-old carpenter and pig farmer, had been badly shaken by events that evening. He was in shock. His subsequent contradictory statements to the press and in court would show how confused and rattled he was. And no wonder. A small child had just died in his arms. His work clothes were saturated in Percy's blood. He couldn't get the image of those neck wounds out of his head. And the boy Husband, standing there in the darkness, not saying a word, just staring at the corpse...

Platt was no doubt furious at Robert's failure to summon the police, and he may have been disquieted by the boy's oddly cold demeanour at the crime scene, but he won't have dragged him across town. For one thing, Robert's father wouldn't have allowed it. He was a brawny coalman, with no love of authority, and if Platt had so much as laid a finger on Robert he would have been quick to defend him.

Earlier, when Robert had shown Platt where the body was lying, he'd been reluctant to approach the murder scene. Now, back at the Pallant, he marched straight up to where Sergeant Knapton was standing over the body. The crowds parted to let him through. He held his hands close by his sides.

'Did you see anyone?' asked the police sergeant.

'Yes, I heard someone crying out, and I saw a tall man.'

'Where were you when you saw him?'

'I was over there by Mr Farnden's house, by the gas lamp.'

'What was he doing?'

'He was doing this—' and Robert passed his right hand backwards and forwards across his throat in a sawing motion.

'How was he dressed?'

'He had on a dark coat.'

'And which way did he go?'

'He ran off that way,' replied Robert, pointing towards the Fair Field.

Sergeant Knapton wasn't entirely convinced by Robert's story, and he made a note to quiz the boy further at a later date.

Dr Florio St Quintin Bond was the next person to arrive at the scene. He'd been in the Public Reading rooms when news of Percy's death reached him about half-past six. Quickly making his way to the Pallant, he found poor Percy lying in a pool of blood, which the rain had diffused over a large area. He later estimated that Percy must have lost several pints of blood. The fact that there were no other traces of blood near the body indicated that the boy had in all likelihood been murdered where he lay. The body was still warm. He saw three wounds on the neck: one of them was a mere scratch on the left side but a more significant injury extended one and a half inches upwards towards the right ear. Beyond ascertaining that the child was dead, there was little he could do there and then. Conditions were not ideal: the light was poor, it was raining hard, and the crowd was pressing in on all sides. Furthermore, the body was absolutely caked in mud and gore. The immediate cause of death was obviously collapse from loss of blood but more than that he couldn't say until he had conducted a proper post-mortem on the body. He directed that the body should be removed to the mortuary.

Dr Bond performed one other duty that evening, which shows his great humanity and compassion. He went round to Bug's Row and gently broke the news of her son's death to Mrs Searle. He stayed with her for half an hour, in her cramped living room, comforting her and calming her distracted mind. Baby Florence mewled continuously in her cradle by the fireside, as if she knew her big brother Percy would never be coming home again.

Most evenings on his way home from work Mr Searle stopped off for a quick drink at the Perseverance Tavern on North Street. He was in there on Monday night around half past six buying some tobacco when he overheard people gossiping about the murder of a young boy in the Pallant. Apparently the victim was the son of a local man who worked at the water works. Fearing the worst, Mr Searle hurried to the Pallant. His son Herbert usually made his way home through the Pallant at this time. Was it Herbie who had been attacked? But on reaching the scene he was aghast to learn it was little Percy. Shy, harmless little Percy who had no enemies in the world. They'd eaten dinner together only a few hours before. He held his son's body in his arms and openly, furiously, wept. A man stepped forward from the crowd and urged Mr Searle to bear up under his great affliction.

A little later, just before seven o'clock, the creak of cart wheels were heard as Martha Burrows manoeuvred her trolley into the Pallant.

5

Across the Fields

Not unexpectedly, the murder of Percy Searle became headline news in all the local newspapers.

Right from the start the press portrayed Percy's murder as a crime almost without parallel in Hampshire. The *Hampshire Post* called it 'as brutal and purposeless an assassination as has ever been recorded'.[20]

The uniquely terrible nature of the case was summed up in an editorial in the *Hampshire Telegraph* on 1 December:

> The tragic occurrence at Havant on Monday evening last has been the all-absorbing topic of the week throughout the entire district, and all agree that the foul crime perpetrated upon the person of the unoffending child Searle, was the most revolting that has been committed in the county of Hampshire for many years.[21]

It continued:

> Seldom indeed have the dread annals of crime contained the record of a murder more hideous or more inexplicable than the one that on Monday evening sent a thrill of horror through the town of Havant and carried consternation into many a home... the news that a little innocent child had on Monday been foully done to death under circumstances of the most revolting cruelty spread far and wide, and created the most intense excitement and the deepest indignation.[22]

Everyone was completely baffled by the crime. It was barely

---

20 *Hampshire Post*, 30 November 1888.
21 However, the Victorian press was in the habit of describing all murder cases as 'without parallel' or 'exceptional'.
22 *Hampshire Telegraph*, 30 November 1888.

conceivable that a man would attack a young lad like Percy with no reason. He was a quiet, well-behaved child, not given to brawling with his schoolmates or companions, so the notion that he had received his fatal injuries in a scrap with another boy was immediately dismissed. And robbery was clearly out of the question – little boys seldom had anything on them worth stealing.

One theory uppermost in many people's minds was that Percy had been lured to the murder spot by a local resident, someone known to Percy and from whom he had no reason to anticipate danger – a neighbour, perhaps, or a shopkeeper. According to Daniel Farson, the *Portsmouth Times* hinted that Percy had been the victim of an attempted sexual assault. Farson quotes the newspaper as stating:

> The murderer attempted to commit another crime, not unknown in Assize calendars, and he stopped the boy's cries by resorting to the knife.[23]

This is not a subject the *Portsmouth Times* expands on at any time during its extensive subsequent coverage of the case, and nor have I been able to track down the original newspaper report which Farson cites. Farson has either fabricated this passage or he has mixed up his sources and is quoting from another unspecified publication entirely. Certainly, there were risks to young boys of sexual violence from men, even if this was a subject the Victorian press was reticent to discuss except in the most general and roundabout terms; but the notion that Percy had been molested by a stranger or by a man (or older boy) of his acquaintance is completely without foundation. Besides, as we have seen, Sergeant Knapton had checked Percy's clothing and there was no sign of disarrangement.

One rumour which came to dominate the early newspaper accounts of the Havant murder, and which still to this day frames many people's understanding of the case, was the notion that Percy was a victim of Jack the Ripper. (Later versions of this theory would state that Percy was the victim of someone merely *imitating* Jack the Ripper.) On the surface, this was a ludicrous suggestion.

---

23   Daniel Farson, *Jack the Ripper* (London: Michael Joseph, 1972), p. 54.

Percy's murder, by all accounts a blundering, amateurish attack, bore no resemblance at all to the efficient handiwork of the Ripper. The idea that there could be any connection whatsoever between the savage slayings of at least five adult female prostitutes in the Whitechapel area of London and the solitary murder of an eight-year-old schoolboy living in rural Hampshire more than a two hour train ride away seems almost risible. Yet it isn't difficult to see how paranoid perceptions about Jack the Ripper might easily have taken hold among the people of Havant.

If the newspaper reports are to be believed, the district of Havant was in a heightened state of turmoil over Jack the Ripper even before the murder of Percy took place. The day after the murder, the *Portsmouth Evening News* observed that:

> The note of alarm sounded throughout the country by the repeated Whitechapel murders has found its way in this direction... rural people living in Brockhampton have for some little time past been in the habit of locking up their houses at an early hour in the evening, and of venturing out as little as possible after nightfall.[24]

Of course, this is scaremongering. As we have seen, Mrs Searle had no qualms at all about sending Percy out on his own in the dark. Yet to some extent it's true that a mood of dread and mounting hysteria prevailed across the entire country, testifying to the power and ubiquity of the Jack the Ripper legend.

The *St James's Gazette* brooded on the notion of contagion:

> The further details which have come to light about the murder at Havant reveal that a crime has been committed not less shocking and certainly not less alarming to the sense of public security than any of the atrocities which have gone unpunished in Whitechapel. There is not much to favour the idea that the crime at Havant may be attributed to the criminal of Whitechapel. It would be more comfortable to believe that we had only one purposeless murderer to catch and punish. Can it be that an infection of bloodshed has spread itself over the country? There is a fashion in morbidness: sometimes it generates a belief in magic, sometimes an outbreak of lust, and sometimes a craving for human blood which operates on

24 *Portsmouth Evening News*, 27 November 1888.

imaginations which have become diseased by drink or by gloating upon the horrors of criminal fiction or criminal reports.[25]

The *Portsmouth Times* drew an illuminating parallel between the highly-charged atmosphere engendered by the Ripper murders and a similar panic experienced in the aftermath of the Ratcliff Highway murders in 1811 when two separate families in London's East End, including a young mother and her baby, were viciously clubbed to death by an unknown assailant. The *Hampshire Post* quoted the reminiscences of Thomas De Quincey:

> For twelve succeeding days, under some groundless notion that the unknown murderer had quitted London, the panic which had convulsed the mighty metropolis diffused itself all over the island. I was myself at that time nearly three hundred miles from London; but there, and everywhere, the panic was indescribable.[26]

De Quincey goes on to relate how a neighbour of his, a lady living alone in a very isolated house, barricaded herself behind eighteen chained and ponderously bolted doors before she felt safe in her bedroom.[27]

According to Robert Husband (if his story could be believed) the murderer had made off in the direction of the Fair Field. Therefore, one of Sergeant Knapton's first actions after leaving the crime scene was to organise teams of local vigilantes to head out into the countryside and track down the child killer.

Each vigilante party consisted of four or five men. The *Evening News* would later refer to them rather grandly as 'volunteer detectives' but in fact none of them had any experience of police work at all; they

---

25 *St James's Gazette*, 29 November 1888.

26 Thomas De Quincey, Postscript to 'On Murder Considered as one of the Fine Arts' (1854). De Quincey misremembers the date as 1812. See John Barrell, *The Infection of Thomas De Quincey: A Psychopathology of Imperialism* (Yale University Press, 1991), pp. 64–66.

27 The garrotting panic of 1862 and the baby farming panic of the early 1870s are other examples where criminal events associated with children were raised to the status of moral panics.

were just regular citizens who had answered Sergeant Knapton's call for able-bodied men to help hunt down little Percy's attacker. They were tradesmen and warehouse labourers, clerks and shopkeepers, a couple of ploughmen, and a large contingent of men from the water works where Percy's father worked.

In 1888 Havant had one police sergeant (Sergeant Knapton) and one constable (PC William Notton). In theory, the 3rd Volunteer Battalion of the Hampshire Regiment, headquartered at Lymbourne, could be called upon if required to lend auxiliary assistance to the police, but on the evening Sergeant Knapton requested their help it seems they were holding an important indoor rifle shooting competition and prize raffle in the drill hall at the Portsmouth barracks, and they resisted appeals to venture out into the rain and the dark. Instead, Sergeant Knapton managed to swell the ranks of the posses by mobilising a crew of off-duty coastguards from Portsea Island.

From the yard behind the Bear Hotel the search parties set off around eight thirty, radiating out across the countryside. Their instructions were to keep a sharp look-out for suspicious persons and to make enquiries at any public houses they passed on the road. Jack the Ripper was out there somewhere, and he needed to be caught.

Three teams headed west towards Bedhampton, Purbrook and Cosham; others headed east in the direction of Emsworth Common, New Brighton and Warblington. The largest contingent flooded the Fair Field. The coastguards had arrived and incredibly they'd brought with them a troop of sea cadets to make up numbers. The cadets were young boys barely much older than Percy Searle. They should have been at home in bed, not out hunting a child killer in the dark. Sergeant Knapton sent most of them down to Farlington Marshes, where their knowledge of coastal waters would presumably help them locate the Ripper if he was hiding in the reed beds and brackish lagoons.

There may have been an element of nervous high-spirits and bravado among the volunteers as they stood around awaiting their orders. What an adventure! Tracking the Ripper in the dark! Each posse was given a single oil lantern, which scarcely cast enough light to illuminate the way ahead. As they headed out into the secluded country lanes along muddy paths sodden with piles of fallen autumn leaves, their cockiness will have quickly evaporated. What the hell were they doing out at night hunting down Jack the Ripper? He'd already run rings round Scotland Yard's finest. There were rumours he possessed supernatural powers: stand him in front of a panelled fence and within seconds his face took on the colour and the texture of the wood. Horribly, the knife he used to carve up women and children made no noise as it sliced through flesh and tissue and bone. It was said he purposely rattled his black bag so that the last sound his victims heard on Earth was the clink of sharp surgical instruments.

One search party made their way north to Rowlands Castle via West Leigh and Staunton. We know the names of these four 'volunteer detectives' — Rogers, Munday, Carter, and Marshall — because their exploits were written up in the *Evening News*.[28] They met several men out and about that evening, all of whom gave satisfactory accounts of themselves. At one point they encountered two women making their way to Barton's Green. The posse was right to proceed with extreme caution: the Ripper was a master of disguise who donned the skirts of midwives to evade capture. However, one of the women was known to the men, so they were allowed to pass on their way.

When they reached the Staunton Arms it seemed for one glorious moment they were actually closing in on their prey. Jack the Ripper had been here the day before! Or more exactly, the children of the neighbourhood had taken a dislike to a stranger seen loitering in the area, probably a vagrant, and had styled him 'Jack the Ripper'. No credence was given to this tale, and the party, perhaps a little disheartened, moved on 'in search of more adventure' to Rowlands Castle.

As the night wore on, the search parties returned one by one to

---

28 *Portsmouth Evening News*, 27 November 1888.

Havant, exhausted and despondent, with naught to show for their fruitless tramping across the wet fields. Some teams returned well after midnight. The coast guards and the sea cadets never returned at all, and one supposes they made their own way home to Portsea Island after hours of trudging across the mudflats. If anything, these search parties had only exacerbated the sense of alarm felt by the rural community, who had watched in disbelief as teams of plucky but frightened men and boys blundered around in the dark hoping to come face to face with Jack the Ripper.

In fact, lots had happened since they'd set out on their frantic hunt for the killer. A wrongful arrest had been made. A murder weapon had been found. And people were now starting to think perhaps it wasn't Jack the Ripper after all. Maybe Percy's killer was someone already known to them, someone who lived in their midst.

PART TWO

6

A Dorset Policeman

The Hampshire Constabulary was formed in 1839, making it one of the oldest forces in the country.[29] In the early years it was a struggle to recruit men of creditable character: many constables were disobedient and neglectful of their duties, and habitual drunkenness was a frequent cause of dismissal from the service. By the mid 1880s the total number of officers in the county amounted to two hundred and twenty-nine constables, twenty-six sergeants, three inspectors, twelve superintendents and Chief Constable Captain John Forrest. National guidelines stated that the number of policemen in any county force was not to exceed one for every thousand inhabitants: Havant had one police sergeant and one constable for a population of just over three thousand.

They dealt mainly with common offences like larceny, disorderly conduct, damage to property, domestic disputes, and desertion from the armed forces (a major problem in a county containing several large army and navy depots). They were also expected to investigate crimes of a predominantly rural and agricultural nature – poaching, fowl stealing, loitering and begging by itinerant vagabonds and pedlars, and the theft and maiming of horses. The passing of the Army Corps Training Act in 1876 imposed additional responsibilities on the police to assist the military authorities with the maintenance of law and order. They were also responsible for detecting and

29 For information on the history of the Havant police, see Ian A. Watt, *A History of the Hampshire and Isle of Wight Constabulary 1839–1966* (Hampshire & Isle of Wight Constabulary, 1967); 'Law and Order' in *The Making of Havant* (2) published by The Havant Local History Group, 1978, pp. 41–46; E.C. Bailey, 'Havant of Past Days: Law and Order', *Hampshire Telegraph,* 29 March 1935.

preventing illegal prize fights and guarding farm workers' cottages left unattended during the summer months. The control of dogs was another of their duties: officers were instructed to dispose of strays by discharging prussic acid from a syringe down the animal's throat. Assaults on the police were regrettably commonplace, most often occurring when constables were summoned to evict drunken customers from beerhouses.

From time to time the police even had to deal with properly serious crimes, such as the shocking 'Son of Satan' murder case of 1862 when twenty-three-year-old Mary Hall from Fordingbridge was strangled on her way home from church.

In 1858 a police station was built in West Street in Havant on a quarter acre of land costing £100. The building contained living quarters for married officers and two detention cells for prisoners with hatches built into the doors. A magistrates' courtroom was also attached allowing the business of the district Petty Sessions to be conducted with solemnity and decorum: until that time the Bench of magistrates assembled in a noisy, overcrowded upstairs room at the Black Dog Inn.

It seems Havant had its own tiny police force prior to the opening of the West Street station. Sergeant Frederick Cavell joined the Hampshire Constabulary in 1841 when he was twenty-one, and moved to Havant in 1851. Later, he became the receiving officer for the Havant Workhouse before eventually transferring to the Water Police in Portsmouth.

Sergeant Cavell was followed by Sergeant Charles Byles, who was stationed at Havant from 1865 until the mid 1880s. He was apparently well-liked by the law-abiding people of the town. Noted for the vigour with which he pursued vagrants and beggars, he was also very strict with small children playing hoops in the roadway, administering sharp raps with his cane if he caught any transgressors. His fearsome-looking truncheon can be seen at the Havant Museum, along with the town stocks and whipping post.

In 1885 the Hampshire Constabulary purchased thirty-three state of the art bicycles at a cost of £289, although they proved practically useless on the muddy rural highways. In the days before telephones, radios and motor cars, urgent communications were despatched by telegraph. Wires were laid along all the main railway lines and a few branch lines.

Police uniform at the time consisted of a top hat, blue frock coat, white (or blue) trousers, a greatcoat or cape and a truncheon. In Portsmouth, the hats had been replaced by helmets in 1868. A constable earned an annual salary of £60 16s. 8d. (£51 14s. 2d. if they lived in the station) while a sergeant earned £76.

William Knapton was born in Gillingham in Dorset in 1842. His father was a dairy farmer with a smallholding of twenty acres. He did his best to provide William with a good education even though he showed no especial promise at school. William was likely put to work around the farm at a very young age, and his parents no doubt expected him (as their eldest son) to eventually take over the running of the farm. But William had other ideas. On leaving school he found work as an errand boy at the General Post Office in Gillingham. Shortly afterwards he became apprenticed to a Dorchester boot- and shoe-maker named Charles Parsons. He married a local girl, Ann, fathered two children, and moved with his family to the tiny village of Piddlehinton just north of Dorchester.

In July 1866, he surprised everyone again by enlisting in the Dorset Constabulary. Perhaps he could see no real future for himself as a shoemaker: boot-making was rapidly becoming a mechanised process with automated factory production set to take over by the 1880s. Possibly, he simply grew bored by the routine and by the five mile hike there and back everyday from his home on the Dorset downs to the Dorchester workshop. Maybe he was attracted by the job security and the police pension.

He met all the constabulary entry requirements: he was twenty-four years of age, stood 5ft 9in tall without shoes, and was able to read and write. A medical examination by the police surgeon certified him fit in health and bodily strength.[30]

---

30 Details of Inspector Knapton's police career taken from his Hampshire Constabulary Examination Book, Hampshire Record Office, reference 200M86.

After serving his probationary period in Dorchester, he transferred in August 1869 to the Hampshire Constabulary. Over the next fifteen years he was stationed variously at Shirley, West End, Twyford, Stockbridge, Sandown on the Isle of Wight, and Lyndhurst, before finally moving to Havant in December 1884 where he succeeded Sergeant Byles.

He appears to have been a rather dutiful, ponderous and rule-bound police officer who pursued miscreants doggedly rather than with any noticeable flair or inspiration. He was bright, but not perhaps gifted with any outstanding detective ingenuity. He was stolid and reliable, which were, in fact, the qualities most prized by commissioners when recruiting men from unskilled or semi-skilled rural backgrounds.[31] He rose steadily through the lower ranks, becoming a sergeant in 1873. The only blot on his service record was a fine of seven days pay in September 1877 for 'conduct unbecoming of an officer of a disciplined Constabulary', but he worked hard to put this embarrassment behind him and in December 1878 he was commended in General Orders. When he left Lyndhurst to take up his new position in Havant, the villagers bought the departing officer a handsome drawing room clock in gilt and black marble with the engraving 'Presented to PS Knapton by the tradesmen of Lyndhurst as a mark of respect and esteem.'

Unquestionably the murder of Percy Searle became the most significant case of his career, and it provided the severest test of his policing capabilities. It is fair, I think, to characterise his outlook and sensibilities as essentially those of a small-town constable, happiest when on regular patrol work and rubbing shoulders with working men and women, but totally unused to elaborate criminal investigations. With the Percy Searle case, he suddenly found himself at the centre of a high-profile, complicated murder enquiry. His actions would be scrutinised in greater detail than at any other time in his career.

---

31   See Haia Shpayer-Makov, *The Ascent of the Detective* (Oxford University Press, 2011), p. 83.

7

Mob Rule

Percy's attacker had apparently made off in the direction of the Fair Field. He may have hiked across open farmland to Emsworth, or perhaps he'd headed down to Langstone and Hayling Island. More likely, though, he'd scarpered up New Lane to the railway station intending on catching the first train out of town.

Indeed, a railway porter named Alfred Steele would later claim that on the evening of the murder, but before he himself knew that a murder had taken place, a 'curious individual' rushed into the station and without buying a ticket leaped into a second class carriage on the 6.35 train bound for Brighton, all the while attempting to keep his face turned away from the porter's view. The fellow's manner was so unusual Steele remarked on it to a colleague. Was this Percy's killer? Was it Jack the Ripper? Whoever it was, he'd given the police the slip. By now he could be anywhere – Chichester, Barham, Littlehampton, or any other stop on the line to Brighton.

Around 6.40 that evening, after Dr Bond had ordered the removal of Percy's body to the mortuary, Sergeant Knapton left the murder scene and hurried to the Telegraph Office at No. 4 East Street. He sent telegrams to all the principal police stations within a twelve mile radius, including Portsmouth, Petersfield and Chichester, urging a keen look-out for suspicious characters and requesting officer backup. He also telegraphed Superintendent George Kinshott at the Osborn Road station in Fareham. Over the next few hours, in response to Knapton's appeal, detectives began arriving in Havant from all corners of south-east Hampshire. Among the officers joining the investigation were Detective Sergeant Urry of Gosport,

Detective Inspector Lawler of Winchester,[32] and a very experienced local officer, Detective William Money, of the Portsmouth police.

As well as coordinating search teams to patrol the back roads and surrounding villages, Sergeant Knapton readily accepted the offer of assistance from a self-styled vigilance committee that had quickly sprung up from among the outraged citizens of the town. They volunteered to scout every outhouse and empty building in the town and check on strangers and suspicious characters staying overnight in lodging houses and in the tramp ward at the workhouse. Sergeant Knapton may have felt he had no real alternative until reinforcements arrived, but it was a mistake to cede authority to lawless bands of aggressive young men fired up in the excitement of the moment. The vigilance committee rapidly turned into an extra-judicial mob tearing through the town, ransacking private property, and committing acts of vandalism and wanton damage. A report in the *West Sussex Gazette* described the mayhem:

> In some cases men were dragged from their beds and compelled to give an account of themselves, while unknown strollers and strangers were put through the same ordeal. So anxious were the vigilance committees for arrests that one man, unknown to them, was pulled up near the parish church, and as his account of himself was not sufficiently coherent, the coastguard, who had volunteered their assistance, were quickly called to form an inquisition. As the man demurred to this inquisitorial examination, a revolver was presented at him, and dreading the consequences, the stranger meekly awaited the arrival of a police sergeant to give him his 'pass on.' A number of men were challenged in this way.[33]

It was even possible that the murderer of Percy Searle was among their number, masquerading as a concerned public-spirited sheriff.

Sergeant Knapton had to interrupt his search party work when

---

32   Lawler was still basking in the commendations he had received for the 'intelligent and persevering manner' in which he had worked the case of Albert Brown, who was sentenced to death at the Winchester Assizes in 1886 for the brutal murder of a fellow seaman. See Ian A. Watt, *A History of the Hampshire and Isle of Wight Constabulary 1839–1966* (Hampshire & Isle of Wight Constabulary, 1967), p. 38.

33   *West Sussex Gazette*, 29 November 1888.

he was urgently summoned to the railway station to deal with an individual acting suspiciously. The man was dressed in a long coat and wore a sealskin cap. He had a thin face, a small moustache and dark whiskers which didn't quite conceal several livid marks or scratches on his cheeks. He was carrying a small bundle. When Knapton ordered him to turn out his pockets, he produced a small knife.

The man was deaf, or almost so, and communication proved difficult, but he readily gave his name as Thomas Clarke, an engine fitter from Paradise Street in Portsmouth, and provided a credible account of his actions that evening: he and a work colleague called Job Hayter had just walked to Havant from Emsworth (a distance of just under three miles) after working all day at the Hipkin's Brewery laying pipes. Hayter had hurried ahead to catch the train to Portsmouth but Clarke was slower and had missed it.

Knapton appears to have had misgivings about Clarke's story, and felt he needed more time to investigate the truth of his statements. On this pretext he arrested Clarke and marched him to the police station as if he were a ruffian. The man was trembling and in a highly agitated state. A mob began following the police officer and his prisoner down North Street, shouting abuse at Clarke and hurling mud at him. At the station Clarke was searched and stripped of his coat and jacket, then locked in a cell.

Sergeant Knapton at once telegraphed details of the arrest to Chief Constable Alfred Cosser at Portsmouth. Hayter was in turn promptly arrested by the Portsmouth police at his home in Riga Terrace in Landport, and taken to the Russell Street police station where he was detained for an hour and a half without being informed of the details of the charge. However, his story tallied exactly with Clarke's, and it soon became clear to the arresting officers in both Portsmouth and Havant that there was no evidence whatsoever against either prisoner. Hayter was discharged and allowed to return home, but curiously Clarke remained locked in his cell all night without food or water. His request for a cup of coffee or cocoa was refused.

Later that evening, around nine o'clock, a significant incident occurred that would dramatically alter the course of the police investigation.

Groups of men and women were still milling around the Pallant, gawping at the puddles of blood in the road. Tom Spurgeon, a master at the Manor House school and the principal's son, decided he too would go out and view the murder scene. With the aid of a lantern, he began searching the ground outside his front gate. Incredibly, he spotted a knife lying in the road about eight or nine yards from where the body had been found. Examining it closely, he saw that it was an ordinary pocket knife, probably of fairly common manufacture, with a buckhorn handle and two blades. The smaller blade was snapped off half-way down; the larger blade was about three inches long. When Spurgeon picked the knife up the larger blade rattled a little in its handle owing to a loose rivet. The edge of the undamaged blade was blunt towards the top but appeared sharper lower down; there were signs that the owner had recently attempted to sharpen the blade by honing it against a rough surface.

There was no doubt in Mr Spurgeon's mind that this was the murder weapon because he could see blood on both blades and on the handle. Perhaps the miscreant had thrown the knife away in a state of panic before fleeing the scene. Spurgeon dashed off in search of Sergeant Knapton. Eventually he found him at the railway station and handed over the knife. Knapton carefully wrapped it in a roll of paper before placing it in his tunic pocket and returning with it to the station.[34]

---

34   Mrs Madeleine Tutton (*née* Bailey), born in 1914, who grew up at the Manor School with her mother and the daughters of Tom Spurgeon, recalls being told about the murder when she was a small girl. Her recollection is that Tom Spurgeon was said to have found the knife in the front garden of the school house rather than in the street outside. This would certainly explain why the knife had not been previously spotted by anyone milling around in the Pallant, but it poses problems: if Tom Spurgeon found the knife in his garden, why did he give evidence in the coroner's court, in the magistrates' court, and at the Assizes in Winchester, saying he found the weapon a few yards outside his front gate? Madeleine Bailey has written a lovely booklet about her time at the school, *Memories of Manor School Havant* (privately published, 2009).

At 10.30 pm Superintendent George Kinshott arrived in Havant to take overall operational control of the murder enquiry. Sergeant Knapton will have immediately briefed him on the state of the investigation. One wonders what Superintendent Kinshott made of it all. There were teams of untrained men and boys haphazardly roaming the countryside looking for Jack the Ripper. Other vigilante groups had gone on the rampage with pistols, invading homes, destroying private property, and causing widespread terror. Even worse, Percy's killer had probably already made his escape by simply jumping on the first train out of town. And there was an innocent man in custody. For his part, Sergeant Knapton may well have been thankful for the steadying presence of a more experienced senior colleague.

The knife was the only clue the police had at this time. Superintendent Kinshott examined it with Sergeant Knapton. It was really just a broken pocket knife, dirty and dull-edged – a boy might prize it and show it off to his playmates in the schoolyard, but it was hardly an instrument an adult would use. Developing the idea, Kinshott wondered if the assailant might actually be a juvenile: the abandonment of the knife in the middle of the road and so close to the murder site suggested panic and lack of calculation on the part of the perpetrator. Or perhaps the weapon had been jerked out of the murderer's hand when he stumbled on some road debris while fleeing the scene. And the fact that the attacker hadn't been strong enough to cut through the cartilage of the windpipe but had resorted to stabbing the throat with the tip of the blade also supported the view that the person they were after might not be an adult.

The policemen decided they would exhibit the knife at the police station the following day and invite members of the public to inspect it. That way someone might identify the weapon as belonging to one of their companions or colleagues. It was their best chance of apprehending the culprit.

Meanwhile, police officers continued conducting house searches far into the evening and well after their usual hours of duty. The residents of Havant will no doubt have slept fitfully that night, brooding over the brutal killer in their midst. Was the maniac already prowling the streets in search of his next victim?

PC John Samuel Wareham was given the unenviable duty of guarding the murder scene overnight, although in truth there was little to see except a large pool of blood in the road, already diluting in the drizzle, and nothing much to protect. He painted a black upright cross on the school wall adjacent to the crime scene, marking the location of the tragedy for future visitors to the town: traces of the cross would still be visible when the old Manor House and the estate walls were demolished many decades later.[35] Residents may well have taken pity on him standing there by himself, at the scene of a grisly murder, in the wet and blustery dark. They began to serve the constable pots of ale to keep him warm.

The cold, rainy weather persisted on Tuesday. Squalls moved in across the coastal mudflats. Gulls screeched as they wheeled above the Pallant. The town looked drab and a little forlorn.

At about a quarter to five in the morning a bricklayer walking from Portsmouth to Rowlands Castle was questioned by a policeman near Havant railway station, but he was allowed on his way after providing a satisfactory account of his movements. Stories were circulating that several arrests had taken place in Portsmouth during the night, including that of a woman, but these turned out to be false reports.

In the morning, at 8 am, the twenty-three-year-old constable Samuel Wareham was still nominally keeping guard over the Manor House murder scene, although by this time he was conspicuously intoxicated. Later that day he was dismissed from the service with the forfeiture of a week's pay.

It is interesting that the earliest recorded killing in Havant involved children. In his historical work *A Topographical Account of*

---

35   Bill Harris, *Manor Close, Havant: A Short History* (Manor Close Residents' Association, n.d.), p. 6.

the Hundred of Bosmere,[36] Charles Longcroft[37] recounts a case dating back to 1264 concerning Geoffrey le Fevre of Havant, not yet ten years old, who killed a boy of the same age, John le Mourier, also of Havant, while they were playing together. Geoffrey was pardoned by the Lord of the Manor because the incident was judged to be an accident.[38]

According to the *Portsmouth Evening News*, there had not been a murder in 'easy-going' Havant for more than 400 years, not since the skeletal remains of a presumed murder victim had been found beneath the Royal Oak Inn when it was knocked down in the 1760s.[39]

Yet it would be wrong to characterise Havant and its neighbourhood as a sleepy backwater where violent criminal activity never took place. As recently as July 1878 the local press had been full of the case of George Mason, a labourer from the town, who attempted to murder his wife Ellen while she was out shopping in East Street. He stabbed her with a knife three times in the shoulder, once over her right breast, and once in the back of the neck.[40] She was fortunate to survive such a savage attack. In June 1862, a couple of miles north of Havant in what is now Waterlooville, a gipsy named Edward Lee sliced his pregnant wife's throat with a razor and threw her out of the covered wagon in which they were travelling. By the time the police arrived at the scene the horse had trampled all over the body.[41] And in the neighbouring village of Purbrook in 1885, a bout of horseplay between two young men quickly turned to manslaughter when one of the youths struck the other a severe blow to the back of the head while he was on the ground, rupturing vessels in his brain and

---

36   Charles John Longcroft, *A Topographical Account of the Hundred of Bosmere* (John Russell Smith, 1856 and 1857 editions).

37   E.C. Bailey describes Longcroft as 'a good sportsman, the best dressed man in Havant, and one of the handsomest'. See his article 'Havant of Past Days: Law and Order', *Hampshire Telegraph*, 22 February 1935.

38   For a brief discussion of this case, see John Reger's article 'Courts in the Dark Ages', *Hampshire Telegraph*, 2 December 1960.

39   *Portsmouth Evening News*, 1 & 5 December 1888.

40   *Hampshire Telegraph*, 3 July 1878.

41   *London Daily News*, 23 June 1862.

causing a fatal blood clot to develop.[42]

Even so, the murder of Percy Searle was a uniquely shocking crime and by all accounts the most momentous event in Havant within living memory.

Rival teams of journalists began arriving in Havant on Monday night, taking up rooms in the Bear and Dolphin Hotels. Next morning they were out in strength around the town, interviewing anyone who claimed knowledge of the murder or who possessed information, however sparse, about the main players in the drama. On several occasions the manoeuvres of the press would outflank police enquiries.

The Searle family had journalists knocking on their door at breakfast time. Mr Searle looked a shattered man, pale and grief stricken. He nearly broke down more than once while he was being interviewed. He told the reporters how he had been drinking in the Perseverance Tavern after work on Monday afternoon and how he had rushed to the Pallant to find Percy lying dead outside the Manor House school. He had no idea who might have committed such a despicable act, especially since Percy was such a mild-mannered boy and popular with all his schoolfellows. On being told that the police had no fresh clues, he gloomily announced that he thought the murderer had got away with it and wouldn't now be caught. Finally, he said his wife had been in a constant swoon since learning of Percy's death, and he feared she would be permanently damaged by the experience.

John Platt gave the newspapers a summary account of his actions on Monday night and suggested to them that the murderer was in all likelihood a stranger to Havant. Dr Bond also spoke briefly to reporters. He told them that the boy had 'bled to the extent of fully a quart'. In the doctor's view the implement used in the attack was a knife or a dagger of some sort. As he had not yet seen the pocket

---

42 *Hampshire Telegraph*, 12 September 1885.

knife found on Monday night he could not say if this was the kind of weapon that might have produced the wounds to the lad's throat, but from its description he supposed it could have been.

Robert Husband, too, was persuaded to talk to the press. He described how his father had sent him to the Pallant on an errand and how he had watched in horror as Percy was attacked up against the garden wall of the Manor House. He said it was very dark at the time but he distinctly saw the form of a man and a boy. He shouted out 'Murder!' as loud as he could and the man ran off. He was perhaps twenty-five yards away when the attack took place.

The Reverend Samuel Spurgeon was a genial old gentleman, a Baptist minister and a preacher at the Dissenting Chapel in the Pallant. He was also headmaster of the Manor House Academy which he ran with his two sons, Thomas and George. It was a private boarding school for around fifteen to twenty boys aged between ten and sixteen, offering a sound education in the Sciences and Art with religious training. Diet was unlimited and of the finest quality. The school stood in extensive grounds and boasted a covered playground, two tennis courts, and a meadow for recreation. Obviously the welfare of his charges was uppermost in the Reverend's mind: he told a representative from the *Portsmouth Evening News* that he knew nothing of the sad affair until Tuesday morning when his son apprised him of events the previous night. He offered the opinion that the recent series of cold-blooded atrocities in London (i.e. the Jack the Ripper murders) might have inspired someone living locally to copy his deeds.

These sentiments were echoed in the *Hampshire Post* a few days later:

> In every town there are persons of mature age, and presumably not insane, who do not hesitate to acknowledge themselves disciples [of the Ripper]; and even in Whitechapel itself men of intelligence, and of apparent respectability, have been detected proclaiming their identity with the butcher, and glorying in the consternation which they have produced.[43]

---

43   'The Havant Murder', *Hampshire Post*, 30 November 1888.

Small groups of men and women congregated in the Pallant all day to discuss the tragedy. Strangers were subjected to intense scrutiny. Most children seemed to have bunked off school and could be seen running up and down the Pallant and chasing each into the yard at the back of the Bear Hotel. Reporters were keen to quiz them about little Percy. He was a quiet, shy sort of lad, they said. Well-liked by all his schoolmates, good at drawing, but sometimes picked on for no reason by older boys.

Shortly after nine o'clock on Tuesday morning Sergeant Knapton and Superintendent Kinshott went round to Robert Husband's house in North Street to question the boy for the second time. They wanted to know if he could tell them anything more about what he'd seen on Monday night.

Robert's original description of the man he'd seen assaulting Percy was fairly vague. Now, after a good night's rest (or after coaching from his father, some people would later allege) he found he could remember a host of other details.

'I heard a boy crying out,' he said, 'and I saw a man – a tall man – with a dark coat and a light patch let in the back.' He described a strap running diagonally across the man's chest from the left shoulder with something like a satchel suspended from his wrist on the right side. He also wore a top hat, he said. He remembered the sound of stones being scuffed on the ground as Percy futilely resisted the attack.

This is the second of at least four or five conflicting accounts Robert would give of his actions on Monday night. Perhaps he was shocked and traumatised by the frightful scenes he'd witnessed so that some form of memory disturbance was to be expected. Or else he was embellishing and exaggerating his story out of schoolboy braggadocio. Or he was simply lying.

In version one (told to Sergeant Knapton at the scene of the crime on Monday night) he said he was standing over by the gas lamp beside Pallant House at the end of the lane leading into the Pallant when he heard a 'gurgling noise' and saw Percy being attacked about twenty-five yards away in the shadow of the school wall.

Now, in version two (told to Sergeant Knapton and Superintendent Kinshott on Tuesday morning) he stated he was just leaving Mr Farnden's house in the Pallant when he witnessed the crime. He also provided additional details concerning the assassin's appearance which seemed designed to make him resemble more closely the Whitechapel fiend.

Both police officers felt they hadn't yet heard the full story from Robert. They would continue their enquiries later, but right now they had other matters to deal with such as the fallout from the Thomas Clarke fiasco.

Late on Tuesday morning Thomas Clarke was finally brought before Captain Boyd and Mr J.E. Cox at a special sitting of the county magistrates. He'd been in police custody for seventeen hours. He'd not been given any food on Monday night and he'd turned his nose up at the mug of tea and the two slices of stale bread and butter offered him for breakfast.

Superintendent Kinshott and Sergeant Knapton were present in court. It was not their finest hour. There was no evidence whatsoever against Clarke. He hadn't been anywhere near the Pallant on Monday evening. All he'd done was dash up North Street to catch a train. Sergeant Knapton had clearly acted precipitously when he arrested the man on suspicion of being involved in the murder, and he'd treated the prisoner disrespectfully by frogmarching him down the high street in front of jeering crowds. Sergeant Knapton told the magistrates that 'there was a deal of excitement going on at the time, and I was anxious to save time for other purposes, and thought it better to detain Clarke until I had a better opportunity of ascertaining the truth of his statements'. The clerk of the court opined that 'it was rather a mistake to take a man into custody before you have made full enquiries'.

At any rate, Clarke was discharged and allowed to leave the court at midday.

At the same sitting, Captain Boyd and J.E. Cox dealt with 'a strange looking man' who had been charged with 'wandering abroad while in an unsound mind'. Sergeant Knapton provided the details. The man, who gave the name of Edwin Rutter, had been seen on Monday afternoon – the day of the murder – acting in a suspicious manner on the road from Cosham to Havant. He seemed to be avoiding the notice of passersby by jumping over a hedge whenever anyone approached. Knapton went off in search of the man and on finding him 'formed the opinion, from his general appearance and strange demeanour, that he had recently escaped from some institution'. Boyd and Cox briefly conferred, and the prisoner was remanded for psychiatric examination.[44]

Throughout the day a steady flow of curious townsfolk had been filing into the police station to examine the pocket knife. But tracing its owner was by no means a simple matter. Several people thought the knife resembled one owned by the father, but this horrible suspicion was quickly discounted; others thought the weapon may have belonged at one time to Robert Husband or to his elder brother George, or to an acquaintance of an acquaintance of the Husband brothers. One man, after inspecting the knife closely, believed he could identify the owner and gave the police a name, but subsequent enquiries uncovered a second, almost identical knife, with similar damage to the smaller blade.

The *Hampshire Post* criticised the police for exclusively exhibiting the knife at the police station: they believed the knife was so obviously the property of a small boy it ought to have been shown around all the schools in Havant and the owner determined that way.[45] But just to complicate matters, not everyone thought the knife was the murder weapon: some people wondered at the unexpected ease with which Thomas Spurgeon had apparently located the knife right outside his garden gate despite hundreds of people having passed the spot earlier in the evening without seeing anything. And they remarked also on the condition of the knife: it was covered in blood, admittedly, but was it Percy's blood? Was it even human

---

44   As in the case of Thomas Clarke, Sergeant Knapton can be faulted for acting precipitously and forming hasty judgments. Medical reports on Rutter's mental health proved satisfactory, and the prisoner was released without charge. See 'A Suspicious Stranger', *Hampshire Telegraph*, 1 December 1888.

45   *Hampshire Post*, 30 November 1888.

blood? And surely, if the knife had been lying in the rain for nearly three hours, why hadn't the blood washed off? Why was there no mud on the blades or on the handle when Spurgeon had found it? These were worrying questions.

A correspondent signing themselves 'An Anxious One' wrote to one of the local newspapers to raise a wider concern:

A JUVENILE JACK THE RIPPER

Hearing children's voices outside my window, I looked out and saw four little children, varying in age from two to five, discussing what the play should be. The oldest proposed 'Jack the Ripper' and said 'I will be Jack. I haven't a knife to stab you, but my slate will do'.

Do you not think it would be advisable for parents to keep such knowledge away from their little ones?[46]

Identifying the owner of the pocket knife was clearly a priority for Sergeant Knapton, but other lines of enquiry demanded his attention as well. The strange man seen hurrying away on the Brighton train just minutes after the murder was committed was one lead that needed following up. Information had also reached the police concerning a suspicious character who had been staying at a hotel in Emsworth for several days and who had travelled to Havant on the morning of the murder but not returned. Items of his luggage remained uncollected at the hotel. His behaviour was so peculiar the hotel staff were inevitably referring to their guest as The Ripper. A later version of this story – almost certainly groundless – had the mysterious guest approaching the hotel, shaking off a pursing crowd, and disappearing in the direction of Chichester.

As dusk fell the streets became practically deserted. Men made their way home from work or strolled to the nearest beerhouse, but there were no women or children to be seen anywhere.

At ten past six, exactly twenty-four hours after Percy had been murdered, Sergeant Knapton and Detective Inspector Lawler went to the Pallant to conduct a little practical experiment. Knapton, who was wearing a light coat, stood at the murder spot under the Manor

---

46   *Portsmouth Evening News,* 3 December 1888.

School wall while his colleague positioned himself at the entrance to Mr Farnden's house (about 38 yards away). In the second of his statements to the police, Robert Husband had claimed that he saw a man attacking Percy from this vantage – he said he could see a light patch set in the back of a dark coat, a chest strap, a satchel, a top hat like Jack the Ripper wore. But when Inspector Lawler looked out across the Pallant, he couldn't see Inspector Knapton at all, let alone distinguish his clothing. He couldn't see anything further than a few feet in front of him.

Then it started raining heavily, driving everyone off the streets, including the two policemen.

8

The Ripper's Pal

On Wednesday morning, 28 November, Mr Edgar Goble, the coroner for Hampshire, opened the inquest into the death of Percy Searle. The setting was the boardroom of the Havant Workhouse on the north side of West Street. Among the thirteen jurors were Mr John Arter, ironmonger and whitesmith, Mr E. J. Stent, of the prominent parchment-making family, Mr Thorburn Stallard, and Mr James Agate: they were all eminently respectable tradesmen and professional middle-class people, and they all knew each other socially as well as through their various municipal and civic activities. Mr Arter was chosen as foreman.

The jury followed the coroner into the mortuary to view the deceased. At one time the mortuary had been within the workhouse itself, but recently it had been moved to a detached spot in the kitchen gardens. Here, inmates grew their own vegetables, and there was a pigsty in an adjacent field. Visits to the mortuary were never popular with jurors: in 1888, at an inquest on one of the inmates, it was reported that

> The offensive smell at the workhouse mortuary elicited expressions from the jury that it should be properly ventilated.[47]

Percy was covered with a sheet which had been drawn up to the top of his chest, although the body hadn't been undressed yet. His head inclined slightly to the left; the forehead and hair were caked in dried mud, and the lower part of the face was slathered in blood,

---

47 Quoted in Robert West, *The Havant Union Workhouse* (Havant Borough Council, 2015), p. 16.

but the neck had been partially washed clean of blood and dirt so that the gaping wound just below the right ear could be clearly seen by the jurors. His hands, which were clenched, were also bloody, 'as though in his last agony the poor little sufferer had attempted to check the flow of blood'.[48] Percy's cap and the blood-stained parcel of shirting he had collected for his mum rested on a bench next to the body. The whole scene must have presented a piteous spectacle.

The boardroom was rather small and cramped, so after viewing the body the coroner decided to move the inquest to the magistrates' court just a short distance away further down West Street, next to the police station. Only a few spectators were admitted into court and witnesses were asked to wait in an anteroom until they were called to give evidence. Captain Boyd, who on Monday evening had walked through the Pallant moments before Percy was attacked, was present in court, occupying a seat alongside the coroner.

The first to give evidence was Mr Robert Searle, who identified the deceased as his son. He told the court Percy would have been nine next April. He had last seen him alive at dinner time on Monday when he had been in his usual health. He was a quiet, inoffensive boy not given to quarrelling. He couldn't think of anyone who had reason to hurt his son, and so far as he knew no one held a grudge against the family either. When he first heard that a child had been murdered in the Pallant, he thought it was another of his sons, Herbert, but rushing to the scene he discovered Percy lying there in the road.

The next witness was fifty-one-year-old Dr Florio St Quintin Bond.[49] He was a house surgeon at Chichester Infirmary but he was also a registered medical practitioner with a private practice at No. 1 East Street in Havant. His unusual forename came about when his godparents opened a book at random at the christening and selected the first name they came to – 'Floriel'. But everyone called

48 *Portsmouth Times*, 1 December 1888.
49 Patricia Cornwell, in her book *Portrait of a Killer* (2002), confused Dr Florio St Quintin Bond with Dr Thomas Bond, the Westminster police surgeon who conducted the autopsy on Mary Jane Kelly, the last of the 'canonical' victims of Jack the Ripper. This error has been corrected in the revised and updated edition of her book, *Ripper: The Secret Life of Walter Sickert* (2017).

him Frank.

He described how he was summoned to the Pallant on Monday evening around 6.30 pm. He found Percy lying in a semi-supine position on the road next to the Manor School wall. He was surrounded by a large pool of blood issuing from wounds in the neck. He estimated Percy had been dead perhaps a quarter of an hour. Dr Bond hadn't yet conducted a full post-mortem on the body, but he had examined the injuries carefully and was able to present some preliminary findings:

> There are three wounds. I should say the cause of death was haemorrhage caused by those wounds. The most severe wound was a punctured gash behind the angle of the right lower jawbone. In all probability the wound penetrated a large blood vessel in the neck. The wounds had apparently been inflicted by a sharp instrument and considerable force must have been used.[50]

The knife recovered from the murder scene was then handed to the witness, and Dr Bond offered the opinion that the injuries he was describing might well have been caused by just such a weapon. Mr Arter asked the doctor if he could tell how the fatal wound was executed – was it with an upward or downward thrust of the knife? 'Downwards and inwards' came the confident reply. He continued:

> On the left side of the middle line of the neck I found a small wound, apparently a mere abrasion. On the right side there is a similar wound which has penetrated the skin. These wounds were across the throat. I should assume that they were inflicted by some person attempting to cut the throat across, neither of which wounds would prove fatal. The punctured wound on the right side of the neck is about three inches in depth, and corresponds exactly with the length of the blade of the knife produced.
>
> The direction of the wounds is from left to right, as if inflicted from behind by a right-handed person... It looks as though the murderer at first made an attempt to cut the throat, and failing in that, drew up his knife and plunged it downward, inflicting the fatal wound. It

---

50 Inquest deposition of Dr Florio St Quintin Bond, 28 November 1888. See the client papers of Longcroft and Green (Havant solicitors), Hampshire Record Office, reference 96M92/C14.

appears as though the knife has been forced in and torn out. It is not a clean cut like a razor cut, but more like the cut from a bayonet.[51]

The doctor could not be certain, but he felt the victim had been standing when the wounds were inflicted because the blade had been drawn across the throat. He did not think the attacker would necessarily have got blood on his hands or wristbands. In all likelihood, he said, the knife was drawn out quickly and the hand removed before the blood started spurting.

The coroner then asked if a boy as well as a man could have inflicted the wounds. 'Yes,' answered Dr Bond. 'I think a boy would have sufficient strength to do it.'

Mr Chigwell, another of the jurymen, asked as a matter of formality if the injuries could have been self-inflicted. No, said Bond. The mortal wound could not have been self-inflicted.

In reply to a question from the coroner, the doctor told the court that the light from the gas lamp situated at the end of the Pallant fell about 8 yards short of the spot where the body was lying. The body was therefore in total darkness, and it was raining, both of which hampered his examination at the scene.

Mr Searle was briefly recalled. He said he had never seen Percy carrying a pocket knife, nor had he ever seen the knife produced in court.

John Platt, of North Street in Havant, was the next person to give evidence. He related how he had passed through the Pallant on Monday evening at around twenty minutes past six. It was very dark and pouring with rain. He described how Robert Husband had run up to him and told him about a small boy being murdered by the school wall, and how they had walked back up the Pallant together. Platt knew Percy by sight and to speak to at times, and he faltered as he recounted how the child had died in his arms. Percy's clothes were covered in mud and he judged a scuffle had taken place before the boy was overpowered. He'd told Robert to run off and quickly fetch the police, but it transpired the boy had simply gone home for his tea. He described calling round at Robert's house to bring him back for questioning by Sergeant Knapton. He said the boy had just washed his hands and was wiping them dry with a towel hanging on the door.

Sergeant Knapton then spoke to the court, describing his actions at the crime scene. Perhaps wishing to allay public fears of a sexual prowler, he emphasised that Percy's neckerchief was not undone, nor his clothing disarrayed. He recounted how Mr Spurgeon later handed him the clasp knife, and he summarised the two statements he had taken from the accused boy.

Other witnesses were still waiting to be called, among them Robert Husband, but after conferring with Superintendent Kinshott the coroner announced that he proposed to bring the inquest to a close for the day. He wished to give the police more time to continue their investigations, plus Dr Bond had still to complete his post-mortem examination which might throw additional light on these tragic events. The inquest was therefore adjourned till Tuesday morning, 4 December. The jurors and the witnesses were bound in the sum of £10 each to appear on that date.

While her husband was giving evidence at the inquest, Mrs Searle was speaking to press reporters at Bug's Row, or at least she was trying to. Overwhelmed with sorrow, she sat in a low chair beside the fire, resting her head on her arm, surrounded by relatives and sympathising neighbours. The only person who did not seem affected by recent events was four-year-old Sydney, who continued to run noisily around the front room. Percy was a quiet little fellow, she told the newspapermen. He enjoyed painting and drawing pictures. She did not believe he was capable of reading sensational literature or playing at murders with the other boys.[52] In a shaking voice, she alluded to a disagreement a few weeks previously between her boys and the Husband boys over the supply of coal. It seemed a trifling matter, but the pressmen eagerly scribbled down the details, sensing that something important was being revealed.

52   See *Portsmouth Times*, 1 December 1888.

Mr Arthur Fogden was the proprietor of a drapers and outfitters shop at 11 High Street in Emsworth. On Wednesday morning, just as the inquest was beginning, he opened his shop as usual and was puzzled to see a plain brown envelope lying in his post box; it wasn't addressed to anyone in particular and had obviously been delivered furtively overnight. He was shocked by its contents:

> On the envelope being opened it was found to contain a square piece of paper upon which was a rough illustration of a man brandishing a knife in his hand and striking at a woman, who is depicted as exclaiming 'Oh dear!' At the top of the sketch was the following 'Mr Lockyear, I am not Jack the Ripper, but I am Jack the Ripper's pal. I have done a murder or two, but the next one I intend to do will be a woman at Emsworth. Look out'[53]

The *West Sussex Gazette* claimed that the text of the letter read:

> 'I am not Jack the Ripper, but his pal. I killed the boy at Havant and shall do for a woman at Emsworth next.'[54]

A 'rude drawing of a man killing a woman' illustrated the note.

The 'Mr Lockyear' referred to in this letter was Fred William Lockyear, the Emsworth postmaster. He knew all about Jack the Ripper: only the day before he, too, had received a letter from the killer, sent directly to his home and personally addressed to him. It contained drawings of the recently-resigned Metropolitan Police Commissioner Sir Charles Warren, the Home Secretary Henry Matthews, and a few other policemen, along with the stark warning message 'We intend to get the best of them'.

Both missives were quickly dismissed by the *Portsmouth Times* as being 'in all probability the handiwork of some leisured idiot who thinks he is playing off a capital practical joke',[55] yet the Emsworth letters (or the 'Ripper's Pal correspondence' as they came to be

---

53   Ibid.
54   *West Sussex Gazette*, 29 November 1888.
55   *Portsmouth Times*, 1 December 1888.

known) are important for several reasons.[56]

Firstly, they are interesting in their own right as examples of the kind of communications sent by Jack the Ripper (or persons claiming to be Jack the Ripper) in the first weeks and months after the Whitechapel murders. Many hundreds of such letters were received by the police and local press: in their definitive work on the Jack the Ripper letters, Stewart Evans and Keith Skinner estimate there are around 300 letters in the official police files that were 'signed' by the Ripper,[57] although countless more were sent directly to local dignitaries, to the Fleet Street offices of the national press, and to the news desks of provincial newspapers and other organisations. At the height of the Jack the Ripper frenzy, approximately 1,000 letters each week were being received by the police alone.[58] The majority of these letters were viewed as the work of cranks, attention-seekers, or plain nuisances. Even the most notorious of these letters – the 'Dear Boss' letter which used the name 'Jack the Ripper' for the first time, and the 'From Hell' letter which contained a portion of a human kidney supposedly taken from one of the victims – are considered by most commentators today to be hoaxes. The Emsworth letters, however, are particularly notable because, as we have seen, they contained illustrations and sketches.[59] Roughly one in ten of all letters supposedly sent by Jack the Ripper included visual elements – red ink penmanship, fake splashes of blood, drawings of knives, coffins, and mutilated body parts, etc.

Secondly, it is well worth asking: who wrote the Emsworth letters,

---

56   Letters signed 'Ripper's pal' (or similar) were not uniquely sent to residents of Emsworth. For example, in late November 1888 a Nottingham man received a letter from 'Jack the Ripper's Pal' threatening to resume his murder spree among the 'filthy dens' of Whitechapel. He claimed he had been taught his hideous calling by a Bavarian man he met on board a steamship returning to England from Colorado (see *Belfast Telegraph*, 26 November 1886).

57   Stewart P. Evans and Keith Skinner, *Jack the Ripper: Letters From Hell* (London: Sutton Publishing, 2001), p. 199.

58   Donald Rumbelow, *The Complete Jack the Ripper* (London: Penguin, 1988).

59   Dirk C. Gibson, in his study of the Ripper letters, found that roughly one in ten of them were embellished with art work. *Jack the Writer: A Verbal and Visual Analysis of the Ripper Correspondence* (Bentham Science, 2016), p. 149.

and why were they sent to Arthur Fogden and Fred Lockyear in particular? In the end, the Ripper's Pal letters may tell us nothing at all about Jack the Ripper and very little about the death of Percy Searle, but they are certainly revealing about the grudges and the long-standing disputes and petty resentments that inflicted the residents of Emsworth in the 1880s.[60]

Thirdly, we must consider the psychological effect of these letters on a community already whipped into a state of febrile apprehension by lurid newspaper speculation about Jack the Ripper, by Robert Husband's description of a Ripper-style figure disappearing into the night, and by stories already coming out of Emsworth of a mysterious Jack the Ripper hotel guest. In such a climate of suspicion and dread, the letters from Jack the Ripper (or his pal) threatening to extend his activities along the south Hampshire coast will have rendered superficially plausible the connection between the Whitechapel butcheries and the Havant murder.

In fact, the Emsworth letters were not an isolated incident. In recent weeks the police had received several letters from Jack the Ripper (or similar) threatening to murder children or announcing his plans to switch operations to the Portsmouth area, or both.

On 6 October a letter was sent to Metropolitan Police Commissioner Charles Warren from someone signing themselves 'The Whore Killer'. It stated:

> If I cant get enough women to do I shall cut up men, boys, & girls. Just to keep my hand in practice. Ha! Ha![61]

Just over a week later, on 15 October, another letter arrived at Scotland Yard from 'Jack Ripper':

> ... I am going to take my Knife with me it is nice and sharp & I will kill 10 more mid-ages women and 8 children the oldest shall be 18.[62]

On 14 November, a sick, boastful letter from 'Jack the Whitechapel

---

60   See Interlude: The Ventriloquist, the Butcher, and the Dying Child.
61   Gibson op. cit. p. 49.
62   Gibson op. cit. p. 52.

Ripper' was discovered outdoors in Plumstead in south-east London:

> Dear Boss I heard last week that you had caught me but you will find I am not yet you will hear of me and my work again I am going to commit 3 more 2 girls and a boy about 7 years old this time I like ripping very much especially women because they don't make a lot of noise.[63]

Five days before Percy's murder – on Wednesday 21 November – Mr Thomas Saunders, the presiding magistrate at the Thames Police Court in London, received a letter purporting to come from 'Jack the Ripper'. Chillingly, the envelope bore the Portsmouth postmark. The *Portsmouth Evening News* of 22 November and the *Portsmouth Times* of 24 November published the full text of the letter:

> 'No. 1, England, 1888
>
> 'Dear Boss, – It is no good for you to look for me in London, because I am not there. Don't trouble yourself about me till I return, which will not be very long. I like the work too well to leave it long. Oh, it was such a jolly job the last one. I had plenty of time to do it properly. Ha! Ha! The next lot I mean to do with a vengeance – cut off their head and arms. You think it is a man with a black moustache. Ha! ha! ha! When I have done another you can catch me, so good bye, dear Boss, till I return. – Yours, 'JACK THE RIPPER.'

Earlier that same morning, a tradesman in Hanover Street, close to the Portsmouth dockyard, was opening his shop when he discovered the words 'Jack the Ripper is in Portsmouth, signed 'Jack the Ripper.'' written in chalk on his shutters. According to the *Portsmouth Times*:

> Without a moments hesitation the writing was expunged, and nothing more was thought of the matter until Mr Saunders, a metropolitan police magistrate, announced that he had received a letter from, it would appear, the individual who 'embellished' the shutters. It is therefore obvious that there is some lunatic at large in the borough, and the sooner he is in safe custody the better.[64]

On the same day Percy was murdered, an unknown penman threatened to kill 'some young youth':

---

63   Gibson op. cit. p. 115.
64   *Portsmouth Times*, 24 November 1888.

> Just a line to tell you that I shall do another murder on some young youth such as printing lads who work in the City... I shall do them worse than the women I shall take their hearts/and rip them up the same way ... I will atack [sic] on them when they are going home.[65]

Yet another letter was received a few days after the murder by Mr George Fellows, editor of the *Isle of Wight Herald*, published in Cowes:

> Cowes was in a state of excitement on Thursday night [30 November] when it was noised abroad that Mr G Fellows, the editor of a local paper, had received a letter from Jack the Ripper, stating his intention of carrying on his malicious practices in Cowes. On inquiry it appears that the letter was signed 'An Avenger', and the writer stated that he has come to Cowes, and that he intends following up his vengeance as before on a certain class. The envelope bears the Cowes postmark, the writing on it being entirely different from that of the letter. The affair is, of course, treated as a hoax.[66]

Weeks had passed since the last murder in Whitechapel, yet the police were still no nearer to catching the culprit; in the meantime Jack the Ripper had become the focus for all manner of threats and anxieties in the country and his letters, with their sick graveyard humour and crude sexual innuendo, served to perpetuate his legend and keep him in the public eye.

But the senior police officers investigating the murder of Percy Searle weren't the least bit interested in Jack the Ripper or in the hoax letters or in the 'tall dark man' theory. Their suspicions were pointing in a different direction entirely.

Enquiries were continuing to trace the owner of the pocket knife found at the scene. Some intelligence had come through, as yet unconfirmed, that the knife may at one time have belonged to a youth called William Stevens, who worked at the Smiths & Son's bookstall

65 Stewart P. Evans and Keith Skinner, *Jack the Ripper: Letters From Hell* (London: Sutton Publishing, 2001), p. 265.
66 *Portsmouth Times*, 1 December 1888.

at Havant railway station. On Thursday last, Stevens may possibly have given the knife to George Husband, the brother of Robert.

On Wednesday afternoon, Sergeant Knapton, Superintendent Kinshott and Sergeant Urry went round to see Robert Husband again. This time they were interested in the clothes he was wearing. They noticed what appeared to be spots of blood on the right wristband of his shirt, although Knapton couldn't be certain if it was human or animal blood. Kinshott asked Robert to account for the stains. Robert hesitated for half a minute before turning his hands over to show the police officers two small scratches on the front of his wrist. 'That's how it came, sir,' he said. Robert's father backed his son up, mentioning he had had a little pimple there.

But Sergeant Knapton thought the grazing looked several days old and barely sufficient to account for the blood stains. He left the house for a short while, presumably to confer with other senior colleagues, leaving Superintendent Kinshott and Sergeant Urry to continue their questioning of the boy.

The circumstantial evidence was certainly mounting up against Robert. He had plainly been lying when he said he saw a man attacking Percy from Mrs Farnden's front door – from that position the murder spot was in complete darkness. He had lied when he said he heard the scuffling of stones as Percy resisted his attacker – there was no gravel or loose stones in that part of the Pallant. And then there was his own suspicious behaviour – his failure to summon the police, his urgent hand-washing just after the murder. Also, it had emerged that Robert was the youth who had stepped forward to fiddle with Percy's limbs when Martha Burrows was positioning Percy on her mortuary cart – was that a kindly gesture brought on by sorrow, or some darker, sickening act of necrophilia? It seemed the murder weapon could be traced to the Husband family, and now there was blood stain evidence (if blood it was) on Robert's clothes.

Knapton returned and after communicating with Superintendent Kinshott he touched Robert lightly on the shoulder, and in the presence of his stepmother and father said to him,

'Robert, I now charge you with the murder of Percy Knight Searle on Monday night last.'

Robert burst into tears and replied, 'I never did it.'

According to several newspapers (such as the *Star* of 6 December 1888) Robert's father reacted to the arrest of his son by saying to Sergeant Knapton, 'If ever I see a person committing a murder I'll be buggered if I say anything about it'.

Sergeant Knapton asked Mrs Husband to hand over the towel Robert had used on Monday night to dry his hands after returning home. Mrs Husband fetched it but said it had been washed since then.

Robert was then escorted up North Street and through the recreation ground fields to the police station, where initially he refused to hand over his scarf. Knapton noticed that this garment, too, was marked with possible blood stains.

Robert was locked in a cell. He sobbed bitterly and refused the meal that was offered him at tea-time. The aperture in the cell door through which food was passed was left open for him all evening so that the light from the gas lamp in the corridor outside would shine into the cell. In the evening his father paid him a brief visit, and after he had gone, Robert continued crying well into the midnight hours.

Earlier that afternoon Knapton returned once again to Robert's home to take possession of the remaining items of clothing worn by Robert on the night of the murder. He took away with him a shirt, a jacket, a pair of knickerbockers, a pair of stockings, and a cap. There was also a pocket handkerchief carried by Robert on Monday. It was itself of a dark red colour, but it bore staining, too – dark red stains on a dark red piece of cloth.

At six o'clock that evening the skies were clear and the stars shone brightly. Once more, a group of men were gathered in the Pallant to repeat the practical tests conducted by Knapton and Lawler the previous night. There was Mr Stephenson, the Deputy Chief Constable of Hampshire (described by the *Portsmouth Times* as the *beau ideal* of an experienced and cautious police officer), Superintendent Kinshott, Sergeant Knapton, a Mr Hellyer of Havant, and Mr Arter, the foreman of the jurors at the inquest. One senses a slightly jubilant almost festive mood amongst them: Sergeant Knapton and Superintendent Kinshott waved their arms at each other from across the Pallant as if signalling by semaphore. Mr Arter rolled up his coat to expose a freshly laundered clean white shirt sleeve and pulled it open across the chest to reveal his shirt front. Another juryman, Mr James Agate, was also in attendance: he had brought along a white dog which leapt on the lead, presumably revelling in this exciting new game in the dark. Even then, in the fairer weather conditions and with the extra illumination from the night sky, it was still too dark to see across the Pallant. On such evidence – waves in the dark, a white shirt sleeve, a pale dog – might hang a boy's life.

Much later that night, Mr Husband was interviewed by a correspondent from the *Portsmouth Evening News*. He said his son was with him all day working in the coal yard. He was only gone a few minutes to collect 3d from Mr Farnden. When he returned home he was shocked and frightened by what he'd seen in the Pallant, as any boy would be. There was no blood on him at all. He willingly returned to the Pallant to be questioned by the police sergeant. He'd told the officer exactly what had happened; he'd told him all about the man he'd seen in a top hat scurrying off across the Fair Field. He didn't allow his boys to play with knives. His son was innocent.

Interlude

The Ventriloquist, the Butcher and the Dying Child

Fred Lockyear came from East Devon originally. He worked for a while as a telegraph operator at Southampton before moving to Emsworth in 1877 to take up his appointment as local postmaster. He threw himself with vigour into the social life of the community, getting involved in civic affairs and making a name for himself as a talented and versatile stage performer. His 'Funny Festivities' routine consisted of comedy magic, ventriloquism, mind-reading experiments, and solo recitals on the fairy harp, banjo and musical goblets.[67] He developed a version of the act suitable for Sunday School audiences, so there is every chance he may have performed in front of Percy and his brothers at some point or other. In 1883 he wrote a little booklet called *The Practical Ventriloquist*,[68] which sold rather well. That may be him on the cover, a handsome, well-groomed fellow with a fine moustache that doubtless helped conceal the movements of the upper lip during his voice-throwing routine.

Yet Mr Lockyear was not a totally likeable man. The genial children's entertainer had a cruel, vindictive streak. Beneath the wacky comedy magic there was an unsavoury personality.

He served on the committee of the Emsworth Regatta. In 1880 the Hampshire coroner accused him of being 'hard-hearted and inhuman' when he allowed the event to continue after a fatal accident involving one of the vessels. He was rebuked for 'allowing

---

67   *Portsmouth Evening News*, 3 January 1881 & 22 December 1883.
68   Fred W. Lockyear, *The Practical Ventriloquist* (London: Hart & Co, 1883).

boats to sail nearly over the same spot where [a] lifeless corpse was lying'.[69]

In June the following year, he wrote a rather unpleasant letter to the *Hampshire Advertiser* describing in detail a protracted fight he had witnessed between a mouse and a snake. He seemed obscurely excited by the fact that the mouse had bitten off an inch and a half of the snake's tail, which, as he phrased it, 'still pulsated' in the rodent's jaws.[70]

In February 1885 he mirthlessly pursued a vexatious civil action against an auctioneer from Stratford who had sold him two broken ventriloquist automata the year before.[71] The story goes that Lockyear turned up at the county court with the dummies in a hamper, intending to call them as witnesses. He won this case and the auctioneer was ordered to reimburse the plaintiff £2 12s. 6d. We can imagine Lockyear smirking rather unpleasantly outside the courthouse, although maybe he had perfected the technique of smirking without moving his lips.

Lockyear wasn't a stranger to the legal system. In March 1883 he had witnessed an injured bull being driven past the post office. It was practically lame from a swollen leg and a missing hoof. Blood was streaming from the damaged foot. The bull hobbled on a little further before keeling over in the road, exactly opposite the grand driveway of Emsworth House, the imposing residence of magistrate Charles Boyd. As we have seen, Captain Boyd was in the submarine corps, engaged in classified research into underwater ballistic missile systems; his military training exerted itself, and he went outside and immediately took control of the situation. Aided by police sergeant William Russell, who had just arrived on the scene, he gravely examined the injured bull and began taking measurements of the blood markings on the road.

The owner of the bull and the herdsboy who had driven the animal through the town were duly charged with animal cruelty. When the

69 *Hampshire Telegraph*, 18 September 1880.
70 *Hampshire Advertiser*, 8 June 1881.
71 *Portsmouth Times*, 19 February 1885.

case came up at the Havant Petty Sessions, Lockyear was one of the witnesses called to testify to the ill-treatment of the bull. He gave a slavering performance, full of gratuitous bloodthirsty details. But astonishingly, in the run up to the court case, no one had thought to ask the herdsboy, Charles Yateman, how exactly the animal had injured itself. It was easily proved that the bull had been in fine health that morning and had simply damaged its hoof when it blundered through a hedge: it was a typical 'degloving' injury that occurs all the time with cattle. Captain Boyd and the police looked a trifle foolish (they'd look foolish again during the Percy Searle murder investigation), and Lockyear's evidence was ridiculed. The case was rightly dismissed.[72]

From that day on, it seems Lockyear pursued a bizarre, indiscriminate hate campaign against butchers in the Havant and Emsworth area. He was already a satirical columnist for one of the local newspapers; now he used this platform to regularly lampoon the 'butchers of Emsworth', making them out to be a bunch of uncouth, venal buffoons, and worse.

All this came to a head in August 1886 when a butcher called William Newman violently assaulted Fred Lockyear in the Crown Inn at Emsworth. He'd had enough of Lockyear's sick jokes and his endless disparaging remarks: he punched Lockyear in the face, bloodying his nose, then struck him across the forehead, threatening to 'break his neck'. The landlord restrained Newman, and revived the unconscious Lockyear with some brandy. In September the case came before the magistrates. Lockyear may have been relieved to see the familiar figure of Captain Boyd sitting on the Bench that day. The court deliberated for some time – no doubt carefully weighing up the extent to which Lockyear's relentless baiting constituted an aggravating circumstance. Newman was fined £4 plus costs for an unprovoked and cowardly assault, and bound over to keep the peace for six months; Lockyear was prevailed upon to cease writing about the 'butchers of Emsworth' in his newspaper column.

72   *Portsmouth Evening News*, 19 March 1883.

Interestingly, Arthur Fogden, the draper, who would later receive a letter from Jack the Ripper's pal, stood surety for Newman both at the previously adjourned magistrates' hearing and as bail bondsman for his continued good behaviour.

In 1889 Lockyear left Emsworth to take up a position as postmaster at Arundel. While there, he turned to writing poetry, and in 1894 the Guildford publishers Biddle & Son brought out a small miscellany of his verse entitled *Fireside Poems*. Lockyear described it as 'a collection of impulsive inspirations reflecting human nature as it is', but the arts critic for *The Era* dismissed the work as 'commonplace' and 'unexceptionable'.[73] One of the poems, which recalls the style of George R. Sims, is 'The Conjuror and the Dying Child'. It relates how a children's magician (Lockyear himself) is summoned to the bedside of a dying boy to ease his passing with a few simple conjuring tricks. Grotesquely, Lockyear conceptualises this mise en scène as an act of murder:

THE CONJUROR AND THE DYING CHILD

A smile of contented pleasure illumined his gladdened face.
There was nobody there but the mother, the sick boy himself, and I:
It seemed such a gruesome process to thus help a child to die.
Before I commenced my programme I felt I could scarcely speak,
And I twice kissed the dear fellow on his withered and pallid cheek.
I started my funniest items – the bundle of wood from the hat,
And then I compounded a pudding with a rabbit –
he pleased was with that.
I smashed a gold watch to atoms, and the youngster
quite trembled with glee
As I burnt up a splendid kerchief which his mother
had lent to me.
I could see he was getting weaker, and so could his mother too:
'Twas murder that I was committing, but what else was I to do?
They buried the dear little fellow, but before they had
laid him away
I placed a white rose in his coffin – the one that I wore that day.

73   *The Era*, 15 September 1894.

INTERLUDE

It has made me a different man, Sir, and now, when I've
nought to do
I think of the dying child, Sir, and the way that I killed him, too.[74]

---

74   Fred W. Lockyear, *Fireside Poems* (Guildford: Biddle & Son, 1894).

9

The Boy Assassin

Most days Robert Husband helped his father in the coal yard near the bottom of North Street. He filled and weighed the sacks, loaded them onto barrows, chopped wood, and sometimes assisted his older brother George serving customers in the shop out front. It was arduous, unceasing work, especially in winter when the queues stretched up North Street almost as far as Elm Road. The yard reeked of ash and the air resounded with the scraping of shovels. At the end of the working day Robert would leave the yard smeared in a thin layer of coal dust like black cloth.

The Husband family lived in a tumbledown cottage located within the yard. Almost certainly it was tied accommodation linked to the job of coal yard keeper. The yard and cottage were hidden from the main road by the houses fronting the west side of North Street: pedestrians could reach the yard via a narrow passageway off North Street, but the main trade entrance for customers and delivery vehicles was round the back through wooden gates. The coal merchant Mr Samuel Clarke, who owned the depot and was therefore Robert Husband Sr's employer, had lived at one time at No. 32 North Street, which overlooked the yard. In June 1873 Martha Burrows took possession of the house and began running her tobacconist and carrier business from there.

The bottom end of North Street and parts of West Street were prone to flooding. Before it was culverted in 1910, the Lavant stream ran open and uncontrolled down North Street with bridges across it. Following heavy rainfall, or when the Lavant rose on the Downs, the stream would 'break', resulting in thousands of gallons of water sweeping down North Street. The ground floors of many houses, including the Husbands' cottage and Martha Burrows's home, would became submerged in flood water, exceptionally up to 18 inches deep.[75]

From her upstairs back windows, Martha will have often gazed down at Robert as he toiled among the trolleys and the heaps of coal. Robert was a surly, disrespectful child, but Martha took a shine to him. She often employed young boys, aged twelve or thirteen, to run errands for her and perhaps to assist in the collection of bodies. Maybe, under different circumstances, if his father had permitted it, Robert might one day have worked with Martha as a mortuary helper. But his destiny lay elsewhere.

Robert Husband Sr was a fairly short man at 5ft 5in, but he was heavily built and broad-shouldered with immense upper body strength. He had a full head of brown hair and a neatly-trimmed sea captain's beard streaked with salt. He worked in the coal yard twelve hours a day, Monday to Saturday, and was also expected to patrol the yard in the evenings and at night and all day Sunday to deter folk from sneaking in and grabbing a few handfuls of coal.

He was born in Wincanton in Somerset on 15 July 1836[76] but grew up in the village of Street near Glastonbury. Surrounded by meadows and small areas of peat moorland, Street was a rather sparsely populated settlement in the 1830s and 40s until it developed as a shoe-manufacturing town in the late nineteenth century. Mother and son lodged in a terrace of cottages known as Teetotal Row on the west side of the village; Rhoda worked as a shoebinder and Robert was an apprentice shoemaker. But the boy was gripped with the desire to travel, and when he turned eighteen he left home and made his way to Portsmouth.

On 24 October 1854, he joined the Royal Navy as a volunteer on board HMS *Myrmidon*. Four years later he became a sail-maker's

---

75 *Hampshire Post*, 10 January 1879.

76 Some sources suggest the Husband family had links to Truro in Cornwall, but Pigot's Commercial Directory for Cornwall has no mention of any Husband in any trade whatsoever at any period in the 1830s.

mate responsible for maintaining canvas work aboard ship.[77] He served on several vessels including HMS *Algiers* (1859–61) and HMS *Challenger* (1869–71).

Robert may have joined the navy to see the world, but from March 1871 onwards it seems he didn't travel anywhere. He served on board HMS *Asia*, a hulked ship in Portsmouth Harbour that had been converted into a shore establishment providing administrative headquarters for the Admiral Superintendent. Thus, he will have spent his final years in the Royals on dry land. He retired in November 1874 after twenty years' continuous service. His RN service record shows a hard-working, dutiful seaman.[78] He was awarded a pension of £34 12s per annum.[79]

While serving on HMS *Asia* he began courting Ellen Hammond, a twenty-year-old domestic servant who lived with her brother and his wife on Flying Bull Lane in the Cherry Garden Field district of Portsmouth.[80] This was a rapidly urbanising working-class area of the city that had developed alongside the expansion of the docks in the mid 1850s. On 6 July 1872, Robert and Ellen were married at St Mary's church in Portsea. Shortly afterwards the newlyweds set up home in Cherry Garden View, just round the corner from where Ellen's family lived. A year later, on 17 July, their first child, Jane, was born. A second child, George, arrived on 4 February 1875. With these growing family commitments, Robert may have sought work as a labourer at the dockyard where his brother-in-law worked.

A third child came along on 22 February 1877. This one was named Robert after his father and grandfather, although the family always called him Bob or Bobbie. (One day, he would be known publicly by an entirely different set of epithets – the Boy Assassin; the Youthful Ripper; the Boy Ripper.) Like his brother and sister, he was born at

---

77   Robert's father, also called Robert, was a tailor, so there was some family aptitude for work with needle and thread.

78   ADM 139/162/16156.

79   *Portsmouth Evening News,* 18 January 1889.

80   This road is supposedly named after the first balloon flight in Portsmouth around 1784, which took off from fields close by. To ensure no danger to human life, the balloon's only passenger was a bull.

Cherry Garden View, and the birth was registered by Ellen on 31 March at the Portsea Island Register Office.

Later that summer, or perhaps early in 1878, Robert Husband Sr landed the job of store keeper at Clarke's coal yard in Havant. Though Ellen may have been reluctant to leave her sister and brother-in-law behind, the Husband family relocated seven miles east along the coast, and settled into the tied cottage behind Martha Burrows' house on North Street.

There is a portrait of Mr and Mrs Husband dating from around 1878. It looks like it has been taken in the coal yard. Robert is looming over his wife who is sitting demurely with her hands folded across her lap. Ellen is staring stolidly into the camera while her husband's attention has been distracted to one side. It is a dark, rather joyless picture, as if soot from the yard has blackened the image. Ellen is twenty-seven, perhaps twenty-eight, but she looks much older.

Indeed, Ellen may already have been dying when this photograph was taken. Lately she had been suffering excruciating abdominal pains, but it was still a shock when the doctors diagnosed peritonitis. And then the fever began – nausea, vomiting, anxious breathing, and heavy dull throbbing pains in the head. She had flatulence and disgust for food. Towards the end she will have been bedridden and semi-delirious. On 16 February 1879, aged only twenty-eight, and with her husband at her bedside, she died.[81]

We can only imagine the impact these terrible events must have had on her three small children, then six, four, and two. Not just her death, but the prolonged and debilitating manner of her dying. The children will have heard her raving and picking frantically at the bedclothes. There would have been stench and shrieks of pain. As Robert grew up, would he retain any memories of his mother? Would he recall her face, or remember the sound of her voice calling him from another room? Or would it forever be the awful smells of

---

81   The attending physician was Dr Quintin Bond. The date of Ellen's death is formally recorded on her death certificate as 16 February 1879. However, Martha Burrows, in her diary, states she collected Mrs Husband's body from the coal yard on 16 January 1879.

the sickroom that brought his mother back to him?[82]

The Hammond family will have rallied round, offering practical help and emotional support to their bereaved in-laws. Maybe, too, there were concerns, privately expressed, that Robert Sr might not cope without his wife. But within weeks he was wooing twenty-one-year-old Fanny Louisa Ryves, a millwright's daughter originally from Baker Street in the Kingston area of Portsmouth but now living in the Cherry Garden Field estate.

Unconventionally, Fanny may have moved in with Robert as a sort of 'housekeeper' or children's nurse. Then, rather suddenly, on 28 December 1879, Robert and Fanny were married at the Havant Register Office. On the marriage certificate Fanny has given her age as twenty-five, but in fact she was twenty-one. Robert is listed as a widowed pensioner. Clearly, this was a wedding of expediency because three months later, in the first quarter of 1880, Fanny gave birth to Albert. Fanny may have been more religiously devout than Ellen, for Albert was to be baptised; this seems to have prompted Robert to add his elder children to the ceremony, and so Jane, George and Robert, by then seven, five and three, were finally christened, at St Faith's church in Havant on 29 August 1880.

We don't know much about Fanny. She seems to have been a fairly diffident young woman, moon-faced and matronly in appearance even in her early twenties. Robert appears to have been her first male friend of any significance. Pregnancy would be a more or less constant state for Fanny over the next sixteen years as the ever-growing Husband family took over the bottom end of North Street. Ellen was born in 1881, followed by William (1883), James (1884), Harry (1886) and Arthur (1888). With only his navy pension and the pittance he earned as a coal yard keeper, Robert will have struggled to support his family. Crammed into that small ramshackle cottage, life would have been burdensome with no privacy for the parents and few luxuries or treats for the children. Clothes would be darned

---

82 In 1894 a fever hospital opened in Potash Terrace in Havant, but far too late, of course, for Ellen. It closed in 1939.

and re-darned and handed down from one child to the next. The Husband brood will have scavenged on the fringes of the coal yard, bathing irregularly, rarely wearing a clean change of clothes.

The two oldest boys, George and Robert, as full blood siblings, may have formed a special bond that set them apart from their younger half-brothers and half-sisters.

Robert was initially a pupil at the National School in Brockhampton Lane – the same school Percy attended – but at the insistence of Fanny he later began receiving instruction at the much smaller two-room St Joseph Catholic School in West Street, adjoining the presbytery. It had fewer than 30 pupils, some of whom walked nearly five miles there and back each day to attend.[83] Robert was a bright boy, perhaps not academically gifted but 'able to read well and an intelligent scholar generally'.[84] While the 1880 Elementary Education Act had made school attendance compulsory between the ages of five and ten, on reaching eleven Robert will have been promptly taken out of school and put to work in the coal yard with his father and elder brother. His parents could ill-afford to forego the income from an extra pair of hands.

A photograph of Robert taken when he was ten and a pupil at St Joseph's shows him in his front buttoned tunic with dark bowtie and detachable white collar.[85] He is wearing a serious expression that carries with it a hint of sullenness and truculence. Probably he resents the charade of the school photograph ceremony.

He inherited his short stature from his father. Aged almost twelve

---

83 Christine Houseley, *A History of the Catholic Church in Havant* (St Joseph's Church, 134 West Street, Havant, 1975).

84 *Portsmouth Evening News*, 29 November 1888.

85 The author was Samuel Whitbread, a former baker who had turned his hand to photography in the late 1880s. He had commercial premises on West Street. In April 1887 Whitbread was sentenced to three months in prison for embezzling the monies of the Pride of Havant Oddfellows Lodge, of which he was the secretary. He subsequently resumed his career as a photographer, and on Thursday morning, 29 November, he was out in the Pallant taking pictures of the murder scene for the inquest jury. The photograph of Robert Husband was registered by Whitbread on 7 December 1888, but not before several newspapers had accessed the image and used it to create unflattering caricature drawings.

he was only 4 feet 2 inches in height. The *Portsmouth Times* described him as 'diminutive' and 'a little undergrown fellow'. When he finally appeared in court, the *Hampshire Telegraph* noted that the rail of the dock was on a level with his eyes. Indeed, although Percy was his junior by nearly four years, the two boys were almost exactly the same height. Robert's youth, his short size, and his presumed emotional frailty were repeatedly sensationalised by the newspapers covering the Havant murder. He is depicted as constantly sobbing, always in need of a chair; in an engraving entitled 'The Arrest of the Boy Husband', the *Illustrated Police News* shows Robert being escorted to the police station by two tall, burly constables. Robert is dwarfed by the officers, and one of them is holding his tiny hand in a bear-like paw, like a father guiding his tender son.[86]

In fact, Robert was a healthy, robust lad. He had been working in the coal yard for nearly a year, and was putting on muscle. He was lean and tough, strong for his size and his age. And when representatives from the *Portsmouth Evening News* and other papers began digging a little deeper into Robert's disposition, a darker, far more sinister side to his character began to emerge.

Everyone spoke about his quick, brutal temper. Lately he had been 'frequently reproved for his cruelty to animals'.[87] He was a brawler, a bully who picked on smaller boys and enjoyed hurting them. 'He wasn't content with fighting,' reported the *Evening News*, 'but would kick you after you were down.'[88] Giving evidence at the magistrates' court, John Platt described Robert as 'a daring lad who was rather given to fighting. His father had thrashed him on numerous occasions to stop him from doing harm, but he could not break him'.[89] Robert and his brother George always seemed to be involved if there was

---

86   This is dramatic licence. As we have seen, Robert was arrested by Sergeant Knapton and Superintendent Kinshott.

87   *Western Times*, 30 November 1888. Robert Husband was in the same gang as John Sparks: at the Havant Petty Sessions on Thursday 6 December, Sparks pleaded guilty to torturing a cat. He stamped on it till its eyes were hanging out before throwing the body into a hedge. *Hampshire Telegraph*, 8 December 1888.

88   *Portsmouth Evening News*, 29 November 1888.

89   *Portsmouth Times*, 1 December 1888.

trouble in the town. The night before Percy was attacked, there was an affray between rival gangs of youths in the yard behind the Bear Hotel, and the Husband lads were right in the thick of it.

Robert had cunning and a sharp instinct for survival. He could cry and pretend sorrow if it served his purpose, or he could turn nasty in a flash, meting out violence to boys much younger and weaker than himself, prolonging the punishment long after his victims were cowed and beaten. He was vicious with an unforgiving memory for wrongs real or imagined. But he was also diligent and hard-working with a reputation for singleness of purpose, and his boyish good looks will have lent him superficial charm. There were two sides to him: the cherubic Catholic schoolboy in a dickie bow and white collar grafting all day in the coal yard with his father, and the grubby young thuggish animal abuser camouflaged in coal dust, lurking in the shadows with his pocket knife. For many people, it was this second image – the Monster Boy, the hobgoblin, the Boy Assassin – that came to dominate their view of Robert in the winter of 1888.

When the *Dundee Evening Telegraph* published a picture of the alleged boy Ripper, they took Samuel Whitbread's familiar portrait of him and cruelly manipulated it, giving the cherub in bowtie and collar an ugly, sneering expression – the countenance of a murderer.[90]

THE ALLEGED MURDERER—AGED 11.

90   See *Dundee Evening Telegraph*, 6 December 1888.

10

Questions and Answers

Thursday morning broke dull and cloudy. It had drizzled overnight and more rain was expected before midday. Already the gardeners were hard at work in the Manor House grounds, pruning the gooseberry and blackcurrant bushes and sweeping the driveway clear of fallen leaves. The cows in the Fair Field had been left out all night and now they were making their way lugubriously towards the byres.

There was activity in the Pallant, too. The land surveyor Mr A.C. Lewis was preparing a new large-scale plan of the murder spot for the coroner and the inquest jury; he was taking field sketches, measuring roadway widths, and noting the position of surrounding buildings and the lines of sight from doors and windows. He paid special attention to the gas lamp outside Pallant House, calculating the range and angle of its illumination. He nodded greetings to Samuel Whitbread, who was busy taking pictures of the murder scene, also for the coroner. In 1888 Kodak brought out the first box camera ('You press the button, we do the rest!'), but Mr Whitbread preferred his trusted half-plate studio equipment.

Adding to the street theatre was Captain Charles Boyd. Accompanied by Inspector Lawler, the captain was pacing up and down the Pallant, timing his movements and taking meticulous measurements. He could now confirm that on the night of the murder he had walked through the Pallant at exactly nine-and-a-half minutes past six. He had continued on his way down what is now East Pallant towards the town hall and fifty-three paces later he had passed a man (a navvy, Captain Boyd supposed) heading in the direction of the Pallant. Captain Boyd and Inspector Lawler will have reflected gravely on the significance of this sighting, for it partly corroborated Robert's version of events. A strange man had definitely been in the Pallant when Percy was attacked and murdered.

Meanwhile, the draper Mrs Sarah Randall was seeing an unexpected boost in trade:

> That those actuated by curious rather than sympathetic motives have been attracted to Havant... is shown by the fact that several strangers to the town have made purchases at Mrs Randall's shop with the stated object of carrying away a memento of the tragic affair from the establishment where the first alarm of the murder was received.[91]

At eleven thirty that morning a special sitting of the county Bench got under way at the police court in West Street. All morning a crowd had been gathering outside the court, and when the doors were finally opened there was an almighty jostle for seats.

The courtroom was soon packed. A row of reporters stretched across the front of the gallery. All the public seats were taken, mostly by women, and spectators lined the walls at the back of the room. The tall, willowy figure of Captain Forrest, the chief constable of Hampshire, occupied a seat on the Bench between Mr William Snell, the presiding magistrate and Mr Charles Stephenson, the deputy chief constable.

Captain John Henry Forrest was a formidable and imposing character: for a quarter of a century he had ruled the Hampshire force with an iron fist: harsh, despotic, often unfair and unreasonable, he constantly berated his officers for their slackness, ineptitude and lack of imagination. A strict disciplinarian, he had a horror of filth and untidiness, and he abhorred incompetence and inefficiency. He often turned up unannounced at county police stations and flew into a tantrum if the cupboards in the dormitories weren't spotless.[92]

---

91 *Portsmouth Evening News*, 1 December 1888.
92 For details of Captain Forrest and examples of his vivid rebukes, see Ian A. Watt, *A*

Captain Boyd was also in court, although not in an official capacity since it was expected he would be called to give evidence later in the proceedings. As a justice of the peace, it felt strange for him to be sitting in the public area. He was a little out of puff, having just dashed over from the Pallant.

The murmur in the court quickly died down as Robert was ushered in.

> The boy, a little undergrown fellow, described by those who know him as an 'old-fashioned little chap', was touched on the shoulder by the police-sergeant and pointed his way into the dock near the door. He walked in firmly, without hesitation, placed his hands for a moment on the front of the dock, quickly dropped them to his sides, and then glanced round the Court with an air of quiet curiosity. His face bore traces of a severe outburst of grief, but was otherwise stolid in its calmness, and at times the lad even appeared unconcerned.[93]

His mother had insisted he wear his Sunday best. He looked quite dapper, in fact, in his dark grey tweed tunic buttoned up to the throat, offset with a red neckerchief spotted with white. In hindsight, perhaps the scarf was a mistake, since it conjured up images of Percy's torn and bloody throat. Someone must have had words because Robert didn't wear it again at later hearings. He seemed composed and relatively relaxed, although his eyes were red-rimmed and swollen from constant weeping. His face was pale and his cheeks were slightly flushed. He'd scoffed a good breakfast that morning at the station, but then he'd started complaining of severe pains in his leg, claiming he'd fallen out of bed during the night. He was in such agony he regretted he didn't think he'd be able to attend the magistrates' hearing. But the police were having none of it.

The boy's father was brought into court, and ushered to a seat next to his son George in front of the dock. He looked 'careworn and sorrow-stricken'.

History of the Hampshire and Isle of Wight Constabulary 1839–1966 (Hampshire & Isle of Wight Constabulary, 1967).

93 *Portsmouth Times*, 1 December 1888.

Mr H. Martin Green, the clerk of the court, got to his feet.

'Now, Robert Husband—is that your name?'

'Yes, sir.'

'You are charged with having, on the 26th November 1888, in the parish of Havant, in this county, feloniously and with malice aforethought, killed and murdered one Percy Knight Searle. It is proposed to take sufficient evidence now to justify a remand.'

The hearing would last for two and a half hours. Half way through, Robert was provided with a chair in the dock. He sat sideways in it, with his left arm draped over the back of the chair and his head tilted to one side into the bend of his arm. It was a mannered pose, perhaps a little too casual and insouciant for the liking of the Bench. Yet behind the studied indifference, Robert was following proceedings with keen interest:

> During the greater part of the hearing his glances were mainly directed to the witness-box, but his eyes moved with a restless frequency. Outwardly, he maintained a stolid composure from first to last.[94]

The first witness was Sergeant William Knapton. No doubt the presence of Captain Forrest and the other bigwigs put extra pressure on him. They'd be watching him carefully to see how he conducted himself, so it was important he gave his evidence clearly, accurately, and without malice or favour. He couldn't afford any more embarrassments like the fiasco earlier in the week with the deaf engineer from Portsmouth.

He told the court how on Monday night he'd been summoned to the Pallant. He described finding Percy's body in the road, and related how the prisoner had been brought to him for questioning. The court wanted more details. Had Robert's clothes been covered in blood? What condition were his hands in? But Sergeant Knapton hadn't noticed. Captain Forrest shifted in his chair. 'The prisoner held his hands straight by his sides,' said Knapton, by way of explanation. But it didn't explain anything.

94 *Hampshire Telegraph*, 1 December 1888.

Sergeant Knapton then spoke about his two visits to Robert's house on Tuesday and how he'd arrested the boy on Wednesday and secured his clothing for forensic examination. At the inquest Sergeant Knapton claimed that Robert had said he'd heard stones being scuffed on the ground as Percy resisted his attacker; now, in the magistrates' court, the police sergeant admitted he couldn't swear whether the boy had said anything about stones at all. Captain Forrest looked down and made a note in his pad.

At this stage, Robert was without legal representation. His father, however, was permitted to ask questions on his behalf. Mr Husband was clearly anxious, and perhaps intimidated by the legal pomp; he might not have fully understood his role in court and he certainly didn't understand the rules of evidence relating to cross-examination. And why should he? He was a sail-maker, a coal yard keeper. Could Mr Snell double stitch a mizzen royal and rope a new reef band in a fore-and-aft sail? He launched into a rambling general defence of his son, but the clerk stopped him.

'That is a statement. Strictly speaking you cannot ask questions, but I have no doubt the court would permit you to put any question on behalf of your son bearing upon what has been said by Sergeant Knapton.'

Mr Husband didn't understand. If he couldn't ask questions, why was he being told to put questions to the witness and then stopped from doing so? Rather weakly he said, 'I don't know anything.'

The first stirrings of public unease at the way the authorities were handling this case can perhaps be traced back to this exchange.

The next witness was Henry Shirley, the assistant at Mrs Randall's draper's shop on the corner of the Pallant and North Street. He identified the parcel of shirting produced in court as the same one that Percy had collected on Monday evening, and he told the court that ten or fifteen minutes after Percy had left the shop, Robert Husband came tearing down the Pallant on the opposite side of the road. Mr Shirley had the impression – and that's all it was, an impression – that Robert was intending going past the shop, and only stopped when he realised he'd been seen. This was a damning statement, for it implied that Robert had been guiltily fleeing the scene. Again, Mr Husband was given the opportunity to put questions to the witness. Again, he launched into a general defence of his boy. Once more he was shut down, this time by Mr Snell, the magistrate. 'You must not make a statement. Put questions to the witness.' But Mr Husband had no questions to ask, and Shirley's testimony went untested.

John Platt was up next. He repeated the evidence he had given at the inquest. He said when he went round to Robert's house the prisoner's hands were wet. The unspoken accusation hung in the air. *The Boy Ripper caught red-handed, rinsing away Percy's lifeblood.* Or was it normal behaviour for a boy who'd spent all day working in a coal yard to wash his hands before sitting down to his tea?

Then it was Mr Tom Spurgeon's turn in the witness box. He whooshed into court in his black academic gown. It was an unnecessary flourish, but no one seemed to mind. His bald head glistened with raindrops. He deposed how he'd found the knife in the street outside his gate and taken the weapon to Sergeant Knapton. And then he whooshed out.

There were several young boys waiting to give evidence. For them it meant a day out of school or unpaid time off work. For the magistrates, though, child witnesses presented all manner of legal and philosophical difficulties. Were they able to distinguish between truth and falsehood, between real and imaginary events? Did they understand the meaning of the oath? Could they comprehend the seriousness of the charges against Robert and appreciate the absolute necessity of speaking the truth? And then there were issues of suggestibility and malleability.

The police pressed on. They believed they could trace the knife back to Robert Husband, or at least to his brother George.

Henry Wheeler was fourteen and he worked as an errand boy at Mr Joseph Agate's grocery and tea dealing shop on North Street. Charlie Searle, Percy's oldest brother, also worked for Mr Agate, although his employer had granted him compassionate leave in consequence of the family's bereavement. Charlie had attended the inquest hearing on Wednesday and after the adjournment he popped into the grocer's shop and described the appearance of the bloodstained knife to his manager. Henry Wheeler overheard the conversation and immediately remarked that Robert Husband had tried to sell him a similar knife on Monday. Charlie hurried off and told Sergeant Knapton. As a result, Wheeler was shown the knife by the police sergeant and a positive identification was made.[95] His evidence in court was that on Monday morning, the day of the murder, Robert had met him in the street and tried to sell him the clasp knife for a penny. He was sure it was the same knife produced in court because he recognised the worn blade. Mr Snell wanted to be certain.

'Have you any doubt at all about the knife?'

'No, I am sure that is the knife Robert showed me.'

Henry Wheeler was then handed over to Mr Husband for cross-examination. For a moment the father seemed to grasp what was required of him.

'Where did you see my boy in the morning?'

'Standing against Mrs Burrows's, in North Street.'

'He was working with me all the forenoon, and was in the yard all day.'

[From the Clerk] 'Mr Husband, that is statement. You must ask a question.'

'He was working with me all the forenoon, and was in the yard all day, wasn't he?'

Exasperated, Mr Snell let it go.

George Husband was next to enter the witness box. He admitted that the knife belonged to him. He said he'd last had it on Sunday evening when he went for walk with his family, but the knife must have fallen out of his jacket pocket. He'd gone to whittle a stick, and the knife wasn't there.

Another young lad giving evidence was William Thomas Stevens, who worked at the bookstall at Havant railway station. He said the knife in question was his but he gave it to George Husband on

95   *Portsmouth Evening News*, 3 December 1888.

Thursday last. He was able to identify the knife by the broken small blade and because he recognised the brass name plate on the handle.

The last witness was Albert Ferrell, the thirteen-year-old son of a chimney sweep. He described himself in court as a houseboy. He said his duties involved 'cleaning knives and forks and boots and shoes'[96] for his employer. The court found this rather comical and laughed at the boy. His evidence was that on Wednesday or Thursday of last week – he couldn't be sure which day it was – Robert Husband had tried to sell him a knife for a penny, but he had no money on him.

And that completed the police case. The evidence was weak and it had been poorly presented. The main problem was that the witness statements contradicted each other. If Stevens had owned the knife up to the point when he gave it to George on Thursday, Robert couldn't have been trying to sell it to Ferrell on the same day or the day before. If George had lost the knife on Sunday, then assuming Robert hadn't found it, how can he have been trying to sell it to Wheeler on the morning of the murder? At least two of the witnesses (George and Stevens) needed to be lying or mistaken for the statements of the other two witness (Wheeler and Ferrell) to be truthful. And was it reasonable to suppose that hundreds of people (including the police) had not noticed the knife lying so conveniently right outside Tom Spurgeon's front gate, covered in fresh blood that the rain ought to have washed away?

The Bench was asked to remand the prisoner, and Mr Snell appears to have done so casually and mechanically. 'Very well,' he said. 'We will remand the prisoner till Wednesday next.' And Robert was taken back to the cells.

He bawled continually for the next few hours, out of frustration more than anything else. He clearly hadn't understood what the clerk had told him about the purpose of the hearing. Robert probably thought if he and his dad turned up and denied the charge he would be released and life would go back to normal. More than anything, it was boring being locked up in the cell. There was nothing to do. He

96   *Portsmouth Times*, December 1 1888.

wanted to be out with his mates like Charlie White, Alfie Ward, and Johnny Sparks the cat killer.

Sergeant Knapton had to visit the boy frequently during the afternoon and evening to pacify him. At length, when he was supplied with reading material, he seemed to settle down and gave his captors no more trouble. He ate heartily at dinner and tea-time.

In the afternoon, Dr Bond conducted the post-mortem on Percy's body. The mortuary facilities at the workhouse were fairly basic – just a cramped, poorly-ventilated shed equipped with wooden slabs, some drainage buckets, and a bench. There was no dissection room for autopsies, and the building was without mains water supply; water for sluicing away blood and rinsing instruments came from well pumps in the workhouse grounds.[97]

Dr Bond recorded that the body was spare and rigor mortis had set in, the lower jaw and the fingers being tightly clenched.[98] However, the examination revealed nothing of material importance; Dr Bond was not swayed from his earlier opinion that the cause of death was due to loss of blood resulting from the injuries to the neck and throat.[99] The body was placed in an elm coffin ready to be transported to the parent's home.

Later that evening, the bearers arrived at the mortuary:

> 'The removal was effected quietly at seven pm on Thursday, the coffin, which is covered with blue cloth, and ornamented with lace and white metal mountings, being carried through a bye-lane to Mr Searle's residence.[100]

The breast plate bore the inscription —

> 'Percy Searle, died November 26th, 1888, aged eight years'

---

97 Robert West, *The Havant Union Workhouse* (Havant Borough Council, 2015), p. 17.

98 Inquest deposition of Dr Florio St Quintin Bond, 4 December 1888. See the client papers of Longcroft and Green (Havant solicitors), Hampshire Record Office, reference 96M92/C14.

99 Percy's death was registered on 14 December 1888 after the inquest had reached their verdict. The death certificate gives the cause of death as 'Wilful murder against some person or persons unknown'.

100 *Hampshire Telegraph*, 1 December 1888.

Percy was taken across the fields to avoid drawing the attention of morbid crowds. The bearers will have crossed the recreation ground behind the Union Workhouse, turned right along Market Lane, and taken a footpath through the deer park to reach New Lane and Bug's Row. It must have been an unbearably sad procession, the wind tugging at the cloth and the blaze of the oil lamps signalling the coffin's steady progress across the dark fields. The coffin was placed on two kitchen chairs in the Searles' front room and draped in a tablecloth. For two nights, relatives and personal friends of the family, neighbours, and folk from town, came to pay their respects.

The coffin must have dominated the tiny front room. The lid of the coffin was left unscrewed, allowing the body to be viewed. According to the *Portsmouth Times*, 'the little fellow looked very pleasant in his prettily made coffin, and the features gave scarcely any sign of his cruel death'.[101] The corpse may have rested on a layer of sawdust to absorb moisture. Candles and flowers helped mask the unpleasant odours beginning to seep from the coffin. At night, the rats and crawling insects scurried behind the walls.

The funeral was entrusted to Mr John Staples, undertaker, of West Street. The Staples were a family firm going back three generations; son Frank was personally superintending the arrangements for Percy's service. One of the Staples children was Frederick, born in 1877, the same year as Robert Husband. In a small town like Havant, you couldn't avoid these kinds of connections and associations.

As far as practicable, many working-class families tried to set aside money for future funeral costs by contributing weekly or monthly sums into burials clubs. But it appears the Searles had no such insurance, and the family would have been unable to afford an adequate and respectable funeral for Percy. The provision of the elm coffin and its fittings, the rent of the hearse and the carriages, the hire of mourning clothes and funeral drapes, and so on, will have been well beyond the means of Mr Searle.

Almost from the start, the people of Havant gathered round to

---

101 *Portsmouth Times*, 1 December 1888.

offer support and practical help to the grieving family. The first move came from William Stewart, the projectionist at the Band of Hope meetings where Percy had revelled in the magic lantern shows. The day after the murder he wrote to the *Portsmouth Evening News*:

> 'Percy's mother is poor and has a large family. We cannot give her back her darling, but we can show our Christian sympathy by helping her to bury her little lamb. Any subscriptions sent to me, I shall be glad to hand to her.'

His appeal collected well over £5. Another correspondent, Mr George Long from Landport, collected 'penny' subscriptions from the tradesmen of the town. 'It would do a great deal of good,' he wrote, 'and no one would be the poorer.'[102] Mr John Munday of Bedhampton Lane, who on Monday night had been one of the 'volunteer detectives' scouring the countryside for Jack the Ripper, offered help in a more practical direction: he had received just over £2 from sympathising townsmen, and this sum would more than cover the expenses of the interment.[103] The Sunrise Minstrels, a charitable organisation in Havant, voted 5s. to Mr and Mrs Searle, and a musical service held at the Wesley Chapel in Portsmouth contributed £2 5s. by an offertory. Mr J. Bowles, the principal at Brougham House School in Kingston, called round in person and presented the sorrowing parents with a contribution of £1 5s. 6d. from himself and the pupils. A whip round at the game between Havant FC and local rivals the Southampton Pirates would raise twelve shillings for the appeal fund.[104] The profits from a concert to be held at the town hall the following week would also be donated to the bereaved family. An exceptionally generous undertaking came from the members of the Ancient Order of Foresters, to which Mr Searle belonged; they would relieve the family of the full costs of the funeral.

Most of the contributions came from Havant, Emsworth and Portsmouth, but money also came in from as far afield as Brighton

---

102 *Portsmouth Evening News*, 4 December 1888.
103 *Portsmouth Times*, 1 December 1888.
104 Havant lost 3–0. Mr J. Agate, one of the jurors at the inquest, played in goal.

and the capital. Mr F. Perkins of Old Jewry, London, sent a cheque for £1 with a note which read, 'It is but a poor way to show one's sympathy to those so deeply afflicted, but it is all that is left for us to do'.[105]

Wreaths and crosses began to arrive at the door of Mr and Mrs Searle, among them a beautiful display from Mrs Horrell, the matron of the Havant Workhouse. But perhaps the most touching tribute came in the form of a simple white lily wreath from the Havant National School, paid for by the children themselves from their penny subscriptions. A little card said, 'With the schoolboys' deepest sympathy'. It would take pride of place on the coffin when Percy was laid to rest on Saturday.

Of course, there was no one who begrudged the Searle family this charity or mocked the outpourings of public sympathy. But in other parts of the town, disquiet was fomenting at the way the Husband family and young Robert in particular were being treated by the police and judicial authorities. Many people thought there was no evidence against the lad at all. He was being victimised, even framed for the murder. Soon they would be reaching into their pockets to pay for the accused boy's defence fund.

105 *Portsmouth Evening News*, 4 December 1888.

11

An Old Line of Gravediggers

When Captain Forrest left Havant late on Thursday afternoon, he was in an uncharacteristically amiable frame of mind. Although the case against Robert was evidentially weak, he seemed generally satisfied with the way the police investigation was going. In consequence, he had ordered a scaling down of operations. Officers who had been drafted in for special duty on Monday and Tuesday were now starting to move out; Superintendent Kinshott had already packed his bags and returned to Fareham, while the deputy chief constable had caught the ferry back to Newport.

The evening newspapers were congratulating Sergeant Knapton and his fellow officers for their intelligence and vigilance:

> From the first the police have acquitted themselves in the face of a most difficult task. They have followed up every clue, actual and supposed with unremitting industry, and while manifesting throughout a desire not to act with undue precipitancy.[106]

Not unexpectedly, the *Portsmouth Times* were outspoken in their praise of the police:

> Of course, now that suspicion has fastened upon the boy Husband, busybodies of the soi-distant superior sort express their wonder that the fact was not ferreted out before. It should, however, be remembered that on the night of the murder the accused boy disarmed suspicion for an hour or two by setting the police on the wrong track.
>
> The police did remarkably well and credit is especially due to P.S.

106 *Portsmouth Evening News*, 29 November 1888.

Knapton for the smartness he has displayed in connection with this crime.[107]

And Havant itself was slowly getting back to normal:

Though still in a state of inward excitement, the town of Havant has to the eye of a casual beholder settled down into its customary quiet routine of daily life. In most quarters, the alarm and vague suspicion aroused by the mysterious nature of the murder have been allayed since the arrest of the boy Husband.

The theory of the foul deed having been the work of Jack the Ripper, which was from the first entertained only by a minority composed of the most nervous and credulous inhabitants, may fairly be said by this time to have been exploded.[108]

Friday morning dawned bright and clear. The clouds had lifted after an evening of rain, and winter sunshine brought a cold yellow light to the Pallant.

An early riser was Sergeant Knapton. He was catching the first train up to London for a meeting with the Home Office analyst Professor Charles Tidy. The knife and the garments worn by Robert on the night Percy was killed were going to be scientifically examined at Somerset House. If the stains on the articles proved to be blood – that is, human blood of recent origin – then the case against the accused boy would be significantly strengthened. Knapton rarely got the opportunity to visit the capital, so he will have relaxed in his compartment and enjoyed the ride through the Hampshire and Surrey countryside into Waterloo.

In contrast, Robert was grumpy and bad-tempered at daybreak. He had spent another restless night in the cells. On Wednesday he'd supposedly fallen out of bed and injured his leg; now he claimed to have banged his head while sleeping. He insisted that a visit to the doctor was needed. But the police dismissed his complaint as 'purely mythical', and indeed, after a good breakfast, Robert forgot all about his supposed injury.

With Sergeant Knapton away in London, and Constable Notton on

107 *Portsmouth Times*, 1 December 1888.
108 *Portsmouth Evening News*, 29 November 1888.

duty in the town, the station was eerily quiet. It was an ideal time for Robert to put into action his daring escape plan. The evening before he'd made a fuss about wanting to speak with his father. When Mr Husband arrived at the station, he was only allowed to see his son in the presence of an officer, which presumably thwarted Robert's intention of discussing the details of his breakout scheme with his father. Bizarrely, Robert just stood in the cell with his head down, not saying a word.

After breakfast on Friday he made his move. Using the dessert spoon he'd been given the evening before, he tried first to force back the bolt of the cell door by inserting the handle of the spoon between the spring lock and the doorpost. But the spoon snapped at the handle and jammed in the door. Undeterred, he now focused his attention on the hatch and trap.

The communications hatch in the cell door, through which food and drink was supplied, was about 14 inches by 12 inches in size and 4ft from the ground. When opened, the trap door formed a sort of ledge or table projecting into the corridor. Robert had previously requested that the hatch be left open to allow light and air into the cell. Now, as quietly as he could, he reached through the hatch and began working the trap backwards and forwards, gradually weakening the hinges. He was meticulous about covering up all traces of his work, gently easing out the splinters that came away from the woodwork and brushing up the flakes of paint from the metal hinges. He disposed of the debris in the cell toilet.

After several hours' strenuous effort, the bolts finally gave way, allowing Robert to wrench the hatch and its wooden frame completely away from the door. He wasn't able to pull the hatch into the cell, so he had to let it fall to the corridor floor. The aperture was now wider by nearly two or three inches – big enough for him to wriggle through. He landed on the floor outside his cell. He just needed to tiptoe along the passageway to the door at the end of the corridor, and he would be free! But Mrs Knapton had heard the clatter of the falling hatch, and upon investigating she was astonished to see the boy crouched on the corridor floor like a feral animal, preparing to flee. Immediately, she summoned help from the police house, and Robert was quickly locked up in the neighbouring cell, this time with the communications hatch firmly locked in an upright position.

The police had been very fortunate: Robert was only seconds away from breaking out, and it was only the quick wits of Mrs Knapton that had foiled his plan. It was just as well that Captain Forrest had left town the day before, because leaving a boy prisoner unattended all day in a cell with the serving hatch open was exactly the sort of grossly incompetent behaviour that was bound to incur the captain's wrath.

As it was, Robert raged and bawled continually for several hours until Sergeant Knapton returned from London by the 5.12 train and heard all about the lad's attempt at escape.

Even though the police presence in Havant had been significantly reduced, there were still witnesses to be interviewed and new lines of enquiry to follow-up. In fact, the arrest of Robert Husband had encouraged new witnesses to come forward and speak openly. A number of children, among them a seven-year-old girl, were now providing additional details about Robert's movements on the day of the murder. The reports needed checking out, but apparently Robert had been seen loitering outside the draper's shop and peering through the windows when Percy was inside; he had been seen brandishing a knife in North Street on the day of the murder; and most significantly of all, information was emerging of an alleged feud between the Searle family and the Husband family that might provide a motive of sorts for the attack on Percy. All told, the police case against Robert was beginning to mount up.

On Saturday afternoon, 1 December, Percy was buried in Havant Cemetery. The burial ground and mortuary chapel occupied an acre of land at the northern end of New Lane, just beyond the railway line and the gas works. It was only a couple of minutes' walk from Bug's Row to the cemetery.

The elm coffin remained open until the cortège was ready to depart. Mr and Mrs Searle took one final look at their son, then the coffin was sealed and the body taken outside head-first. The procession set off up New Lane. The remains were borne on the shoulders of four members of the juvenile branch of Court Concord. Wreaths and other tributes rested on the coffin. Percy's classmates and a large number of Mr Searle's brother foresters accompanied the mourners to the cemetery. A crowd of more than 500 spectators had gathered to pay their respects. Mrs Searle was so overwhelmed with grief she could barely walk without assistance.

The gravel path from the cemetery gates to the mortuary chapel was lined with masters and pupils from the National School, each child holding a bunch of white flowers. The funeral service was conducted by the rector of Havant, the Reverend Canon Renaud, who spoke movingly about the sacrifice of a young and innocent life. Afterwards, the mourners gathered around the open grave on the north side of the mortuary chapel where Percy would be buried beside his sister, Ethel Kate, who had died in infancy in September 1874. The *Portsmouth Evening News* reflected on the scene:

> The pretty little Cemetery presented a series of strange contrasts. The peacefulness of God's Acre disturbed by the tramp of many feet, the outbursting sorrow of the living and the quiet restfulness of the dead, the somber [sic] garments of the chief mourners, and the unaccustomed brightness of the weather – all must have induced in a sensitive mind a keener realization of the disjointed state of things that alone could have led to this terrible murder of a child.[109]

The coffin was lowered gently into the ground and Canon Renaud uttered a few words of prayer over the grave. Nearby, the parish gravedigger waited with his shovel. He would later be interviewed by the *Evening News*. He and his ancestors had been digging graves in Havant for over a century, he said. First at St Faith's Church, and later at the cemetery. But his son showed no interest in such work, and the family line of gravediggers would die out with him.[110]

109 *Portsmouth Evening News*, 1 December 1888.
110 'An Old Line of Gravediggers', *Portsmouth Evening News*, 1 December 1888.

12

Telling the Truth

On Tuesday morning, 4 December, the adjourned inquest resumed at the police court. Before proceedings got under way, the Bench had to decide if Robert should be allowed in court. There were differing views on this. Superintendent Kinshott said he didn't want the accused boy in court because the warrant stated he should be detained in the police station and the police court was not the police station (although the buildings abutted each other and were connected internally). This rather petty argument didn't convince the coroner, who felt it would be fairer to have Robert attend the inquest. Kinshott appealed to the deputy chief constable, Mr Stephenson, who was sitting next to the coroner; Stephenson said it was highly irregular having a prisoner before the coroner's court, but if the coroner wished it, he would not object. The coroner asked Robert's father if he'd like his son to be in court, but Mr Husband, non-committal as ever, said he'd leave it up to the coroner. In the end, the matter was settled by the jury, who conferred briefly and decided that Robert shouldn't be brought into court. And so it was that Robert stayed locked in the police cell throughout the proceedings, except when he was ushered into court, briefly, to be identified by one of the witnesses.

Sergeant Knapton was the first witness to give evidence. He may have been feeling a little ill-tempered that morning after reading a letter published in Monday's *Portsmouth Evening News* criticising his actions on the night of the murder. Specifically, a friend of Thomas Clarke, the deaf man who had been taken into custody by Knapton, was kicking up a fuss at the way his colleague had been treated by the police; his grievance was that Clarke had been arrested for no good reason (for the convenience of the police, in fact) and then frogmarched down North Street as if he were a common ruffian; he had been held in custody for seventeen hours without food or drink and deprived of his jacket and coat in an unheated cell. Sergeant Knapton had already been admonished by the magistrates for his conduct, and possibly Superintendent Kinshott had spoken to him about the incident as well, so he will have been irked at seeing the blunder brought back into public notice once again. He may have reflected ruefully on the vicissitudes of public office – one moment the newspapers were commending him for his intelligent and meticulous handling of the case, the next they were publishing letters from members of the public criticising him for his overzealous policing.

He tried to put his grumpiness to one side as he addressed the court. He described how he'd taken the knife and the articles of clothing up to London for examination by Professor Tidy. (The analyst was expected to complete his examination on Wednesday in time for the resumed committal hearing.) Sergeant Knapton also told the court what Robert's father had said to him when he'd charged his son: 'If ever I see a person committing a murder, I'll be b——d if I say anything about it'. These words were obviously uttered in anger and Mr Husband hadn't meant anything by them, so it was unfair of Sergeant Knapton to mention this incident in his evidence. It was a crude attempt to besmirch the character of Mr Husband. In different circumstances, away from the pressures and frictions of the court, the two men might have found they had a great deal in common – they'd both been apprentice cobblers in their younger days, and they shared a West Country background.

The coroner next took evidence from Mr A.C. Lewis, who had furnished the court with a detailed plan of the murder scene and the surrounding area. Mr Lewis had been up and down the Pallant with his tape measure: the body was found 112 yards from Mrs Randall's shop and 38 yards 2 feet from Mrs Farnden's house (where Robert said he was standing when he witnessed the murder). The knife was discovered 24 feet from the body. The light from the single gas lamp in front of Pallant House fell at a slanting angle onto the wall of the Manor House school and actually illuminated the spot where the weapon had been found, but it did not reach any further. In other words, assuming Percy had been attacked where the knife was found, anyone standing at Mrs Farnden's house could have seen what happened, but the spot where the body was found was in total darkness.

Was it possible that Percy had been accosted in the light of the gas lamp and his body dragged eight yards into the shadows? The next witness, Dr Bond (recalled), scotched this idea. Bond detailed the results of his post-mortem. In addition to the wounds already described at the previous hearing, he reported a superficial abrasion to the tip of the nose and a recently inflicted cut on the forefinger of the right hand (possibly a defence wound). The fatal injury under the right ear was three inches deep and penetrated the right tonsil. He could not say if the puncture wound had been inflicted when Percy was standing or lying on the ground, but it had bled profusely both internally and externally and he felt sure there would have been a trail of blood if the body had been dragged any distance.

Superintendent George Kinshott then gave an account of the arrest of Robert Husband, his testimony agreeing with the evidence already put before the coroner's jury by his sergeant.[111] He told the court that Mrs Husband had washed the towel Robert had used to dry his hands at teatime on Monday evening. The unstated calumny here was that Mrs. Husband had in some way impeded the investigation by destroying the blood stain evidence.

After lunch the court heard from Henry Shirley, the draper's assistant. Robert was briefly brought into court by PC Notton so that Shirley could identify him as the lad he'd seen running away from the Pallant. A reporter from the *West Sussex Gazette* thought the prisoner looked 'far better than on his previous appearance', although his eyes were still swollen from ceaseless weeping. Robert

---

111 It is a small point, but Sergeant Knapton deposed that Mr Husband had uttered the curse 'buggered', while Superintendent Kinshott remembered it as 'damned'.

stood at the door for half a minute or so, languidly surveying the Bench and the jury and the rows of spectators. He may have vaguely resented the fact that the hall was slightly less congested than on his first appearance.

Shirley gave his evidence a little nervously. He seemed unsure of himself. The coroner wanted to know if there had been blood on Robert's hands that evening. Shirley said he hadn't seen any and Robert had been standing in the light falling on the road from the shop window. Was the boy trying to keep his hands out of sight? No, not really. Was it true that as soon as Robert spotted Shirley in the doorway of the shop he crossed over to speak to him? Yes. So it wasn't really true to say he was trying to run past Shirley and avoid him? No, he supposed not. William Farnden had been leaving the draper's shop when Percy entered, and the two boys had chatted briefly, but Shirley admitted he couldn't remember if Farnden had been in the shop before the murder or after. When John Platt accompanied Robert back to the Pallant, Shirley thought he'd taken hold of the boy's hand, but then he said he wasn't sure. He couldn't say in which hand Platt held the lantern. He hadn't heard any cries of 'Murder!" It all seemed very vague and unsatisfactory. Superintendent Kinshott had just complained about Mrs Husband washing the hand towel (and possibly deliberately destroying incriminating blood stain evidence) yet here was Shirley telling the court that Robert had no blood on his hands anyway just moments after the crime.

Tom Spurgeon was next. Still wearing his black academic gown, he swept into the inquest hall like a vampire hunter, explained how he'd found the knife, and swept out again. If the knife handle was covered in blood (as Mr Spurgeon said it was), wouldn't some of it have been transferred to the murderer's hands? Yet as we know, Shirley said he saw no signs of blood on Robert's hands at all. And how come it had taken three hours for someone to find the knife even though there were hundreds of people milling around the Pallant and the weapon had been illuminated all that time by the gas light? But Mr Spurgeon had gone, and these vital questions were never asked.

William Stevens, the son of a dairy farmer, repeated the evidence he had given to the magistrates. The knife used to belong to him, he said, and to his father before that. His father gave it to him about three years back. He'd given it to George Husband on the Thursday before the murder. He could identify the knife by its 'brown handle with wrinkles over it with a piece of brass in the middle of the handle and the little blade was broken'.[112]

George Husband now came forward to give evidence. He had a busy schedule over the next few days: coroner's court today, committal hearing tomorrow, and star witness in the Johnny Sparks cat killing case on Thursday. First of all, the coroner wanted to make sure that George understood the sin of perjury.

> Coroner: Do you know where you will go to if you don't tell the truth?
> George: Yes, the police-station.
> [This produced laughter in the courtroom.]
> Coroner: Isn't there somewhere else?
> George: Hell.[113]

This second reply was deemed the correct one and George was sworn.

He readily admitted receiving the knife from Stevens on Thursday (23 November). He'd had it in his pocket when he attended church with his mother the following Sunday afternoon, but when he arrived home around four o'clock he noticed it was missing. He couldn't explain it. There was no hole in his trouser pocket.

The coroner wanted to know why George had originally denied owning the knife when Sergeant Knapton showed it to him the day after the murder.

> George: I forgot.
> Coroner: Now tell me truly, what did you do with the knife?
> George: [after considerable hesitation] I lost it.

---

112 Inquest deposition of William Thomas Stevens, taken on 4 December 1888. See the client papers of Longcroft and Green (Havant solicitors), Hampshire Record Office, reference 96M92/C14.
113 *West Sussex Gazette*, 6 December 1888.

Coroner: Then why didn't you tell the sergeant of police that when he asked you?

[George burst out crying and gave no answer.]

Coroner: Who told you to tell the sergeant you never had the knife?

George: Nobody.

Coroner: Why, then, didn't you tell the sergeant that?

[No answer]

Coroner: Crying will not help you. You must answer the question. If you do not I shall have to send you to prison.

George: I was afraid to tell.

Coroner: What were you afraid of?

George: I thought he would take me away.

The coroner then turned to events on the night of the murder. Apparently, George came home between eight and nine o'clock, just as Robert was getting ready for bed.

Coroner: Did any conversation take place between you and him?

George: No.

Coroner: Didn't you sleep in the same room?

George: In the same room but not in the same bed. I was asleep before he came up.

Coroner: Do you mean to tell me that your brother did not wake you to tell you that Searle was dead?

George: Yes.

Coroner: In the morning, who got up first?

George: Bob and me got up together. Father called us and we got up together.

Coroner: What conversation took place between you and your brother about the death of this boy Searle?

George: He never spoke to me, Sir. I never knew a boy had been murdered.

Mr Goble was incredulous. Surely the family had spoken of the murder at breakfast time?

Coroner: What did Bob say about what had taken place the night before?

George: He never spoke at all.

Coroner: What did your mother say? Did she speak about it?

George: No.

Coroner:	Are you entirely speaking the truth?
George:	Yes.
Coroner:	Remember, if you are not I will go hard with you. Do you mean to tell the Jury that nothing was said about the murder from the time you sat down to breakfast to the time you got up?
George:	Yes.[114]

George was adamant that no one in his family – mother, father, Robert, Albert, Ellen, William, James or himself – had discussed the murder either at breakfast time or the night before. And he was adamant that the knife went missing on Sunday.

Edward Goble changed tactics.

Coroner:	Do you know a man named Smith?
George:	No.

John Smith, a builder from nearby Bedhampton, was briefly brought into court so that George could see him. It was a slightly devious move on the coroner's part, designed to snare George into lying. He repeated his question a little more sternly.

Coroner:	You know this man, don't you?
George:	I know the face.

It is entirely feasible that George didn't actually know the man's name, so the coroner's ruse proved nothing. It transpired that John Smith thought of himself as a bit of an amateur detective. Under continued questioning from the coroner, George admitted that he had tried to sell the knife to Smith on Friday but the man didn't want to buy it. A few days later, after the murder, John Smith called in at the police station to examine the knife. He recognised it at once as the same item George had tried to sell him on Friday. He went to speak with George and asked him where his knife was. George told Smith he'd lost it and then changed his mind and told him his brother Robert had it to cut wood with. The coroner pounced:

---

114 *Hampshire Post*, 7 December 1888.

Coroner: Then Bob had the knife really?
George: He had it at one time and I at another.
Coroner: Did you ever see your brother with the knife?
George: He had it for cutting wood. I don't know whether that was before or after the murder.[115]

The last witness was Henry Wheeler, the grocer's errand boy, who repeated what he'd said at the magistrates' court about Robert trying to sell him the knife on Monday, the day of the murder.

It was now late in the afternoon, so Mr Goble adjourned the inquiry till Friday. He must have felt satisfied at the day's developments. The chain of ownership of the knife – the murder weapon – was becoming clearer. The knife had passed from William Stevens to George Husband to Robert Husband, who (if Henry Wheeler's evidence could be believed) had the knife in his possession on the day Percy was killed.

Further revelations were promised at the resumed magistrates' hearing on Wednesday.

---

115 *West Sussex Gazette*, 6 December 1888.

13

More Questions
and Answers

Early on Wednesday morning, 5 December, Robert had another of his crying fits and temper tantrums. Sergeant Knapton went to see him in the police cells but on this occasion he didn't caution him. Miraculously, it seems Robert was now able to remember further details about the events on Monday night. This was version three, and it was a mixture of truth, exaggeration and pure invention.

> There was another boy I saw, Charlie Rogers, when I was crying 'Murder!' He works for Mr Carrell, in the Pallant. He said, 'What's the matter, Bob?' I told him there was a murder, and I ran on into Mrs Randall's shop, and nearly jumped over the counter.[116]

According to one version of his story, Robert hadn't entered Mrs Randall's shop at all that evening. In another version, he'd put his head round the door and alerted the customers to the murder. In this latest iteration, he'd actually entered the shop and nearly scaled the counter. But the information that another boy was abroad in the Pallant and had allegedly spoken with Robert was potentially of great interest. Sergeant Knapton despatched an officer to interview Charlie Rogers and evaluate his significance as a witness; possibly his testimony could be heard at the magistrates' hearing later that day.

The magistrates' hearing resumed just before ten o'clock on Wednesday morning. The Bench was crowded with dignitaries: as usual Mr William Snell was in the chair, and alongside him

---

116 *Portsmouth Times*, 8 December 1888.

sat Captain Boyd and General Napier. The Chief Constable of Hampshire, Captain Forrest, had returned to Havant to keep abreast of developments. Also present were the Deputy Chief Constable Mr Stephenson, Colonel Charles Hunt of Cosham (formerly a captain in the 19th Foot), the Reverend A.J. Richards, and others. It was a formidable panel of county magistrates, senior police officers and general observers.

Reporters from all the local newspapers were in court, too, with their pencils and notepads. Every seat in the public gallery was filled. At the back of the hall there was additional standing room for perhaps twenty or more spectators. In an anteroom, Percy's mother, a Home Office scientist, an amateur detective, and lots of children were waiting to give evidence. It promised to be a dramatic day.

Robert Husband was brought over from the police cells by PC Notton. He looked 'tolerably calm' in the words of the *Hampshire Post*,[117] although a little pasty. He wore the same tunic as on his previous appearance, minus the blood-red neckerchief. A journalist from the *Hampshire Telegraph* observed that

> His hair, which did not look as though it has been subject to much careful grooming, was disordered, but his general appearance was rather more favoured than on Thursday week. For one thing, he did not appear to have been weeping so copiously, although his eyes were somewhat swollen from that cause. He was provided with a chair in the dock, and he seated himself in it rather sidewise as at the former hearing, and in a somewhat listless attitude, with his arms by his side.[118]

First into the witness box was Sergeant Knapton, who repeated the evidence given at the inquest on Tuesday. Again, he detailed what the father had said when Robert was arrested – 'If ever I see a person committing a murder, I'll be b——d if I say anything about it.' Quite rightly, Mr Green, the magistrates' clerk, picked the sergeant up on this:

---

117 *Hampshire Post*, 7 December 1888.
118 *Hampshire Telegraph*, 8 December 1888.

Clerk: How is that evidence against the boy?
Knapton: It was said in his presence by his father.
Clerk: Did the boy make any reply?
Knapton: No.[119]

The father had spoken in a fit of rage. That's all it was. Knapton looked small and vindictive for bringing the matter up a second time. He moved on quickly, informing the court of Robert's fresh evidence with regard to Charlie Rogers. The clerk wearily recorded the deposition in his book.

Chairman   (to the prisoner): Do you wish to ask this witness any questions?
Robert: No.
Chairman   (to Knapton): Where is the prisoner's father today?
Knapton: He has been ordered to attend. (To George Husband): Where is he?
George: Father says he can't come.
Knapton: I told him before he left the court on Tuesday that he ought to be here to watch the interests of his son.[120]

A constable was sent to fetch Mr Husband, and shortly afterwards he appeared in court in his coalman's overalls, bib, and heavy working boots. Rather frostily, Mr Snell made his opinion clear:

I wish you to be present, if you please. Your boy is in peril of his life, and some friend should be present on his behalf.[121]

No doubt Mr Snell had Robert's best interests at heart and his remarks echoed the concerns already expressed in the coroner's court at the prisoner's continued lack of legal representation. But it was grossly unfair to portray Mr Husband as uncaring about his son's predicament. There were good reasons why Mr Husband couldn't attend the resumed hearing. It was wintertime. The owner of the coal yard, Samuel Clarke, a wealthy property owner in the town, was primarily interested in maximising profit from his businesses.

---

119 *Portsmouth Times*, 8 December 1888.
120 Ibid.
121 Ibid.

With the two Husband boys and their father tied up in protracted court proceedings, work was piling up at the yard; delivery wagons weren't able to offload their supply, customers were queuing up for coal and leaving unserved. And a coal yard left unguarded for most of the day encouraged people to scramble over the gates to pilfer lumps of coke. It seems Samuel Clarke had denied Mr Husband permission to leave the yard under threat of dismissal. What could he do? He had a family of nine to support on a meagre navy pension and the paltry wages of a coal yard keeper; he couldn't afford to risk losing his job and the tied house that came with it.

Dr Bond was called next. He gave details of the post-mortem examination, largely repeating what he had said at the inquest. He was shown the knife discovered on the night of the murder and he stated that in his opinion it could have been the weapon that inflicted the fatal wounds. But equally it might not have been. He couldn't be certain. The wounds, he said, might have been inflicted when Percy was standing up, or possibly when he was lying on the ground. He couldn't be certain. They might have been inflicted by a left handed person standing in front of Percy or by a right handed person standing behind him. His assailant might have been taller or shorter than Percy. He couldn't be certain. It all seemed pretty vague and catch-all. All the witness could say with confidence – or with near confidence, at least – was that it wasn't suicide.

Robert and his father were then given the opportunity to cross-examine the doctor.

Clerk	(to prisoner): Is there any question you wish to put to the witness?
Robert:	No.
Chairman	(to Mr Husband): Do you wish to ask anything?
Mr Husband:	I have no question. I don't know anything about it.

Perhaps the next witness would provide less equivocal evidence. It was Dr Charles Tidy, professor of chemistry and forensic medicine at the London Hospital, and for many years the official analyst to the Home Office. Since 1885 he had also been a barrister-at-law. He had travelled down to Havant that morning from his home in Manchester Square in London. Tidy was widely regarded as one of the leading forensic physicians in the country. His specialities were sewage treatment and poisons; he had served as an expert witness in many famous poisoning cases, such as the trial of Adelaide Bartlett in 1886, and he would soon be appearing for the defence in the trial of Florence Maybrick. He was the author of the monumental textbook *Legal Medicine* (1882). A charismatic public speaker, his lectures to students at the Inns of Court were enlivened by his mimicking in gesture and movement the ghastly effects of certain poisons on the muscles of the body.

Dr Tidy had a modest and gracious courtroom manner, and he delivered his evidence slowly and with great precision:

> I received on Friday, the 30th of November, at my house, from Sergeant Knapton, the following articles: A knife wrapped up in paper, a shirt, a necktie, a pocket handkerchief, a jacket, a pair of knickerbockers, a pair of stockings, and a cap. I produce all these sealed by myself, for identification. Numerous stains on all these articles were examined for blood. Excepting on the knife and on the shirt, no trace of blood could be detected on any of them. About 35 stains were examined. On the right wristband of the shirt were some five or six small stains. I was obliged to use these for the purposes of the examination ... The entire stains measured about one-sixteenth of a square inch. I found them to be blood, but I am of the opinion they were old blood – I should say at least a month old.[122]

This was devastating testimony. The police case essentially revolved around the bloodstain evidence, yet in the opinion of the Home Office analyst most of the stains on the items of clothing weren't blood at all. And the few stains that were blood predated the murder of Percy Searle by at least a fortnight.

The Bench was thrown into turmoil. An air of desperation, impertinence almost, tinged their follow-up questions.

> Chairman: You say in your opinion it was old blood?
> Tidy: Yes, sir.

---

122 *Hampshire Post*, 7 December 1888.

Chairman: Can you say positively it was old blood?

Tidy: I have no hesitation in saying that the blood was old. I may say, in passing, we know perfectly well the changes blood undergoes by age, and we know fairly well the time required for these changes to take place.

Chairman: If the boy had washed his hands, would it be possible for the soap and water to have effected the stains?

Tidy: No doubt, sir.

Clerk: Does the shirt bear the appearance of having been recently washed?

Tidy: No, it does not.

[Gasps from the court]

Chairman: It has been proved that the boy was washing his hands soon after the murder.

Clerk: We have not that in evidence.

Chairman: I think we do.

Clerk: It was stated that the boy's hands were wet, and the inference was that he had been washing them.[123]

Professor Tidy was a busy man. He was far too courteous to let his frustrations show, but he may well have been irked by Mr Snell's sceptical tone. And an open disagreement between a senior stipendiary magistrate and the court clerk was never conducive to the ordered administration of justice. His testimony was clear and unshakeable: the blood stains on the boy's shirt wristband were older than the murder. This was sensational evidence, and the courtroom was still reeling from the implications. Mr Snell let the matter drop and the court's attention moved on to the knife.

Tidy: The knife had two blades. Both blades were covered with blood. I am of the opinion that the blood upon the knife was living blood. I am unable to say whether the blood was human blood or not.

Clerk: Were the marks of blood recent?

Tidy: Yes, recent.

Clerk: Was the knife wrapped in paper?

Tidy: Yes, and that was stained with a quantity of blood, too.

123 *Portsmouth Times*, 8 December 1888.

Clerk: It does not alter your opinion?
Tidy: Not in the least.[124]

A test to reliably determine the presence of blood in dried stains had been devised in 1835 by the Polish physician Ludwig Teichmann, but a test to reliably differentiate between human and animal blood wouldn't emerge until 1901 when the German scientist Paul Uhlenhuth developed the species precipitin test. As a result, in 1888, criminal suspects with blood on their clothes could get away with claiming it was of animal origin. In his textbook *Legal Medicine* (1882), Professor Tidy quoted the opinion of Professor Richardson of Pennsylvania that

> At present (1875) there is no method known to science for discriminating microscopically or otherwise, the dried blood of a human being from that of a dog, monkey, rabbit, musk-rat, elephant, lion, whale, seal, or in fact any animal whose corpuscles measure more than one-four thousandth of an inch in diameter.[125]

This was another disappointment for the police. Many ordinary people in the town felt the knife had been 'planted' outside Mr Spurgeon's house so that he would run into it as soon as he stepped outside his gate with his lantern; there was a view that the knife had been liberally coated in animal blood so as to incriminate Robert. The police, however, genuinely felt it was the murder weapon soiled with Percy's blood. Professor's Tidy's evidence gave weight to neither side, and therein lay the force of his testimony, for if the stains on the knife could not be indubitably identified as human blood, then the artefact was useless as evidence of a crime: it might be Percy's blood or it might be the blood of a cat mutilated by Johnny Sparks.

---

124 Ibid.
125 Charles Meymott Tidy, *Legal Medicine* Part 1 (London: Smith, Elder & Co., 1882), p. 231. Tidy also highlights Dr Neumann's research into chemical 'blood pictures', which tentatively suggested that 'human blood can be distinguished with the greatest exactitude from the blood of animals, and the blood of one animal from that of another'. This research was in its early stages and presumably insufficiently developed in 1888 to allow Dr Tidy to apply the process with confidence to the bloodstained knife in the Searle case.

Robert was asked if he had any questions for the witness. Rising from his seat, he drew back his right tunic sleeve and showed the court his wrist.

Robert: I had a scratch on my wrist here, which had been bleeding.

Mr Husband: He had two spots on his arm as I have now. The only question I can say is I know he had one spot on his arm.

Mr Snell fell back on his familiar procedural quibble.

Chairman: You will be able to give evidence to that effect by-and-by.

Mr Husband: I told Sergeant Knapton and the Inspector.

Chairman: That is not a question.

Mr Husband: I told Sergeant Knapton and the Inspector, didn't I?[126]

Professor Tidy may have been relieved to board the train back to London.

The prosecution case was now in disarray. Given that the blood evidence could not be used to support a link between Robert and the crime, the focus of the Bench subtly shifted. Dr Bond was recalled.

Chairman: Could the fatal blow have been struck without any blood coming upon the clothing of the murderer?

Dr Bond: That is quite possible. The hand might have received some blood and not the clothing. The shirt wristbands might have been pulled up.

Chairman: Do you think the wristbands would escape it?

Dr Bond: I think so. The blow may have been rapidly made.

Capt Boyd: Supposing the wristbands had not been turned up?

Dr Bond: The blood might have spurted downwards and the wristband escaped.[127]

The sleeve of the attacker might have been stained with blood or it might not. The blood could have spurted this way or that. Once

---

126 *Portsmouth Times*, 8 December 1888.
127 Ibid.

again, Dr Bond couldn't be certain. The one detail Dr Bond did feel certain about was that Percy hadn't staggered from one spot to another. At the murder scene the blood was concentrated over an area extending 2ft or 3ft in diameter and there was no blood trail leading away from the body.

Mr Snell was determined to establish a link between Robert and the crime.

> Chairman: Could a boy of that size have inflicted such a wound with such a knife?
> Dr Bond: Yes, I think so.
> Clerk: It would be no evidence against the boy.

Again, the clerk of the court had to intervene to counter the magistrate's handling of the case. There's no doubt Robert had sufficient strength to inflict the fatal wound, but then so too did every man in the courtroom and every man in Havant. Exasperated, Mr Snell rounded on Mr Husband:

> Chairman: Can't you manage to have a professional man to act in this case for your son?
> Mr Husband: I am going to try on Friday, sir.

Mr Husband couldn't afford to engage a solicitor; he lacked a benefactor, and there were no poor man's lawyers in Havant willing to give free legal assistance.[128] He was doing the best he could to secure funding to provide for his son's defence and it was rather disparaging of Mr Snell to suggest otherwise.

Henry Wheeler was also recalled. At the earlier hearing on 29 November, Wheeler had deposed that on the day of the murder Robert had tried to sell him the knife produced in court. Now, in the light of Professor Tidy's evidence, Wheeler was brought back for further questioning. Was he absolutely sure the knife was the same? Yes, he said, he was certain, although he admitted he hadn't actually

---

128 The first tentative steps towards providing effective legal aid for the indigent came about at the turn of the twentieth century with the passing of the Poor Prisoner's Defence Act of 1903.

held the knife, and he'd only seen one side of the long blade. He hadn't noticed the smaller blade at all and wasn't aware it was broken. His identification now seemed very tentative and unreliable. At the coroner's inquest, a member of the jury had dismissed Wheeler's evidence out of hand, saying 'Wheeler wouldn't be surprised to know that the knife had four blades instead of two'.[129]

Mightily peeved at the way things were going, Mr Snell called a twenty minute adjournment for lunch.

---

129 *West Sussex Gazette*, 6 December 1888.

14

Threepence for Coal

Wednesday afternoon, 5 December, and the case before the magistrates continued to falter.

Anthony Lewis entered the witness box and spoke about his measurements at the crime scene. At the coroner's inquest the day before he had stated that the spot where the knife was found was illuminated by the gas lamp outside Pallant House. Now he gave evidence to the contrary, stating that the spot was 'shrouded in total darkness'.[130]

Superintendent Kinshott repeated his evidence of the day before. Since lunch, Robert had adopted a characteristically languid pose in the dock, his right arm draped over the railing and his chin resting wearily on his arm; but when the superintendent spoke of the prisoner's arrest and how he had accounted for his bloodied wristband by scratches on his wrist, Robert leapt to his feet, rolled up the right sleeve of his tunic, and exposed the marks on his forearm to the astonished view of the Bench, turning his arm this way and that to enhance the display. It was a melodramatic gesture, neatly calculated to recapitulate Professor Tidy's s evidence earlier in the day. It proved beyond doubt that Robert, despite his listless air, was watching the case avidly.

William Farnden Sr was next into the witness box. He was thirty-three and a general labourer. He was the father of young William, who had spoken with Percy at the door of Mrs Randall's shop on the evening of the murder. The Farndens lived at No. 1 in the Pallant, next door to the smithy; it was from outside their house that Robert

---

130 *Hampshire Telegraph*, 8 December 1888.

claimed he had seen Percy being attacked.

Mr Farnden may have been reluctant to give evidence and get involved in the court proceedings. He didn't want the publicity. As a family the Farndens (and fifteen-year-old stepdaughter Ellen Albury in particular[131]) were trying to live down their own recent disgrace in a strange affair that became known locally as the 'Havant Abduction case'.[132] In front of William Snell and the other justices, Mr Farnden stated that, on the day of the murder, around ten minutes past four, he went to the yard in North Street and bought coal from young Robert Husband.

Again, the prisoner leapt up from his chair in the dock and contradicted him, saying it was George who served him. The chairman rebuked him explaining he would have his turn to speak

---

131 Ellen's mother, Sarah Taylor, married William Albury in Alton in 1871, when she was sixteen, and they had produced Ellen. At some point she began to cohabit with William Farnden, who raised the girl as his own.

132 Ellen had been employed as a laundress and domestic servant at the home of Mrs Caroline Chambers, who lived next door to the White Hart Inn in East Street in Havant. On the evening of 2 July 1888, a travelling illusionist called William Monk, aged twenty-four, was performing 'optical delusions' in the stable yard at the rear of the White Hart; he was assisted by Charles Edwards, a thirty-year-old painter. Monk used electric lights, mirrors and lenses to produce curious visual effects: the head and bust of a young lady (seemingly without arms and legs or lower body) conversed merrily with the audience from a coffin; women grew fish tails and appeared to swim in a basin of water; young girls were turned into blocks of stone then returned to human form. Ellen was entranced and seems to have entertained the fantasy of joining the troupe and running away with them. She visited the show the following night, and Edwards was alleged to have acted indecently towards her in a barn. On the third day, she crept out of Mrs Chambers's house and caught the train to Fareham with Monk, his girlfriend, and Edwards. At Fareham they took lodgings at the Robin Hood Inn, the two women being represented as the men's wives. But Sergeant Knapton, having been alerted to the 'abduction' by Ellen's mother, journeyed to Fareham and arrested the two men for conspiring and abducting an underage girl.

At the Hampshire Assizes on 4 August 1888, Monk and Edwards were acquitted of the charge. Ellen had clearly forced herself on the two men and voluntarily travelled to Fareham with them. In court she was also given a very indifferent character reference by her erstwhile employer Mrs Chambers, and by the landlady of the Robin Hood Inn, who took exception to her 'disgraceful behaviour'. But Ellen will have been hurt most by Monk's snubbing of her; she was, he told the court, too plain and too short to be of any use to him as a glamorous assistant in his illusion act. Humiliated and out of work, Ellen went back to living at her parents' home in the Pallant. Details of the case and the trial are reported in the *Hampshire Telegraph*, 14 July 1888 and the *Hampshire Telegraph*, 4 August 1888.

later. However, when pressed, Mr Farnden conceded it could have been George. (Indeed, this was more likely because Robert generally worked in the yard and George in the shop.) Mr Farnden then deposed that, at about a quarter past five, he returned to the yard and paid one of the brothers threepence, although he admitted he couldn't be positive which one.

The chairman then put it to Mr Farnden that Robert had visited his house that evening to collect the threepence. Farnden denied this, stating that he was home 'from half-past five till bedtime, and no one called'.[133]

Farnden was then cross-examined by Robert who, speaking very rapidly, detailed his version of that evening's events. He reiterated most insistently that his father had instructed him to call at Farnden's, which he did, Farnden handing him threepence on the doorstep.[134]

Was Mr Farnden telling the truth? He doesn't come across as a slippery or manipulative figure, and what reason did he have to lie about this incident and make a false statement under oath? When Mrs Farnden's turn came to give evidence, she backed up her husband fully, saying no one had called all evening.

A third Farnden was brought into court – William, aged eight. He was close to tears and came across as a bit gormless, although probably he was just dumbstruck by the occasion. Mr Snell gently asked him a few questions to establish whether he understood the nature and meaning of the oath, but the child failed to reply one way or the other. Consequently, he was sent out of court without being sworn in order that his mother might explain to him the nature of an oath.

There was now a flurry of witnesses. First, Tom Spurgeon of the Manor House Academy hurtled into court once more in his black gown. He indicated on Mr Lewis's map where exactly he'd found the knife. He was followed by John Platt, who pointed out on the

133 *Portsmouth Times*, 8 December 1888.
134 Ibid.

same map where Robert had told him he'd been standing when he witnessed the murder. Then John Smith, the sleuthing builder from Bedhampton, testified that he'd seen the knife produced in court in George Husband's possession on the Friday previous to the murder.

Ethel Whitbread was next. She was the seven-year-old daughter of Samuel Whitbread, the photographer who had supplied the coroner and the magistrates with pictures of the murder scene and the vicinity. Although a year younger than William Farnden, she convinced the Bench that she understood the meaning of an oath, and throughout her testimony she presented as a bright and very self-assured witness.[135] She told the court that at half-past eight in the morning on Monday week she had seen Robert Husband sharpening a large pocket knife against the wall of Miss Burrows's house. She was standing on the opposite side of the street at the time, hence could only see the blade part of the knife. Even so, she confirmed it was similar to the knife produced in court.

Ethel did not seem unduly bothered when cross-examined by Robert:

Robert:	Did you see me with that knife?
Ethel:	I saw you with a knife.
Clerk:	She does not say it was that knife. She says it was a knife like it.
Robert:	Well, I never carried a knife there.

At this point the Farnden lad was again called into court. Mr Green was just about to swear him in when the chairman intervened. The boy's evidence had already been refused, he said.

---

135 A cynic might argue that Ethel Whitbread's precocious ability to grasp the essence of truth and falsehood, right and wrong, derived partly from the fact that her father had served a three month prison sentence for embezzlement and accountancy fraud in 1887. He embezzled money belonging to the 'Loyal Pride of Havant' Lodge of Oddfellows, of which he had been the secretary, and wilfully omitted material particulars from the accounts (*Hampshire Telegraph*, 6 April 1887). It is significant, too, that Mr Snell, while willing to hear Ethel Whitbread's evidence, nonetheless conceded to the court that the judge might reject her deposition at the trial. This expressed intention to commit the prisoner for trial was made before he had heard all the evidence and before the Bench had retired to consider its decision. See *Portsmouth Times*, 8 December 1888.

Clerk:	But he is older than the last witness.
Chairman:	That is nothing to do with the matter at all. It is simply a question of intelligence.
Mr Stephenson:	His mother has since explained to him the nature of an oath.
General Napier:	Yes, crammed him, in fact.

[Applause from the gallery.]

Mr Snell may have relished getting his own back on the bothersome clerk.

The ability of child witnesses to recall events accurately and to distinguish between truth and falsehood were not the only issues that concerned magistrates. Children were also malleable: there was a risk of them regurgitating in court what their parents or other adults in authority had told them to say; equally, children could be taught rote responses to magistrates' questions about the nature of an oath without necessarily understanding the concept of perjury.

For the second time that day Mr Snell asked William if he knew the meaning of an oath, but despite his mother's tutoring the boy still failed to reply. The magistrates conferred, and William's evidence was rejected.[136]

The proceedings were beginning to drag on; Mr Snell was no doubt eager to complete business that day without having to adjourn the hearing for a second time. There were two witnesses left to call.

Mrs Elizabeth Searle, the victim's mother, was brought into court. She was a small, frail woman in her fortieth year. Recent events had aged her terribly, though; she appeared raddled and much distressed, and a reporter for the *Portsmouth Times* described her as looking 'very pale and ill'. She was provided with a seat in the witness box. Her testimony would prove crucial, for it posited a possible motive for the murder.

About five weeks ago, she said, she sent Percy to Mr Clarke's yard to buy some coal. Robert Husband had been working in the yard that

---

136 William's evidence would have been that he remembered seeing Robert Husband peering through the windows of Mrs Randall's shop from outside when he and Percy were inside talking.

day, but he refused to serve her boy. The reason he gave was that the Searles had previously kept the coal trucks too long, which was untrue.[137] Percy had had to traipse to a different supplier. A fortnight afterwards, Mrs Searle visited the coal yard and made a complaint about Robert to Mr Husband. Robert had been present.

Mrs Searle:	By that, I believe that the prisoner owed my little boy a grudge.
Clerk:	But did the prisoner say anything then?
Mrs Searle:	No.
Clerk:	Neither then nor at any other time, to your knowledge?
Mrs Searle:	I have never heard anything of it since.[138]

Such a trifling quarrel, and one so quickly forgotten. Yet motives for murder can often be small and tawdry, and who is to say this grievance didn't smoulder like coal in a grate, catch fire, and become an obsession.

Mrs Searle's evidence in court was actually a watered down version of the story she had told representatives of the press a few days earlier. On that occasion, she also alleged that Robert Husband had angrily confronted her son Frederick outside the grocery shop where he worked, demanding to know why he had told his mother (Mrs Searle) that Robert had threatened to kick Percy out of the coal yard. Frederick denied saying any such thing, whereupon Robert uttered the warning, 'Well, if it was not you it was your Perce and I'll—'.[139] But at that moment he was summoned by his father back into the yard.

We need to be cautious about accepting this story. The fact that Mrs Searle didn't repeat it under oath, suggests that perhaps it never happened.

The last witness was Charlie Rogers. He was fifteen years old and worked as an errand boy for Mr Hezekiah Carrell, a builder, who lived in the Pallant. Most nights Charlie finished work at around

---

137 Many merchants sold soft and hard coal to domestic customers by the truck or hand-cart.
138 *Hampshire Telegraph*, 8 December 1888.
139 *Portsmouth Evening News*, 1 December 1888.

6.15 pm, so he must have walked through the Pallant towards North Street shortly after Percy was attacked. He testified that he saw the prisoner talking to Mr Shirley outside the draper's shop. Robert said to him, 'There's a man murdering a boy round there. Come and see'. But Charlie replied 'No fear' and ran off. When questioned, Rogers stated he hadn't noticed any blood on Robert's hands or clothes.

And that was it. At 3.40 pm the Bench retired to confer in private. Ten minutes later they were back. Mr Snell announced that the prisoner must be committed for trial in order for a jury to decide his guilt. Robert was asked if he had anything to say. In a 'cool and collected manner' he made the following statement:

> Father sent me round to Farnden's, and after I came out from the house I was going on my way home. Suddenly, I heard a cry and I walked up a little way to the lamp. I saw a man in the shadows doing like this [moves his right arm as though stabbing] swinging his arms backwards and forwards, and when the man saw me he ran away and the boy tumbled down. I ran away and hollered out 'Murder'. I was across the other side of the road towards Watson's[140] side. I was just going into Randall's, and I went in and fell against Shirley when he was at the door. I told him that there was a man killing a boy. Then when I was coming out I saw John Platt and I told him and he had a lantern with him. I went up with him too. That is all, sir.[141]

With one or too small variations and additions, it was essentially the same story he had stuck to all along.

The Bench then formally committed Robert Husband for trial at Winchester on a charge of wilful murder.

The following day, on Thursday 6 December, Robert was taken to Winchester Gaol to await trial. To avoid the inevitable crowds, the police kept the hour of Robert's removal secret. Just after 9.00 am Constable William Notton[142] escorted Robert to the railway station

---

140 Preston Watson's Wine and Spirits Merchants on the corner of North Street and the Pallant.
141 *Portsmouth Times*, 8 December 1888.
142 Some press reports inaccurately name him Constable Pronten or Prouten.

via the lane leading from behind the police station. It crossed the recreation ground and connected with Market Lane at the top of North Street. For part of the way they will have followed exactly the same route taken by Percy's coffin bearers. At the railway station they were joined by Sergeant Knapton.

They had arrived in good time. The 9.20 train for Cosham was due shortly. At Cosham they would catch the 9.38 connecting service to Winchester. A journalist from the *Portsmouth Evening News* observed the scene:

> [Robert] seated himself in the waiting room, and appeared to watch what was going on around him with the unconcern of one who had nothing else to think about. When the train drew up to the platform, the prisoner, who was wearing a brown overcoat and a frieze cap, was taken by the hand by Constable Prouten and ushered to a third class compartment. He stepped to the farther side of the carriage, and seated himself in the corner with his back to the engine; and Sergeant Knapton took a seat immediately opposite. The door of the compartment was then locked on these two occupants. About a minute elapsed before the train steamed out of the station, and during this time the prisoner regarded with perfect nonchalance the knot of about a dozen onlookers who had assembled on the platform. As the train moved away it was noticed that a faint smile was on his face. Among the few persons who assembled on the platform to witness the departure of the accused was Charles Searle, an elder brother of the murdered boy.[143]

Was that 'faint smile' a smirk aimed at Charlie Searle? Is that what the reporter is telling us, that Robert was so evil he even mocked the brother of the deceased? In all likelihood this was Robert Husband's first time on a train, and what eleven-year-old boy wouldn't be thrilled at the prospect of a steam train ride? He may also have smiled because he knew his family were fighting hard for him. His dad would sort things out. Yesterday evening his mother and father, George and sister Jane, had visited him in the cell at Havant police station. His father told him not to worry: he was going to Portsmouth on Thursday to find a solicitor and see about a barrister. Many people

---

143 *Portsmouth Evening News*, 6 December 1888.

in the town and further afield were sending in money to help pay for his defence fund. It would all turn out okay in the end, and before he knew it he'd be back in the coal yard humping sacks around.

As the train pulled out of Havant and picked up speed on its way to Bedhampton and Cosham, Robert will have looked out the windows at the chalk ridges of Portsdown Hill rising to his left, and no doubt the thought will have crossed his mind that perhaps he'd never see this part of the world again.

15

The Defence Fund

As Robert was making his way to Winchester Gaol, his brother George was donning his Sunday best for yet another appearance in court – this time as a witness in the Johnny Sparks cat-killing case at the Havant Petty Sessions.

John Sparks, who was eleven, was summoned by Inspector Bartholomew of the Royal Society for the Prevention of Cruelty to Animals. On 21 November a bricklayer called William Rogers, working on the roof of a property nearby, had seen young Sparks stamping on a cat. Before running away, the boy picked up the still-living animal, writhing in agony on the street, and chucked it into a hedge. By the time Rogers reached the cat a few minutes later, it was dead. There was a second boy in the company of Sparks who witnessed the cruelty without intervening; this may have been George Husband or it may have been Robert Husband, or perhaps it was another playmate entirely. The nature of George's testimony isn't recorded. At any rate, Sparks pleaded guilty. His father, a gardener, expressed regret that the boy had acted so cruelly. The Bench dealt with the incident comparatively lightly: they imposed a fine of 19s. on the understanding that John's father would give his son a 'good flogging'.[144]

True to his word, Robert Husband Sr travelled to Portsmouth on Thursday to organise legal representation for his son. Given that Robert had already been committed for trial, it was a rather belated move, but the boy's interests needed protecting at the ongoing coroner's inquest, and there was an urgent need to hire a lawyer to

---

144 *Hampshire Telegraph*, 8 December 1888 & *Hampshire Post*, 7 December 1888.

act as defence counsel at the forthcoming trial in Winchester.

Mr Husband called first at the offices of Francis J. Sansom on Commercial Road in Landport. Sansom was an auditor and public accountant running his own business. He was a young chap in his early twenties, very much a self-made man, and full of 'indomitable energy and perseverance'.[145] An inveterate joiner of organisations, he tended to throw himself wholeheartedly into incessant committee work. We don't know whether Francis Sansom already knew the Husband family in some capacity, or if they were meeting for the first time on recommendation; either way, he proved an extremely valuable contact. It was through Sansom that Robert Husband was eventually put in touch with the well-known Portsmouth solicitor, George Feltham.

Feltham was only thirty-nine, but he had already built up a successful and lucrative practice in the local police and county courts.[146] Although Feltham would become known as a shrewd, forceful defender, in his early career he had done a good deal of prosecution work for the Corporation and the Portsmouth Constabulary. No doubt his skills as an advocate were strengthened by this experience as both prosecutor and defender.

The Havant murder would prove to be an important, high-profile case for him. One imagines he didn't hesitate for long before agreeing to act for young Robert. For Robert's father – an ordinary man unaccustomed to being in the public eye and faced now with an extreme crisis in his life – it will have been a great relief to finally secure a respected professional man to conduct his son's defence.

Fred Sansom also worked tirelessly to raise funds to cover the Husband family's legal costs. With the Hampshire Winter Assizes due to be opened by Mr Justice Stephen at Winchester Castle on 14 December, there was no time to spare.

The first appeals for subscriptions were announced in the *Portsmouth Evening News* that evening:

---

145 *Portsmouth Evening News*, 5 May 1903.
146 *Hampshire Telegraph*, 8 October 1892.

The Prisoner's Defence

A Fund Proposed

Sir, — Aid has been solicited in your columns on behalf of the parents of the murdered boy at Havant, but up to now no notice has been taken of the very serious position in which the boy Husband is placed – without friends and funds. I hoped that ere this a more powerful pen than mine would have appealed for funds to secure counsel to defend him, but as no one has come forward, I willingly step into the breach and appeal to all to send me a mite towards the Defence Fund of Husband. Irrespective of the question of guilt or otherwise, surely no one with a particle of feeling would allow a poor, helpless boy of eleven years of age to go for trial without an adequate defence. All subscriptions sent will be acknowledged. I have started the list with a donation of 10s. 6d. Who will follow?

Yours truly,

FRANCIS J. SANSOM[147]

Sir, — Without in any way wishing to deprecate the efforts made on behalf of the murdered boy's parents, I think, in the interest of justice, that a fund might be opened on behalf of the accused, thus enabling his parents to engage counsel for his defence. Judging from their position, I should say it would be almost impossible for them to do so without assistance. I shall be pleased to receive any sums, however small, towards this object.

I remain, faithfully yours,

ALFRED AMATT[148]

Alfred Amatt was a jeweller and watchmaker. He unsuccessfully contested a seat in the 1886 municipal elections for the St John's ward in Portsea ('Action Not Words' was his campaigning slogan).[149] His left-wing sympathies were clearly evident in his speeches and electioneering pledges: he resented, for example, the squandering of ratepayers' taxes on the town hall and the canoeing lake in Southsea, arguing that the money would be better spent financing

---

147 *Portsmouth Evening News,* 6 December 1888.

148 Ibid.

149 *Portsmouth Evening News,* 19 October 1886. He was elected a town councillor for the Portsea ward from 1898 to 1903. Always a colourful figure, in 1906 he was charged at the Assizes in Winchester with receiving a quantity of watch chains stolen from a jeweller's shop in Southsea, but on the direction of the judge a 'Not Guilty' verdict was returned.

a recreation ground for ordinary working families at North End. St John's ward was a largely working-class district with strong ties to the dockyards, so his overt support for Robert Husband and his son, while perfectly genuine, was also an astute political move.

It made sense for Sansom and Amatt to act jointly in this venture, even if they made a rather unlikely pairing – Amatt the Liberal rabble-rouser and Sansom the staunch young Conservative. Effectively, they merged their individual appeals to form the 'Husband Defence Fund', with both men acting as honorary secretaries. Over the next few days, letters of appeal were circulated to all the local and national newspapers:

> Sir, — A Defence Fund is being raised on behalf of the boy Husband who has been committed for trial accused of murder. His father is a working man and has eleven children[150] to provide for, so that he is able to contribute but little towards the cost of defence. The evidence that has come to light during the past few days makes the occurrence more a mystery than ever. This poor boy stands in a most serious position, without friends or funds. We hope to remedy this.
>
> Will any kind reader send a mite towards increasing the Fund? The smallest subscription will be thankfully received and acknowledged by
>
> Alfred Amatt
> Francis James Sansom[151]

It was a time for friends and former work colleagues to step forward and show their support. One who did so was George Bartholomew from Lymbourne Terrace in Havant. He was a retired engine fitter who had worked for many years as a millwright in the dockyards at Portsmouth. In 1866, aged forty, he was forced to retire after sustaining severe back injuries in a fall while working on board HMS *Warrior*.[152] Bartholomew was a neighbour of Robert and Ellen Husband when they were bringing up their young family at Cherry Garden View in Portsea; he would have remembered Robert Jr as a babe in arms.[153] The two men stayed in touch even after the

---

150 In fact, in 1888–89 he had nine children.
151 *London Evening Standard*, 10 December 1888.
152 *Hampshire Telegraph*, 21 April 1866.
153 George Bartholomew and family lived at 15 Cherry Garden View.

Husband family moved to Havant; in time, Bartholomew also found work in Havant when he became licensee for a while at the Fountain pub on West Street. Now, as a contribution to the Husband defence fund, he had collected £2 13s. from the townsfolk of Havant. He called round at his friend's cottage on North Street and handed over the money in person.[154]

Robert and Fanny Husband must have been overwhelmed by these kind and generous gestures. A published list of subscribers appeared almost nightly in the *Portsmouth Evening News*: many donations were anonymous and for relatively small amounts, suggesting it was mainly from among the poorer sections of society that support was at its highest. But contributions came from many other quarters: for instance, there was 19s. from the Dorset Regiment; 5s. from the servants at the Dolphin Hotel in Chichester; 17s. 6d. was collected among friends at Fareham; Miss Morris on the Isle of Wight sent 2s. 6d; the blacksmiths at the Portsmouth dockyards contributed 4s; the Reverend Morris gave £4 4s; a subscriber signing himself 'an old shipmate of the Boy's father' reached into his pocket and handed over 10s. 6d; two friends in London gave 7s. Perhaps most movingly of all, a group of schoolboys collected £2 8s. 6 1/4d. One lady from Newport on the Isle of Wight even sent a gold ring.

When Mr Husband returned home from Portsmouth in the late afternoon, there was a stack of letters and postcards waiting for him on the kitchen table. Many were from friends and well-wishers expressing support. However, two in particular caught his attention. The first, signed with the writer's initials, accused a resident of Portsmouth of complicity in the murder.[155] The other, clearly a sick hoax, came from someone purporting to be 'Jack the Ripper'.[156] Mr Husband handed both missives to the police, although not in any great expectation they would do anything with them. It was his view, and the view of many people in Havant, that the police had made up their mind about Robert's guilt almost from the start, and had failed

154 *Portsmouth Evening News*, 13 December 1888.
155 *Portsmouth Times*, 8 December 1888.
156 *Portsmouth Evening News*, 7 December 1888.

to properly investigate clues that might have led in other directions.

The spectre of Jack the Ripper returned to complicate the hunt for Percy's killer. Information had already reached the police in November about a suspicious Jack the Ripper-style guest staying at a hotel in Emsworth in the days leading up to the murder. Now, this story rose to the surface again in a slightly different form.

At one time there were as many as thirty pubs and beerhouses in the port of Emsworth, reflecting the importance of the town's position on the turnpike road between Cosham and Chichester. By 1888 this number had been reduced to about fourteen. The Royal Oak in the Hermitage district of the town was established around 1830. An older pub of the same name had been demolished in the 1760s to make way for a new road. According to one historian, during demolition 'some bones were found ... and it was currently believed that someone had been murdered and buried there'.[157] It is a curious coincidence that, some 125 years later, the new Royal Oak would also become associated with murder.[158]

In 1888 the pub boasted ten rooms, a yard and stables, a skittles lawn and an indoor games room. Coroners' inquests used to be held there at one time, but not in recent years. The pub's roadside frontage and its charming spot on the coast ensured a regular trade.

The licence was transferred from James Hogan to James (or George) Kynvin in October 1887,[159] and from Kynvin to Enos Ruddock in January 1888.[160] But by March 1888 Ruddock had gone, and in January 1889 the Royal Oak and all its business furniture and utensils were put up for immediate sale.[161] In between these dates the licensee was a married man whose name has proved elusive,

157 Charles John Longcroft, *A Topographical Account of the Hundred of Bosmere* (John Russell Smith, 1851 edition).
158 The pub was renamed The Millpond in 1998. It closed down in 2005, becoming a B&B.
159 *Chichester Observer,* 12 October 1887.
160 *Chichester Observer,* 18 January 1888.
161 *Portsmouth Evening News,* 4 January 1889.

which is a shame because his wife's tale of a customer who could have been the Havant killer is one of the strangest elements in the Percy Searle story. Great importance was attached to her statement by those interested in defending Robert Husband, and for a while it seemed she would be called as a witness at the adjourned inquest.

The landlady was induced to tell her story on 4 December after she read a newspaper account of the inquest. She was struck by the 'very startling' similarity between an individual who recently called at the Royal Oak and the description of the murderer given to the police by the boy Husband. It is worth giving the text of her statement in full, as recorded in the *Portsmouth Times*:

> Three weeks ago an eccentric individual, of medium height, visited the hotel. His conduct immediately excited suspicion. He was dressed in a dark frock coat, and had a satchel of light material, in a position which in a bad light would resemble a patch across the shoulder. It was supported by a light strap across the shoulder. He also wore a high hat, and answered the description given by Husband. It was noticed that he possessed a pocket knife. He pursued infants with murderous threats, and at his lodgings stated that he had murdered several children, and would do for more. On a previous visit two weeks before, the same individual took a knife from his pocket and threatened to stab the other customers. He was then thrown to the floor and disarmed. The man was seen in Portsmouth within a few days of the murder.[162]

The landlady's statement was supported by her husband and daughters. The formal language suggests that the statement was a collaborative effort put together by the reporter and the witness. This is not to say that the events described by the landlady did not happen in the way she said they did, only that her account of them was a carefully constructed journalistic narrative.

Reporters from several other local newspapers quickly descended on Emsworth to gather more details about these peculiar events. The landlady did not disappoint.

It seems that the mysterious guest first visited the Royal Oak on Friday, 22 September. The landlady could recall the date exactly

162 *Portsmouth Times*, 8 December 1888.

because she made a note of it in a little almanac distributed by the manufacturers of Siegel's Syrup.[163] During the afternoon he sat in one of the rooms drinking stout and mild and eating his lunch out of a newspaper with the aid of large old-fashioned clasp knife. He was wearing a morning coat and a satchel made of light canvas material – just as Robert Husband had described it. He had a peculiar habit of muttering and murmuring to himself. The guest returned at nearly ten o'clock in the evening and got into an argument with several other customers at the bar, threatening to 'rip up' one of them. He stormed across the road to his room at Treagust's lodging house, then came back moments later with a table knife. The knife had a blade of about three and a half inches in length, stated the landlady – just like the weapon found by Tom Spurgeon outside the Manor House on the night of the murder. The stranger was quickly overpowered and disarmed by Henry Wood and other patrons.

The following evening the man was again causing a disturbance, this time outside Treagust's, where he was seen chasing a group of boys and threatening to cut their throats, adding that it would not be the first time he had murdered a child.

A fortnight afterwards, or it could have been in the middle of October, he returned to the Royal Oak, still wearing a dark coat and his distinctive light canvas satchel, although on this occasion he had on a high hat. The landlady refused to serve him, and after muttering violently for a while, he went away. But she heard him outside giving chase to a number of boys who were calling him 'Jack the Ripper'. Once, he looked back and scowled at her as she stood watching him from the doorway. 'He had small dark eyes,' she said, 'and heavy eyebrows.'

The landlady's daughter confirmed to the reporters that the man's conduct was 'violent and very much dreaded'. The pressmen went down to the little harbour and spoke to Henry Wood, who was working there on a boat. He told them he had subsequently seen the

---

163 A product made by A.J. White in London. It purported to promote good digestion and regular bowel movements. Its principal ingredients were aloe and sodium borate, used nowadays in detergents and in the manufacture of fibreglass.

stranger in Portsmouth in the company of a second man carrying a dulcimer. Wood felt sure the troublemaker was an old soldier who had served in India, since he seemed to be muttering into his full, bushy beard in Hindustani.[164]

It is difficult to know what to make of this story. The landlady informed the police of these events when they chanced to call at the Royal Oak in December on another matter, although one wonders why she didn't volunteer her statement earlier. The police obviously didn't treat her story with any seriousness, or if they did they quickly dismissed it out of hand. Even though the landlady made a point of denying that she knew Mr Husband and his family, and even though she expressed willingness to substantiate her claims by drawing up an affidavit, there were misgivings in some quarters over certain aspects of her story, and a general feeling that her account was too obviously contrived and partisan. And yet, if Robert Husband's description of Percy's killer was accurate and truthful, and the mysterious guest at the Royal Oak proved indeed to be the perpetrator, then you would expect the details given by the landlady and Robert to match. Besides which, her story was corroborated not just by her husband and daughters but by Henry Wood and other men like Ernest Ruffell, a sweet shop owner in Havant, who were present in the pub at the time the stranger visited.

But true or false, it was a juicy story, and the image of Jack the Ripper muttering in a foreign tongue into his bushy beard and strolling around the streets of Portsmouth with a companion carrying a dulcimer has a certain baroque appeal to it.

Meanwhile, young Robert was spending his first night in Winchester Prison.

By the late nineteenth century there was a view among many policy makers and welfare campaigners that youthful offenders

164 This account of the landlady's story is taken from the *Hampshire Telegraph*, 8 December 1888.

ought not to be imprisoned alongside adult convicts. Legislation between 1854 and 1857 had begun replacing prisons with reform and industrial schools for persons under sixteen years of age, yet the new system was slow to develop. In 1880 there were still around 6,500 children under sixteen in adult prisons.[165]

But children charged and convicted of wilful murder were exceptional cases, and they needed to be dealt with differently from other juvenile offenders. For boys (or girls) charged with the higher offences (especially murder), and tried at assize sessions, there was no real alternative to sending them to county prisons, either on remand or after conviction. Indeed, because the reform school movement resulted in fewer children being detained in adult prisons, there was decreasing financial justification for prisons to create separate wards for juveniles.

Winchester Prison was built in 1846–49. It housed around 300 male and female prisoners. Frederick Baker, the murderer of Fanny Adams in Alton in 1867, was the last person publicly hanged at Winchester. The prison had five wings radiating from a central hub with a ventilation tower. Each cell had its own gas burner to supplement the natural light entering via windows at the end of each wing and through large skylights in the pitched roof.[166] Hard labour consisted of treadmills and hand cranks (boxes with a handle that needed to be turned by the prisoner), oakum picking and mat making. In 1881 prison warders were issued with staves for their own protection, or with firearms if supervising parties of convicts outside the prison. While there was a separate annexe in the prison grounds for debtors, there does not appear to have been any special accommodation for juvenile prisoners. Robert, therefore, is unlikely to have been segregated from other male prisoners awaiting trial. He may have appeared unconcerned on the train leaving Havant, but

---

165 See Peter King and Joan Noel, 'The origins of "the problem of juvenile delinquency": the growth of juvenile prosecutions in London in the late eighteenth and early nineteenth centuries', *Criminal Justice History*, Vol. 14, (1993).

166 Alan Constable, *Five Wings and a Tower: Winchester Prison 1850–2002* (HMP Winchester, 2002).

unquestionably he will have been in utter and abysmal despair at Winchester.

In his pamphlet 'Children in Prison' (1897), Oscar Wilde wrote about the inhumane practice of incarcerating children with adult felons.

> The cruelty that is practised by day and night on children in English prisons is incredible ... To a little child, whether he is in prison on remand or after conviction, is a subtlety of social position he cannot comprehend. To him the horrible thing is to be there at all ...
> The terror that seizes and dominates the child, as it seizes the grown man also, is of course intensified beyond power of expression by the solitary cellular system of our prisons. Every child is confined to its cell for twenty-three hours out of twenty-four. This is the appalling thing. To shut up a child in a dimly-lit cell for twenty-three hours out of the twenty-four is an example of the cruelty of stupidity. If an individual, parent or guardian, did this to a child he would be severely punished.[167]

Winchester was too far away for his family to visit. Robert will have been alone, hungry, and frightened. But he will not have felt abandoned. He knew his father, his family and friends, and well-wishers from all over the country, were thinking about him and doing their best to set him free.

---

167 Oscar Wilde, *Children in Prison and Other Cruelties of Prison Life* (London: Murdoch & Co, 1897), pp. 7–8.

16

Fresh Witnesses

On Friday, 7 December, the county coroner, Mr Edgar Goble, resumed the inquest into the death of Percy Searle. He told the court there would be several fresh witnesses giving evidence. Mr George Feltham, the Portsmouth solicitor, was seated very conspicuously in the front row, next to Mr Husband. He was there to watch proceedings on behalf of Robert.

The fact that additional evidence – very significant evidence, as it turned out – would be adduced for the first time in the coroner's court on Friday suggested that the magistrates had been overhasty in committing Robert for trial on Wednesday. As the *Hampshire Telegraph* put it, the justices 'might have had a clearer idea of the whole case if they had waited'.[168] As it was, their decision to commit Robert for trial on the gravest charge known to English law (that of wilful murder) before the result of the coroner's inquest was known (i.e. before it was determined how the deceased came by his death) created a number of legal anomalies.

One consequence was that Mr Feltham was prevented from calling Robert as a witness at the inquest (should he desire to do so) except by obtaining a writ of *habeas corpus*. For the jury, the problem was slightly different: they knew Robert had already been sent for trial, yet they were being asked to proceed with the inquiry as if the boy had not been committed. It was an unsatisfactory position to be in.

Mr Feltham made his presence felt from the start. He requested permission to address the jury directly. Mr Goble, however, declined the request, saying he had never known such a thing in his

---

168 *Hampshire Telegraph*, 22 December 1888.

experience. But he added he would be happy to summon anyone to appear before him, including members of the press, if they had evidence to tender. 'The jury,' he said, 'wished to have the matter thoroughly thrashed out.'[169]

As the day wore on, and as Mr Feltham warmed to his task, the police case against Robert began to look increasingly ragged and insubstantial.

The first matter brought up by Mr Feltham was the statement made by the landlady of the Royal Oak in Emsworth, which had been published in that morning's newspapers. Feltham read it out to the court. Of course, it was down to the coroner as to whether or not the landlady would be called to give evidence (in the end, she wasn't), but Mr Feltham said he felt it was only proper that the jury should hear about it. Mr Goble concurred, although his phrasing hints at feelings of irritation at the solicitor's interference:

> I am very pleased to hear you read that, because you know as well as possible the gentlemen of the jury want the whole of the evidence brought here that it is possible to bring; and if you have to tender any evidence which you think is desirable in the interest of this boy, we shall be only too happy to hear any evidence you have to bring.[170]

Superintendent Kinshott was recalled, and under cross-examination from Mr Feltham he admitted rather shamefully that he didn't know one way or another if the garments taken away by Sergeant Knapton for analysis in London were actually the clothes the boy had been wearing on the night of the murder. He looked a little uncomfortable at this line of questioning. It was possible, certainly, that Professor Tidy had been given the wrong set of clothes to examine. The coroner told the court that Professor Tidy couldn't attend on the present occasion, but he'd written to him asking him to be present early next week. The jury foreman, Mr John Arter, started moaning:

Mr Arter: Is it necessary we should have Dr Tidy's evidence again?

169   *Portsmouth Times*, 8 December 1888.
170   *Hampshire Telegraph*, 8 December 1888.

Coroner: You don't know what he will prove. [Smiling] You must
          not read the papers or hear anything outside this Court.
Mr Arter: But we have had the evidence.
Coroner: You cannot judge of the evidence given in another Court.
          You would like to have him here for yourselves, and weigh
          his evidence and judge of his demeanour.

Perhaps the coroner's earlier assurance that the jury wished to have
the matter 'thoroughly thrashed out' was a bit of an exaggeration.

Tom Spurgeon was also brought back for questioning. If he was
expecting another lightning appearance in his black academic gown,
Mr Feltham wasn't having it. He had some questions about the knife.
He wanted to know if Mr Spurgeon had ever seen a knife similar
to the one found on the night of the murder. 'I daresay in my life I
have; I could not say yes or no.' And that was the whole point: even
if it could be shown that the knife produced in court was the same
knife possessed by Robert Husband on the day of the murder (and
even that couldn't be ascertained with any confidence), there was
no evidence whatsoever it was the murder weapon. Pocket knives
were commonplace. Lots of boys had them. Professor Tidy might
have been given the wrong knife to examine as well.

Next was the turn of John Smith, the labourer from Bedhampton.
At the earlier hearing Smith had been brought into court simply for
identification purposes; now he was going to testify. The problem
was, he fancied himself as a sort of amateur detective, and George
Feltham was in no mood to humour him. Smith's evidence was that
George Husband had tried to sell him a knife a few days before
the murder. Smith subsequently recognised the knife at the police
station. He had sought George out and questioned him about the
knife, eliciting from him the admission that he had given the knife
to his brother. This was potentially damaging testimony for Robert
because it associated him, circumstantially at least, with possessing
the alleged murder weapon. But Mr Feltham was quick to interpose.
First of all he objected to John Smith's interrogation of George
Husband, which he argued couldn't be used in evidence against
Robert. Then he made Smith look like a fool:

Mr Feltham: Perhaps you will be kind enough to tell the Coroner and the gentlemen of the jury what particular business you had to find out [i.e. by interrogating George]

John Smith: Of course, I went and asked him.

Mr Feltham: You have said that several times.

John Smith: Well, I went and asked him to see whether it was the same knife as he had shown me.

Mr Feltham: What business of yours was it whether he had lost the knife, bought it, or sold it?

John Smith: When I read the description of the knife in the paper I went to see.

Mr Feltham: You went to cross-examine George Husband? Who put you up to it?

John Smith: No one.

Mr Feltham: No one at all! And you went to get information?

John Smith: I went to get information.

Mr Feltham: You didn't get any?

John Smith: No more than what he told me.

Mr Feltham: He didn't satisfy you?

John Smith: No.

Mr Feltham: You are not satisfied now, are you?

John Smith: So far as that goes, I must be, I suppose. [Laughter in court][171]

Little Ethel Whitbread gave a far more credible performance, confidently repeating the evidence she gave at the magistrates' court about seeing Robert sharpening a knife against the wall of Miss Burrows's house on the morning of the murder.

And finally, Captain Charles Purvis Boyd JP stepped forward to give his evidence. Disgracefully, he had sat on the Bench throughout the entire committal proceedings knowing full well that his own eyewitness testimony – never heard in the magistrates' court – cast serious doubt on the case being marshalled against Robert. Worse still, he hadn't spoken out or demurred when Mr Snell sent the boy for trial on a capital charge.

He was a fussy, fastidious man, who took refuge in the small details of his evidence – timings to the second, the exact number

---

171 *Hampshire Telegraph*, 8 December 1888.

of paces between Point A and Point B, the cardinal direction of the wind in the Pallant – rather than reflecting on the responsibility of providing testimony that might save the life of the boy now awaiting trial in Winchester.

He delivered his evidence in short, clipped sentences. He'd arrived at Havant railway station at 6.04 pm. The train was punctual that night. He proceeded down Prince George Street. He passed Mr Spurgeon's school at exactly nine and a half minutes past six. It was pitch dark and pouring with rain. There was a gusting wind. It came from a south-south-west direction. He had trouble keeping his umbrella up.

There was no one lying against the wall of the school when he passed the Manor House. He then made his way down East Pallant towards the town hall. At exactly 6.11 (or 53 paces further on from where the body would be found) he crossed paths with a man heading towards the Pallant. According to Captain Boyd this man was 5ft 9in or 5ft 10in in height and had the appearance of a navvy. He didn't notice the man sufficiently to say whether he was loitering. Nor could he say what the other man was wearing. He heard no screams or cries that night.

This was crucial testimony. If Captain Boyd was correct in his timings – and who could doubt such an upright, impeccable, and punctilious witness – then this man, this stranger, this navvy, had been in the Pallant at precisely the moment Percy was murdered.

The jury foreman, Mr Arter, piped up again.

Mr Arter:	What were you wearing on the night in question?
Captain Boyd:	A long, light great coat with a cape to it, and an umbrella.
Mr Arter:	Nothing like a satchel round your shoulders, I suppose? [Laughter in court]
Captain Boyd:	Not at all.[172]

The captain bristled at the impertinence. He didn't like being the butt of the court's humour. It was okay for a courtroom to poke fun at

---

172 *Portsmouth Times*, 8 December 1888.

child witnesses like George Husband and Albert Ferrell, but he was an important dignitary living in a substantial house in Emsworth with a butler and footmen. He was captain of the 1st Middlesex Militia and a justice of the peace, for God's sake. How dare that scoundrel Arter – a mere ironmonger – insinuate that Captain Boyd was Jack the Ripper. The coroner interjected quickly to calm the situation. He said he presumed the foreman had asked that question to ascertain if the boy Husband might have seen Captain Boyd in the Pallant and given his description as the attire of the murderer. But Boyd was still in a huff.

George Feltham jumped in to capitalise on the significance of the captain's evidence:

Mr Feltham:	I understand you cannot really identify the man?
Captain Boyd:	Certainly not.
Mr Feltham:	He was going in the direction of where you ultimately found the body had been discovered?
Captain Boyd:	The spot which was afterwards pointed out to me.[173]

Why hadn't this evidence been put before the magistrates? Why hadn't Captain Boyd spoken out earlier?

Captain Boyd walked stiffly out of the courtroom, nearly bumping into the next witness who was already coming forward to give his testimony.

Mr Farnden largely repeated the evidence he'd given before the magistrates, and his wife, Sarah, again corroborated him. She also deposed that her eldest daughter Ellen heard a disturbance in the Pallant that evening but saw nothing when she looked behind the blinds.

Their son, William, whose evidence had been disallowed at the committal hearing, was duly sworn in the coroner's court. He had given satisfactory responses to the coroner's preliminary questions. Perhaps his mother had crammed him again.

Young William's evidence was intriguing to say the least.

---

173 *Portsmouth Times*, 8 December 1888.

William:	On the night that Percy Searle died I went out about five o'clock to Mrs Randall's to buy a reel of cotton. When I was in the shop Percy Searle was there too. I did not speak to him. I left the shop first.
Coroner:	Did you see any other boy?
William:	No.

William said that after leaving the shop he went to the Bear Hotel yard, and when he came out he saw Robert Husband peering into Mrs Randall's shop through the door. The coroner clarified his statement:

Coroner:	Was that while you were in the shop?
William:	Yes.
Coroner:	And did you see him when you went out?
William:	Yes.

He and Robert then went into the Bear Hotel yard for a minute. Afterwards, Robert accompanied William home and was standing outside the rails when the younger boy went indoors.

Coroner:	Now, be careful and answer me with perfect truth, my boy. Did you see a knife in the hands of Husband?
William:	No, sir.
Coroner:	Did he tell you whether he had a knife or not?
William:	No, he said nothing about it.
Coroner:	After you had lifted the latch of the front door did you notice in which direction Husband was going?
William:	No.
Coroner:	Have you any means of knowing the exact time when you went indoors?
William:	No, sir. I have no idea.
Mr Arter:	What did you go into the Bear yard for?
William:	There was a bit of a show there.
Mr Arter:	What show?
William:	I don't know.
Mr Arter:	Did Husband say anything about going up the Pallant?
William:	No.
Mr Arter:	He didn't speak to you?
William:	No.[174]

The gormlessness he had shown in front of the Mr Snell was gone; he was revealed as a bright, self-possessed lad. In reply to further questions from Mr Goble, William even felt confident enough to contradict his mother: he was adamant that his sister Ellen wasn't at home the evening Percy died – she was in Alton, he claimed, and he hadn't seen her for a month. Mrs Farnden was brought back into court and questioned on this point. She insisted Ellen was at home that evening – her daughter had heard a disturbance and went to look through the blinds. But William was equally sure his sister was at Alton. It is a mystery – perhaps not a terribly significant one, but it is curious that Ellen was never summoned to settle the matter one way or another. The aftershocks of the Havant Abduction case were possibly still reverberating through the family.

If Robert accompanied William home, why hadn't Robert asked Mr Farnden for the threepence owed when William opened the front door and entered the house? William's evidence came across as sincere and guileless, if a little confused in places. He said he went out to Mrs Randall's at about five o'clock where he met Percy, but Percy didn't arrive at the shop until a few minutes before six. What had he been doing for an hour? Also, there was no show going on in the Bear yard that night – perhaps William was thinking of the illusionist show in the stable yard at the back of the White Hart where his sister had met Monk and his friends.

Henry Shirley was briefly recalled and said he couldn't remember seeing Percy and William together at any time that evening. John Platt was also recalled: in response to questions from the jury, he confirmed he had taken hold of Robert's right hand when being led to the spot where Percy was lying. The boy's hand was perfectly dry, he said. And yes, he would have felt blood on the boy's hands if there had been any.

Mrs Searle followed. She repeated her evidence about a grudge between the accused and her deceased son. Gently, the coroner and the jury elicited from her that Robert's refusal to serve Percy with

174 *Hampshire Telegraph*, 8 December 1888 & *Portsmouth Times*, 8 December 1888.

coals was based on a slight misunderstanding; Robert hadn't been reprimanded by his father and the matter was quickly dropped by all parties. Furthermore, she granted that to her knowledge Percy and Robert had never quarrelled. It was a sad moment: perhaps the death of her son was slightly easier to bear if she could grasp a reason for it, however petty and warped that reason might be. But now she seemed to accept within herself that this supposed grudge offered no explanation for anything.

Eleven-year-old Frederick Searle, a brother of Percy, was a new witness. He related an altercation between himself and Robert Husband two days after the coal incident, but there was no mention of Robert uttering a threat against Percy (as Mrs Searle had initially alleged in her interviews with the newspapers on 28 November).

There were still a few new witnesses to be heard, but Mr Goble decided to adjourn the inquest at this point till Wednesday morning. Dr Tidy would be able to attend on that day and the case could then be concluded. The coroner emphasised again that it was his desire to have all the facts presented to the jury. For instance, he had been told that soon after the murder a man had been seen hurriedly leaving Havant by train. If Mr Feltham wished it, evidence could be given on that point.

Mr Feltham did wish it.

Percy Searle, aged 7

Robert Husband, aged 10

Bug's Row in the 1950s

North street circa 1900, showing Agate's grocers shop

East Street circa 1887

ARREST of the BOY HUSBAND

Manor House, circa 1885

Scene of the opening of the inquest into Percy Searle's death:
Havant Union Workhouse, West Street, circa 1920

Tom Spurgeon, who discovered the murder weapon, and his family circa 1890

Left to right:
Chief Constable Captain John Forrest; Mr Charles Mathews QC; Mr Justice James Fitzjames Stephen

Winchester Great Hall, where the Assizes were held

Robert Husband and Ellen Hammond, Robert's parents, circa 1878

Below: Fanny Ryves, Robert's stepmother, in 1906, aged 48

Right: Jane Husband, Robert's sister, in 1895, aged 22

Middle row: Robert's brothers in later life

Sydney and Herbert Searle, Percy's brothers, in the 1920s

View of the Manor House (1936) by William Grant

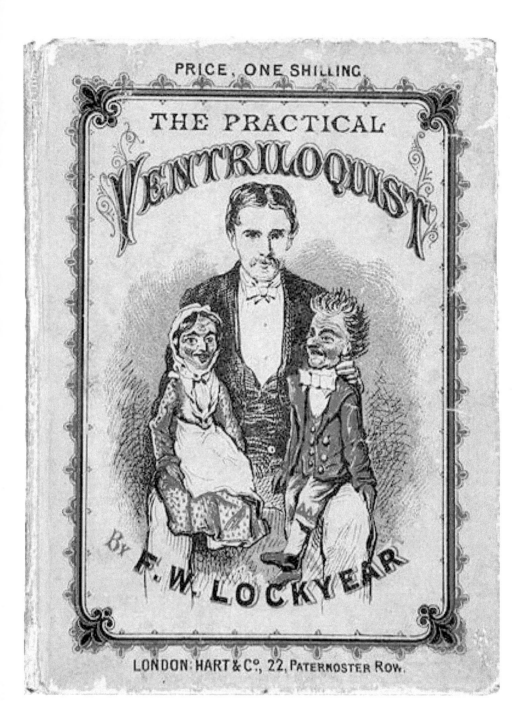

PRICE, ONE SHILLING

THE PRACTICAL

VENTRILOQUIST

By F. W. LOCKYEAR

LONDON: HART & Cº, 22, PATERNOSTER ROW.

Front cover of The Practical Ventriloquist by Fred W. Lockyear

17

Here Comes Jack the Ripper!

With the Winter Assizes due to start on Friday week, there was not much time for George Feltham to appoint and instruct a barrister to act on Robert's behalf. Feltham would have known most of the barristers on the western circuit, and he will doubtless have been impressed by the logic and eloquence of one rising young lawyer called Charles Mathews. The *Hampshire Post* described him as 'one of the cutest men among the Junior Bar on the Circuit'.[175] The two of them were in court together at the Hampshire Sessions in April 1880 when Mathews defended John Crow, an insurance agent, on a charge of wife murder (on this occasion Feltham was instructing the prosecution). Mathews may well have been Feltham's first choice to represent Robert since along with his other qualities of intelligence and forensic thoroughness he showed considerable flair for cross-examination, especially of expert witnesses. Also, at this stage in his career, it is possible that Mathews may have been slightly cheaper than his more senior and experienced colleagues. In all likelihood, Feltham will have contacted Mathews over the weekend of 8 and 9 December. The Husband Defence Appeal had not yet raised sufficient funds to retain a barrister, so Francis Sansom or Alfred Amatt (or both of them) must have stepped in to provide a surety of some description.

Charles Willie Mathews (*formerly* West) was an American. He was born in New York in 1850. His mother's third marriage was to the English actor and playwright Charles James Mathews, whose

175 *Hampshire Post*, 14 December 1888.

name Charles junior later assumed. This stage background must have influenced Charles in many ways, not least in the theatrical often histrionic rhetorical style he brought to the courtroom. It was said he was one of the few members of the English Bar who could draw tears from both the judge and the jury. He had been involved in several celebrated criminal and civil trials: he appeared for the defence in the murder trial of the Stauntons (1879), a shocking case involving homicide by starvation, and again for the defence at the trial of the Wimbledon poisoner Dr George Lamson in 1882. In 1884 he prosecuted in *R. v. Dudley and Stephens*, a notorious case involving cannibalism by shipwrecked mariners. Much later he would go on to become Director of Public Prosecutions.

George Feltham must have been overjoyed when Mathews agreed to take the brief in the Robert Husband case.

The thrice-adjourned inquest was resumed at the Havant Police Court on Wednesday 12 December. Captain Boyd was back on the Bench where he felt more comfortable, sitting next to the county coroner Mr Goble. There were also three (unnamed) 'ladies of distinction' sitting behind the coroner at the front of the court. Mr Husband was present, and George Feltham again watched the proceedings on Robert's behalf. The principal witness was going to be Professor Tidy, who had made another long, weary journey up from London. Several new witnesses were anticipated, too.

Eunice Norris was first to give evidence. She was a young woman working as a domestic servant at the Langstone Lodge hotel on Hayling Island, about a mile from the centre of Havant. She told the inquest that George Husband had called at the hotel on Wednesday morning after the murder to take orders for coal. Speaking of his own accord, he admitted to Eunice that the knife found in the Pallant belonged to him and that he'd last seen it on Saturday night two days before the murder. The knife had been in his old trousers pocket, hanging over a chair in the bedroom he shared with Robert. He had asked Eunice if she thought Robert might have taken the knife out of his pocket, to which she replied, 'How should I know?' The only witness to this conversation was another servant, who was deaf. Eunice's statement contradicted George's evidence given at an earlier hearing in which he claimed he had lost the knife after church on the Sunday morning, not on Saturday night.

Charles Clark, aged ten, was the second new witness. The son of a carter living in the Brockhampton district of Havant, he attended the same school as Percy. He had a dramatic story to tell. He remembered seeing Robert Husband and his gang outside the coal yard at around six o'clock on the night of the murder. Robert had a large knife in his right hand with the blade open. As Charles and some of his friends were running past the yard, Robert cried out 'Here comes Jack the Ripper!'

> He stopped me, but the others ran on. He said he didn't mean any harm. He pointed the knife at me. I had never seen him pointing a knife like that before.[176]

The weapon found in the Pallant was about to be shown to the witness for recognition, but Mr Feltham suggested that several knives should be produced and the boy tested by picking it out from the rest. The coroner elicited from Charles that all he could say about the knife was that it was 'large', so in the end it was decided it would be useless offering the knife for identification purposes. In addition, Charles was unable to say in which direction Robert had headed after the alleged knife incident. And he admitted to the court that he hadn't spoken about these events to anyone (except vaguely to his grandmother) until Sergeant Knapton questioned him earlier that morning. He had seen the body of Percy in the Pallant and he had seen Robert waving a knife about and shouting 'Here comes Jack the Ripper!' only minutes before the murder, and he knew Robert was in custody, but he never had the wit to volunteer his information until today, and only then when questioned by the police. Significantly, none of the boys in Robert's gang – Watley, Stacey and Burchell – and none of Charles's friends were called to corroborate his evidence.

176 *Hampshire Telegraph*, 15 December 1888.

Professor Tidy came forward next. He repeated the evidence he had given before the magistrates on his last visit to Havant regarding the total lack of bloodstains of any kind on the clothes he had been asked to analyse. It is true there were a few small stains on the right hand wristband of the shirt, but in Tidy's view they were at least a month old. In reply to the coroner, he stated his opinion that the attacker was unlikely to have escaped being covered – *smothered* was the word used in many newspaper reports – in blood. This conflicted with Dr Bond's testimony, which was read out to the professor. Dr Bond had argued that an attacker stabbing Percy from behind would probably not be splashed with the victim's blood, but Professor Tidy disagreed:

> The carotid artery having been divided and the knife having been pushed in as far as it could be – three inches – it is extremely difficult for me to suppose that such a wound could be inflicted without the hand and clothes being covered in blood. If the carotid artery had been divided the blood would have spurted out. The artery would have been severed by the insertion of the knife, and some time must escape in pulling the knife out. Some curious circumstance might possibly occur to prevent the immediate spurting, but it is extremely difficult to me to imagine the circumstance.[177]

George Feltham pressed home the advantage.

Feltham: You are of the opinion that anyone using the knife to inflict the wound would have some blood on him?

Dr Tidy: I should have thought a considerable quantity.

And yet no blood at all had been found on Robert's clothes, and John Platt, who held Robert's hand only moments after the crime, reported that Robert's hands were completely dry and unstained with blood.[178] The professor was also asked about the knife itself, and he again observed that he found it difficult to imagine a circumstance in which the blade would be covered in blood but not the hand of the

177 *West Sussex Gazette*, 13 December 1888.
178 Professor Tidy could not be exact as to how long it might have taken the blood to dry, but he said it could not have dried in a few minutes. See *West Sussex Gazette*, 13 December 1888.

person wielding the knife. He agreed that a considerable amount of force must have been exerted to insert such an ill-sharpened blade into Percy's neck, and the fact that the blade was rickety may have been an important factor, but he would not be drawn further on this:

Coroner: I believe you have seen the boy Husband, when he was before the magistrates?

Dr Tidy: Yes.

Coroner: Can you say whether a boy of that age and size would have sufficient strength to inflict such a wound?

Dr Tidy: I cannot say; the question of degrees of strength varies so according to circumstance.

A third new witness entered the court. It was Mrs Alma Taylor who lived at No. 11 in the Pallant. She was in Mrs Randall's shop on the night Percy was murdered. At a few minutes past six she heard running footsteps outside; Robert Husband appeared in the shop doorway with a very excited face, fell against Mr Shirley, and said to the whole shop, 'There's a man killing a boy down yonder'. According to Mrs Taylor, Henry Shirley was in the doorway arranging stock, but Robert addressed the whole shop. This is important because Shirley originally claimed that Husband seemed to be running away and only came over to raise the alarm once he realised that Shirley had spotted him. Now, Mrs Taylor was saying that Robert actually came into the shop of his own accord (before Shirley had seen him) and raised the alarm in a general way. This version of events exactly matched Robert's own account (or at least one iteration of it) given to the magistrates, and it cast a very different, far more favourable, light on Robert's actions that evening.

The final witness tendered by the police was Harry Whitbread, son of the photographer Samuel Whitbread and brother of seven-year-old Ethel who had so impressed the magistrates and the coroner's jury with her confident testimony and unflappable manner in the witness box. Harry was four years older than his sister but he impressed no one and he gave the court something to laugh about at the end of the embarrassingly weak police case. He related how he'd met Robert Husband near the coal yard at 8.30 on the morning after the murder. Robert told Harry that both he and John Platt were going to come into some money. Superintendent Kinshott urged the coroner to ask Harry what the amounts were. Edward Goble humoured him.

Coroner: Did Husband say how much?
Harry: Yes; he was going to have £100 and Mr Platt £105. [Laughter in court]
Coroner: Did he say what for?
Harry: No.
Coroner: I don't suppose the jury have any questions to put. Perhaps Mr Feltham can suggest something? [Laughter]
Feltham: Oh, no. He thought perhaps he was going to be rewarded for assisting justice. [Laughter][179]

This concluded the evidence for the police. Superintendent Kinshott had no intention of calling Robert's father or stepmother to clarify their son's movements on the night of the murder – he had made up his mind about Robert's guilt a fortnight before, almost within hours of taking charge of the investigation, and he preferred to hear silly evidence from Harry Whitbread rather than listen to the parents' side of the story. But George Feltham took the opportunity to call both parents.

The father gave evidence first. He told the court how Robert had been working with him all day in the coal yard. At six o'clock Mr Husband had locked the trucks away, closed the gates, and gone indoors to do the accounting. His wife mentioned that Mr Farnden still owed threepence for coal, so at around five past six Robert was sent to the Pallant to collect the money. Fifteen minutes later he returned and said there was a man killing a boy by the Manor School wall. Robert said he had alerted Mr Shirley and Mr Platt. Robert then took off his hat, retrieved a threepenny piece from it, and placed it on the kitchen table.

Questioned by Mr Feltham, the father explained there was a double-burner lamp burning inside the family cottage but he hadn't

179 *Portsmouth Times*, 15 December 1888.

seen any blood on Robert's hands. His mother told Robert to wash his face and hands before tea. Then Mr Platt arrived and took Robert back to the Pallant. The coroner enquired about the disagreement between the Searle and Husband families. Mr Husband recollected Mrs Searle complaining to him that Robert had refused to serve Percy a quarter of a hundredweight of coal, but he said this was because he did not allow Robert to serve at the counter when he was not there.

The court then adjourned for lunch.

The final afternoon session began with the mother's evidence. Mrs Husband was a small woman, round faced and with a perpetual air of melancholy about her. She had very recently given birth to her sixth child, Arthur, and the stress of the imminent trial on top of her relentless childcare duties had exhausted her. Standing up in court, she looked nervous and ill at ease.

She corroborated her husband's testimony in every detail. The coal yard closed at six o'clock and Robert was sent to Mr Farnden's house to collect threepence owed for coal. When he returned around 6.20 she said his hands were dirty with the coals and nothing else. He washed his hands and wiped them dry on a towel hanging on the back of the washhouse door. Mrs Husband washed the towel the following Wednesday morning and she didn't notice any unusual stains or marks on it. Robert went to bed, she said, a little after eight o'clock. When the family breakfasted the following morning, no mention was made of Percy's death at all. Robert was wearing a clean shirt on the Sunday previous to the murder.

Several of the local newspapers, but not all of them, reported the titbit that Mrs Husband said she took a small penknife away from her son George on the day Percy was killed. Was this a naive attempt by the mother to protect her son by claiming she had confiscated the murder weapon from his brother before Percy was killed? Or was George in the habit of hoarding multiple knives, one of which he lost at church on Sunday (or which Robert had stolen from his trousers pocket), and another which his mother confiscated on the day of the murder? The court was tired, and the implications of this new piece of information, coming right at the end of the enquiry, were not satisfactorily pursued.

The last witness was Alfred Steele, the railway porter, who was on duty at the station on the night of the murder. George Feltham was keen for his evidence to be heard because it tended to shift the focus away from his client and incriminate an altogether different suspect.

Steele related how, at about 6.30 or 6.35 (accounts differ), he saw a man jump into a second-class smoking compartment of the train waiting to leave for Brighton. He described the man as being 'somewhat different from the general run of passengers' (whatever that means): he was around 5ft 9in in height and had a dark moustache. He was wearing a long black coat and a felt hat, although there was no patch in the coat, and the man was not carrying a satchel over his shoulder. In fact, he had no luggage at all. Steele thought his manner was 'strange', and he remarked on this to a colleague, but he had no reason to scrutinise the passenger any more closely because at that time he was unaware a murder had taken place. He closed the carriage door and the train departed, taking the mystery traveller with it.

Superintendent Kinshott was anxious to deflect any implied criticism of the police's handling of the Steele incident. At Kinshott's suggestion, the coroner elicited from Steele that Sergeant Knapton had been at the railway station a little later that evening (when Thomas Clarke has been arrested on suspicion of the murder) but that Steele had not alerted the sergeant to the strange passenger seen leaping onto the Brighton train. Steele said he was busy and it never occurred to him mention the incident to the police. Kinshott added that when the police were eventually apprised of this lead, Detective Lawler travelled up and down the railway line between Havant and Brighton looking for the suspicious-looking passenger, but could not trace him.

Was Steele's 'strange passenger' the same man Captain Boyd had seen heading in the direction of the Pallant moments before Percy was attacked? Was he the same man Robert claimed to have seen stabbing Percy and running off towards the Fair Field? These were questions for the jury to decide. After four hearings and the testimony of twenty-seven witnesses, the coroner's enquiry had come to an end. The case had been 'thoroughly thrashed out', in the words of Edward Goble.

The coroner thanked the jury for their patience and commended them on the intelligent questions they had raised. He then proceeded to give a lengthy summing up.

It had not been a straightforward enquiry by any means, and he conceded that the case had been complicated by the youth of Robert Husband and several witnesses. The jury needed to disregard anything they may have read in the newspapers or heard outside the court and concentrate solely on the evidence presented to them at the inquest. The fact that the boy Husband had already been sent for trial at the Winchester Assizes should not prejudice their deliberations in any way: the magistrates had only to determine if sufficient corroborating evidence existed to support a *prima facie* case, whereas the duty of the coroner's court was to discover how, where and by what means a death had occurred. It was a grave responsibility because if they returned a verdict against a named person, that person must be put in the dock and arraigned.

Mr Goble then turned to the evidence. There were several matters he wished to raise that might help shape the jury's deliberations. Firstly, a strong point in Robert Husband's favour was that he had denied his guilt from the very start. He had been the first to spread news of the crime and had immediately sought assistance at the draper's shop. However, the boy's credibility as a witness had been destroyed when it was demonstrated that Robert could not possibly have seen the murder from any of the two or three different places where he said he was standing, and that if he witnessed the murder at all he must have been much nearer to the location where the body was found. Yet, if he had witnessed the murder then he would surely be very frightened and in an agitated state of mind and might not properly recall where he had actually been standing at the time. Robert claimed he had screamed 'Murder!' as he ran off down the Pallant towards Mrs Randall's shop, but no witnesses reported hearing his cries for help. Mr Goble suggested to the jury they might consider if the high wind blowing that evening had carried Robert's screams away. If the jury chose to disregard the evidence of Harry Whitbread, then no knife was seen in Robert's possession just before the murder was committed.

The coroner addressed the contradictory evidence regarding the payment of the threepence for coal. There was no doubt that Robert had gone to the Farnden's house that evening – young William Farnden had accompanied him to the front garden gate – but it was a matter for the jury to decide if they believed Robert's statement that he received payment from Mr Farnden just after six o'clock that evening or if they believed Mr and Mrs Farnden when they claimed Robert had not called at any time that evening. Mr Goble suggested that Robert might have deceived his father by not telling him that the money had already been paid, but this can scarcely have served as a pretext for the murder of Percy Searle since Robert had no way of knowing that Mrs Searle would send her son on an errand through the Pallant that same night.

It was also for the jury to decide if a grudge over a complaint regarding the serving of coal provided in their view sufficient motive to account for the murder.

In conclusion, Mr Goble alluded to Captain Boyd's important evidence regarding a navvy seen in the area on the night of the murder, and Alfred Steele's testimony about a suspicious-looking man jumping aboard a train shortly afterwards. The jury had before them the full facts of the case and it was down to them to arrive at a verdict.

The court was cleared and the jury allowed privacy to deliberate.

It was a bitterly cold winter's afternoon. An icy wind howled inland from the Solent. The sky shone with a pewter light and seabirds screeched in the rooftops. Outside the coal yard on North Street, queues were beginning to form, stretching almost as far as Elm Road.

Inside the courthouse a large crowd awaited the verdict. Witnesses, police officers, members of the general public and court officials beat their arms and stomped around the unheated outer rooms trying to keep warm as best they could. After two and a half hours, the jury announced they had reached a decision. The court was re-opened and everyone filed back into the main hall. Mr John Arter, the jury foreman, carried a piece of paper in his hand.

Coroner: Mr Foreman and gentlemen of the Jury, are you agreed upon your verdict?

Foreman: Yes, sir.

Coroner: How do you find that Percy Knight Searle came by his death?

Foreman [reading]: We find that Percy Knight Searle was murdered by some person or persons, but the Jury cannot agree as to the sufficiency of the evidence to prove by whom the crime was committed.

Coroner: That is the verdict of murder against some person or persons unknown,

Foreman: Yes, sir.[180]

The inquest then terminated.

George Feltham and Mr and Mrs Husband will have been satisfied with the findings of the inquest. It gave them hope that the jury at the Winchester trial would return a verdict in their favour. For the Searle family, the circumstantial and inconclusive nature of the evidence against Robert Husband will have stoked uncertainty in their minds. A boy murdered, the murderer hanged – that was justice for them. But if Robert Husband didn't kill Percy, who did?

The police, however, remained utterly convinced they had apprehended and charged the guilty person, and that Robert had acted alone. He was a vicious, dangerous child, and he would get his comeuppance at the trial, of that there was no doubt.

A correspondent signing himself 'Sir Ascupart' wrote to the *Pall Mall Gazette* relating an incident he witnessed on Saturday, 15 December, while travelling by train to Southampton. It captures

---

180 *Hampshire Telegraph*, 15 December 1888.

the high spirits and the smug mood of self-righteousness of the Hampshire Constabulary in the run up to the Winter Assizes. (The 'inspector of police' referred to in this letter was most likely Deputy Chief Constable Stephenson, who lived at Newport on the Isle of Wight.)

> On Saturday last I travelled from London to Southampton, and at Winchester the numbers in our carriage were increased by, among others, an inspector of police in uniform – hailing from Newport on the Isle of Wight, I believe – and an elderly divine. The inspector communicative and the divine inquisitive – the divine anxious to know and the inspector only too willing to gratify his curiosity. Was the boy guilty? The inspector was most important. He had had the investigation of the case, 'don't you know.' He knew all the details – had had many of the witnesses before him, described the boy's demeanour, &c. Then, in a dramatic style, he launched into a picture of the trial, as it was going to be, the speeches of counsel for the prosecution, the witnesses that would be called, the speeches for the defence, the judge's summing up, and the inevitable verdict. It would take two days and there could only be one result. Probably you, Sir, will agree with me in considering the remarks of the inspector in a public railway carriage, and in mixed company, with a possible juror in the case, for we were a party of eight men independently of the inspector and divine, in exceedingly bad taste, to use no stronger term.[181]

There was a heavy calendar for the Winter Assizes. It contained the names of 75 prisoners, among the more serious charges being:

2 attempted murders
1 unlawful wounding
4 burglaries
8 housebreaking
2 rapes
4 indecent assaults
4 arson

And there was one charge of murder. It was the most remarkable case in the present assize. It promised to occupy the judge and the

181 *Pall Mall Gazette*, 24 December 1888.

jury for the greatest amount of time. It would attract the biggest courtroom crowds and it would excite the deepest and widest interest among the reading public. It was the trial of Robert Husband for the murder of Percy Knight Searle.

PART THREE

18

Licking the Butcher's Hand

One of the remarkable features of this case is how quickly events unfolded from the murder of Percy Searle on 26 November 1888, to the opening of Robert Husband's trial at Winchester on 19 December 1888. As a result, most of the newspaper coverage of the case came from the magistrates' and coroner's courts rather than from the news columns.[182] Aside from an undertow of lurid press speculation concerning Jack the Ripper, and reports of the deceased boy's funeral, there were few journalistic pieces adding human interest to the pre-trial drama.

The shocking news that an eleven-year-old had been charged with the wilful murder of an eight-year-old was widely reported in both the local and national media, as well as abroad, but little effort was made to broaden the analysis and place the murder in any sort of historical or social context. Previous cases of child-on-child homicide, such as the Breen and Fitz case in 1855[183] and the Barratt and Bradley case in 1861,[184] were not referenced at all in the run-up to the Winchester trial, nor was there any debate on how the Havant tragedy appeared to challenge preconceived notions of childhood innocence and dependency. How children charged

---

182 Judith Rowbotham et al, *Crime News in Modern Britain 1820–2010* (Palgrave Macmillan, 2013), pp. 70–71.

183 Two nine-year-olds, John Breen and Alfred Fitz, murdered another small boy, James Fleeson. After assaulting him and throwing a brick at his head, they pushed him into a canal. They were found guilty of manslaughter and imprisoned for twelve months. See 'The Murder By Boys, In Liverpool', *Liverpool Daily Post*, 23 August 1855.

184 Peter Barratt and James Bradley, both aged eight, tortured an infant named George Burgess before drowning him in a brook. They were convicted of manslaughter and sentenced to five years in a reformatory. See 'Wilful Murder of a Child By Two Boys', *Newcastle Journal*, 18 April 1861.

with manslaughter and wilful murder offences were treated in the criminal justice system went completely unexamined.

In the nineteenth century most murders committed by males under sixteen came about as the result of fighting in the street or in the workplace, and the victims were nearly always boys of their own age and socio-economic background. Murders committed by very young children (under twelve) were exceptionally rare, and remain so today. In his book about the murder of James Bulger, David Smith references only 25 cases from 1847 onwards where children under the age of fourteen feloniously killed another child.[185] Eleanor Betts, in her study, found only four cases in England and Wales between 1816 and 1908 where children aged eleven were charged with wilful murder (i.e. with malicious intent to kill or grievously wounding).[186]

By the late 1880s, the notion of the lawless, 'hoodlum' child was becoming a topic of serious public concern. Newspaper stories tended to amplify these anxieties, personalising the dangers to law-abiding citizens from delinquent behaviour and using terrifying, dramatic examples to typify the problem. These children were frequently characterised as sullen, resentful young ruffians, nearly always male and working class, prowling the streets of major cities armed with knives and pistols, often coming together to form gangs in order to terrorize and run riot.

The Regent's Park Murder of 1888, in which eight teenage boys were charged with the murder of a young man out walking with his girlfriend in the Park, highlighted the growing problem of knife crime and teenage rowdyism in the metropolis. The ringleader George Galletly, aged seventeen, stabbed his victim once in the neck and once in the back, the second injury penetrating the right lung and severing a branch of the pulmonary artery, causing him to bleed to death within minutes.[187]

---

185 David Smith, *The Sleep of Reason* (London: Batsford, 1993).
186 Eleanor Betts, 'From Juvenile Delinquent to Boy Murderer: Understanding Children Who Killed, 1816–1908' (Doctoral dissertation, Queen Mary University of London, 2015). Retrieved from http://qmro.qmul.ac.uk/xmlui/handle/123456789/11902.
187 Proceedings of the Old Bailey online, reference t18880730-759. See also Peter

Gangs of violent working class youths existed in all large urban districts. Even small-town Havant had an issue with juvenile gangs, although obviously on a much reduced scale. Groups of rough boys loafed on street corners, especially in the Pallant, throwing stones, verbally abusing passersby, shouting, and generally making a nuisance of themselves and causing disturbance in the early evenings. Running fights between rival gangs of boys were regular occurrences. Robert and George were involved in many of these affrays; indeed, on the Sunday evening prior to Percy's murder, a fight involving one of the Husband brothers – it isn't clear which one – broke out in the stable yard of the Bear Hotel next to the Pallant.

Predictably, Robert Husband's arrest sparked newspaper fury over the 'pernicious' influence of cheap escapist 'penny dreadful' magazines on the youth of the day. These serial publications were aimed at working class boys and they were full of sensational and horrid excitements. 'How many lads,' asked the *Hampshire Post*, 'are led into crime by the perusal of the lives and adventures of such persons as Dick Turpin, the Pirate King, the Boy Highwayman, and the heroes of what the Americans succinctly distinguish as the Dime Novel?'[188]

Penny dreadfuls quickly became a scapegoat for juvenile crime. They were blamed for all manner of woes and tragedies, from boy and girl suicides to petty crime and murder. In Glasgow, for example, a gang of boy-housebreakers were seen as acting under the influence of these magazines:

> It is believed with good reason that the pernicious 'Charles Pearce' literature which is at present being so persistently sown in the lower quarters of Glasgow by means of certain penny weekly newspapers has much to do with the development of this sort of Jack Sheppardism in juvenile minds.[189]

Stubley, *1888: London Murders in the Year of the Ripper* (Stroud: The History Press, 2012), pp. 214–225. Charles Mathews prosecuted in this case.

188 'The Havant Murder', *Hampshire Post*, 30 November 1888.

189 'Juvenile Housebreakers and Penny Dreadfuls', *Edinburgh Evening News*, 28 July 1888.

The *Ross-shire Journal* recounted the sad case of a lad of eighteen who sought to emulate the adventures of fictional highwaymen who were forever being hanged and cut down alive; his experiments in this direction resulted in his death by strangulation.[190]

Penny dreadful comic books were also blamed when, in 1888, Charles Dobell, seventeen, and William Gower, eighteen, fatally shot a man in Tunbridge Wells. Both men – boys, really – were hanged the following year by the state executioner, James Berry. In his autobiography, Berry repeated the line that, 'There is reason to believe that the lads' natural taste for adventure had been morbidly stimulated by the reading of highly sensational literature— "penny dreadfuls" and the like'.[191]

Robert Husband was 'able to read well' (although the Assize Calendar described him as a 'labourer of imperfect education'),[192] but we do not know what his reading habits were. If he kept a stash of penny dreadfuls tucked away in his bedroom, there would have been nothing unusual about that: after all, most educated working class boys in Britain read the penny dreadfuls. Even though an inquiry in 1888 had failed to establish a link between pulp fiction and juvenile crime, the *Hampshire Post* cautioned that

> An imaginative lad is sadly addicted to fancying himself the hero of impossible adventures, and it is not to be wondered at that he should occasionally attempt to emulate those of his favourites. Ill weeds are more prolific and more easily cultivated than asparagus.[193]

Behind the 'epidemic of murder and bloodshed which has been sweeping over the country', the *Hampshire Post* identified what it believed was a far more depraved and specific corrupting influence:

> The worst of it is, however, that upon feeble or ill-regulated minds the prevalent bloodthirstiness begets a spirit of imitation...a lad yearning for notoriety readily perceives that vice, and not virtue,

---

190 'The Penny Dreadful', *Ross-shire Journal*, 11 February 1887.
191 James Berry, *My Experiences as an Executioner* (London: P Lund, 1892), p. 88.
192 Calendars of prisoners for Assizes (Winter 1888), Hampshire Record Office, reference Q7/2/4.
193 'The Havant Murder', *Hampshire Post*, 30 November, 1888.

supplies the readiest and the easiest highroad to the attainment of his ambition. For some time past, the achievements of the supposed perpetrator of the Whitechapel butcheries have provided the youth of the country with an unexampled fund of excitement. In our own town bands of juveniles may be seen perambulating the streets singing in chorus some doggerel about the exploits of 'Jack the Ripper'. Such of them as can write are also addicted to dropping ill-spelt intimations of approaching tragedies into letter-boxes, with the result that nursemaids decline to go abroad after dark, and our womankind are afraid to be left in the house alone. Whether the alleged murderer of little Searle proves to be an admirer of the great Unknown remains to be seen.[194]

When Robert attempted to break out from the police cells, he was also making a desperate bid to escape the hangman's noose. He will have had a fairly shrewd idea that the case against him was strong enough to justify his committal to trial at Winchester, and he will have known that if he was found guilty at the assizes then the penalty was death by hanging.

Children under the age of seven were considered incapable of voluntarily committing a felony.[195] They were seen as not having sufficient moral or intellectual understanding of right and wrong to be criminally responsible for their actions. They were viewed as *doli incapax* (incapable of harm), which meant they could not be punished for any capital offence, even when the circumstances of the crime suggested that they had been fully aware of what they were doing. For example, in 1866 five-year-old Samuel Case killed his sister by striking her over the head with a brick. There was no question that she had died as a result of injuries intentionally inflicted by her brother, but because he was under seven years of age he was considered not responsible for his actions and consequently he was discharged.[196] In 1882, two-year-old Alfred Burdett from Leicester, the 'terror of all the children in the neighbourhood', killed another toddler by (it seems) ripping open his stomach with a piece of tin

194 Ibid.
195 The minimum age of criminal responsibility had been set at seven since medieval times. It was raised to eight in 1933 and again to ten in 1963.
196 'A Child Killing His Sister', *Dundee Courier*, 22 November 1866.

and throwing him so violently to the ground that he fractured his skull. He then walked away, his pinafore stained with fresh blood.[197] Although baby Burdett was clearly guilty of manslaughter, possibly even of murder, he was not, in the words of the coroner, 'accountable in law for his actions.'[198]

In the nineteenth century fourteen was considered the age of discretion. Unless incapacitated by mental retardation or insanity (idiocy or imbecility), children aged fourteen or older were treated exactly like adults and were sentenced to death if proven guilty of murder. Dobell and Gower, in the case mentioned previously, were both 'hanged by the neck until dead' at Maidstone Prison in January 1889.

The problem area was children older than seven but younger than fourteen. In theory, children of this age were also presumed to be *doli incapax*; but if the prosecution could show that they had behaved with wilful intent and with full knowledge of right and wrong, and with an awareness of the consequences of their actions, then they, too, would be sentenced to death if convicted of murder. For Robert Husband, currently on remand in Winchester Gaol, the law of the land was clear: if he was convicted of wilful murder, the penalty was execution by hanging. The trial judge would have no option but to pronounce the sentence of death.

Yet the thought of hanging young children was a deeply shocking and revolting notion to most people in Victorian society, and throughout the nineteenth century there were repeated calls from penal reformers and opponents of capital punishment to exempt young people from the death penalty.[199]

In fact, very few children were hanged in nineteenth-century

---

197 'The Murder by a Baby', *Yarmouth Independent*, 27 May, 1882. Baby Burdett seems to have been a handful. At the inquest he seized the coroner's papers in an attempt to throw them on the floor. See 'The Blood-Stained Pinafore', *Pall Mall Gazette*, 24 May 1882.

198 'Singular Death of a Child in Leicester', *Leicester Chronicle*, 27 May 1882.

199 The Children's Act of 1908 finally stipulated a minimum age of sixteen for the execution of juvenile offenders, which was raised to eighteen in 1933.

Britain, and in practice what tended to happen was that juvenile offenders found guilty of capital offences were reprieved. Juries had the power to recommend mercy on account of a defendant's extreme youth. The recommendation for mercy would be forwarded by the judge to the Home Secretary, and it was for the Crown to decide if the plea of mercy was justified. In effect, the majority of children convicted of wilful murder had their sentences commuted to penal servitude for life, and served their time in convict prisons alongside adult offenders.[200]

But not all children escaped the scaffold. If the jury declined to recommend mercy, or if the presiding judge refused to forward the plea for mercy to the Home Secretary (as happened in the John Bell case mentioned below), or if the Home Secretary, after deliberation, decided not to grant the reprieve, then the child defendant would hang. In 1831, fourteen-year-old John Bell was hanged outside Maidstone Gaol for the murder of another boy called Richard Taylor, who he had attacked with a knife. The penal reformer Edward Wakefield, putting himself in the place of the hangman, provides a mawkish account of the execution:

> Last year I was called out of town, to hang a little boy for killing with malice aforethought. [He] was the youngest fellow-creature I ever handled in the way of our business; and a beautiful child he was too, as you may have seen by the papers, with a straight nose, large blue eyes and golden hair ... [The crowd] saw the stripling lifted fainting on to the gallows, his smooth cheeks of the colour of wood-ashes, his limbs trembling, and his bosom heaving sigh after sigh, as if body and soul were parting without my help. It was not a downright murder; for there was scarce any life to take out of him. When I began to pull the cap ... over his baby face, he pressed his small hands together (his arms, you know, were corded fast to his body) and gave me a beseeching look; just as a calf will lick the butcher's hand. But cattle do not speak: this creature muttered,—'Pray, sir, don't hurt me.'[201]

Bell was in fact the last child to be executed in Great Britain.

---

200 Up until 1867 children sentenced to death had the sentence reduced to transportation for life, and they would be shipped off to Australia or Van Diemen's Land (Tasmania).

201 Quoted in V.A.C. Gatrell, *The Hanging Tree: Execution and the English People, 1770–1868* (Oxford University Press, 1994), p. 1–2.

If found guilty of murder, Robert Husband would almost certainly be spared the noose; but he would still face imprisonment for life, enduring hard labour and solitary confinement.

The western circuit comprised two assizes each year, one in the spring and one in the summer. Occasionally, if there was a demand for it, there would be an extra assize in the winter. Two justices were sent out from London and they visited all the assize towns on the circuit – Salisbury, Taunton, Dorchester, Exeter, Bodmin, Bristol and Winchester – trying civil and criminal cases. In 1876, the counties of Hampshire, Dorset and Wiltshire were grouped together administratively, and they all shared an assize at Winchester.

For centuries the Great Hall at Winchester Castle had been the location for the Winchester Assizes and Quarter Sessions: Sir Walter Raleigh was tried there for treason in 1603, and it was the scene of the 'Bloody Assizes' of 1685 at which 'Hanging' Judge Jeffreys presided in the aftermath of the Battle of Sedgemoor. Frederick Baker was tried there in December 1867 for the murder of Fanny Adams. In the 1870s, however, new law courts and offices were erected, while the Great Hall itself underwent extensive renovation: new staircases and archways penetrating walls nine feet in thickness linked the Great Hall with the new courts.[202]

The judge appointed to hold the Winter Assizes in 1888 was the Hon. Sir James Fitzjames Stephen. The *Hampshire Telegraph* welcomed the appointment:

> A better judge than Sir James Fitzjames Stephen could not have been selected to try the [Robert Husband] case. He is pretty generally regarded as the best criminal judge upon the Bench, and [can] be relied upon to sift the most terrible charges against the accused.[203]

He arrived in Winchester by train on Thursday afternoon, 13

---

202 Melville Portal, *The Great Hall of Winchester Castle* (London: Simpkin & Co, 1899), pp. 69–74.
203 *Hampshire Telegraph*, 22 December 1888.

December. He was met at the station by the High Sheriff and other officials, and escorted to the aptly named Serle's House for a civic reception. In the old days, before the coming of the railways, the entry of judges into Winchester resembled a royal cavalcade, with carriages and horsemen and a retinue of yeomanry escorting His Lordship and the High Sheriff to the castle; now, the romance had gone and the judge was bustled off the station platform straight into a waiting cab.[204]

At four o'clock, as was customary, the judge attended divine service at the cathedral.

On Thursday, shortly after eleven o'clock, Mr Justice Stephen took his seat in the Courts of Justice at the castle. After empanelling the grand jury, he delivered his charge, dwelling at length on the Robert Husband case before them. It was an extraordinary case, he said, partly on account of the extreme youth of the prisoner. In his career as a judge he had occasionally come across similar cases: he recalled particularly one instance of a little girl tried for murder by poison, and even within the last fortnight he had presided over a trial in Exeter at which a young girl was said to have murdered a four-year-old boy. But in his experience most cases involving children accused of murder did not partake of a very violent nature: in this regard the Husband case was again exceptional owing to the brutal manner in which Percy Searle had been attacked and stabbed in the throat. While Robert was below the age at which people were usually presumed to be aware of the nature and consequences of their actions, Mr Justice Stephen felt sure the grand jury would reach the view that Robert Husband ought to stand trial for murder.[205]

Mr Justice Stephen was coming to the end of a long and eventful career as a judge and writer. Born in London in 1829, he was educated at Eton College (which he loathed) and Trinity College, Cambridge. He was called to the Bar in 1854 and took silk in 1868. He gained an early reputation as a controversial journalist on the

204 *Hampshire Telegraph,* 26 March 1887.
205 *Western Times,* 5 December 1888.

Saturday Review and as a writer of law books. His *General View of the Criminal Law* (1868) marked him out as a legal commentator of considerable stature and originality. Stephen was appointed a High Court judge (Queen's Bench Division) in 1879, partly in recognition of his criminal law reform work drafting the *Criminal Code (Indictable Offences) Bill 1878*. However, his thirteen years on the Bench were not distinguished by any significant contributions to criminal law, and from 1885 onwards there were concerns over his deteriorating physical health.

Notwithstanding the glowing words of the *Hampshire Telegraph*, there were worries, too, about his mental condition and about his capacity to exercise his judicial duties fairly and impartially. His allegedly highly partisan conduct of the murder trial of Israel Lipski in 1887 was one example where his conduct at a trial had come under public criticism.[206] Two years later, in 1889, there would be another furore over his handling of the Florence Maybrick murder trial: he would make a number of errors in his summing up, and in his opening address summarising the evidence against Maybrick he expressed his own personal view that Florence was more likely to be guilty because of her infidelity – 'if a woman does carry on an adulterous intrigue with another man, it may supply every sort of motive ...'.[207] It was highly irregular to bring up a prisoner's moral character in this way, and quite improper for a judge to interject his own opinion even before the trial had begun.

Ironically, it was the public outcry arising from his mishandling of the Lipski and Maybrick trials, rather than his reform work on the *Criminal Code*, that had the greater impact in paving the way for the establishment of a Court of Criminal Appeal.

In 1891, following medical advice, he would resign from the Bench, and two years later he would be in an asylum for the mentally ill. The murder trial of Robert Husband, sandwiched between the Lipski and Maybrick trials, therefore came at a significant period in Stephen's

---

206 See M.W. Oldridge (ed), *Trial of Israel Lipski* (London: Mango Books, 2017).
207 See Kate Colquhoun, *Did She Kill Him?* (London: Abacus, 2017), pp. 204–5.

career; possibly his conduct at Winchester came under especially intense public scrutiny for signs of befuddlement and expressions of prejudice. It may, too, have been a sign of his declining physical strength when he advised the court at Winchester that as a general rule he did not wish to sit after five o'clock.[208]

In his opening address to the grand jury, Mr Justice Stephen mentioned a case he had recently tried at the Devon Assizes involving the murder of a four-year-old boy. This was the Mary Griffin case and it is worth examining it briefly now to see what it can tell us about Stephen's judicial style.

On 9 June 1888, four-year-old William Delafield was playing outside his house in Frankfort Street, Plymouth. A girl called Mary Griffin, aged twelve, who lived close by, approached the boy and lured him away to the Citadel, a seventeenth-century fortress overlooking Plymouth Sound. She was a harmless-looking girl, poorly clad, with long, dirty black hair. They climbed to the ramparts, where it seems she partially undressed the boy, removing his trousers and underwear, before pushing him off the battlements. He fell thirty feet to the stony ground below, dying from his injuries shortly afterwards. Mary was seen fleeing the scene.

Mary wasn't immediately apprehended, but weeks later she was arrested on her own confession for murder. She admitted enticing the boy away from his home, taking him to the Citadel, and deliberately throwing him off the ramparts. 'He went down scat,' she said, adding that she meant to kill him, although afterwards she felt remorseful and started to cry.

Mary was a restless, emotional girl of less than average intelligence, although fully able to distinguish right from wrong. She was described by the newspapers as having a 'strange demeanour'. Her father, a sailor, had deserted the family some years before, leaving Mrs Griffin to bring up Mary and her younger siblings alone. But she struggled to control her eldest daughter, who was running almost wild in the streets, molesting younger children and stealing trifles

208 'Hants Winter Assizes', *Hampshire Chronicle*, 15 December 1888.

from them. In desperation, Mary's mother placed her in the Staddon House Institute for Friendless Girls in Plymouth to 'correct her wild and irregular habits'.

Mary was sent for assessment to Wonford House, near Exeter, a mock Elizabethan lunatic retreat on top of a hill. The grounds of the asylum had no confining walls, and in appearance the House resembled a nobleman's mansion more than a hospital for the insane. It had a rather progressive regime. Maury Deas, the medical superintendent, clearly saw a different side to Mary, or perhaps she was wily enough to deceive him: in evidence at the trial he said Mary was quiet and well-mannered, and he thought it was likely that the boy had accidentally been pushed off the battlements when he objected to having his clothes removed. This was surprising testimony given that Mary had repeatedly confessed to wilfully murdering the boy. The suggestion was also made that Mary partially undressed the child so that she might steal his clothes and sell them, yet the boy's trousers and underwear were discarded over the ramparts as well.

The jury acquitted her of all charges and Mary was free to leave the court. Mr Justice Stephen clearly felt it was the wrong verdict, however. '[The defendant] has had a most merciful jury', was his tactful way of phrasing it. The Griffin case does give an indication, though, of the extent to which juries were willing to give children the benefit of the doubt and acquit them of all charges whenever possible.[209]

The role of a grand jury was to assess the indictment and weigh up if there was sufficient evidence to justify putting the case before a judge and jury. Grand juries often dropped charges against children because of their extreme youth. In principle, though, if sufficient evidence existed, a 'true bill' was returned and the case went to trial.

On 14 December the grand jury met to deliberate on the Robert Husband case. They were still deliberating well into the late evening, at which point the sitting of the court was adjourned. It was resumed

---

209 For details of the Mary Griffin case, see 'The Confession of Murder by a Girl at Plymouth', *Western Times*, 9 October 1888; 'Charge of Murder Against a Child', *St James's Gazette*, 7 December 1888.

next morning at half past ten.

It wasn't too long before the grand jury concluded their business. There was no great surprise in the castle when they returned a 'true bill' against Robert Husband. They had assessed the evidence, formed an opinion as to his culpability, and decided he had a case to answer. On Wednesday 19 December, Robert Husband would stand trial for murder in front of a judge and jury.

19

The Case for the Prosecution

The early morning train was packed with men, women and children making their way to Winchester for the trial. Most of them had boarded at Havant. There was an hour and a half's journey ahead of them in noisy, dark, unheated carriages, yet there was almost a holiday atmosphere among the passengers, as if they were on a works outing to the seaside or a school trip into the countryside. One or two among them had come prepared with hampers of sandwiches, curds and cream. Everyone had dressed up in their Sunday best for their big day in court. The schoolboy Charles Clark looked very smart in his Norfolk jacket and knee-length pants. Always the dapper showman, Tom Spurgeon resembled Jack the Ripper in his top hat and Inverness cape over a grey wool Chesterfield coat. The only scowling face belonged to William Farnden, who resented being forced into a suit by his mother – he continually plucked at the collar of his shirt as if it were a scab. Ethel Whitbread had chosen a stylish sailor dress in pale cream cotton teamed with a wide brimmed hat; she was demure and well-behaved, unlike her older brother who got on everyone nerves by constantly walking up and down the carriage demanding to see people's tickets.

Mr and Mrs Searle and their son Frederick occupied seats near the rear of the train. In silence they stared out at the grey, wintry fields. Mrs Husband and George had selected a carriage near the front of the train, as far away as possible from the Searles. Alas, Robert's father wouldn't be accompanying them: the coal yard owner Samuel Clarke had strictly forbidden him from taking any further time off work, forcing him to stay behind to look after the depot while his son fought for his life at Winchester.

Large crowds had already gathered outside the County Hall on Castle Hill. The police were having difficulty restraining them behind makeshift barriers. Eventually, at half-past nine, the vestibule door was opened and there was an almighty stampede. Within one or two minutes, after much shoving and elbowing, the pubic gallery was occupied to capacity with spectators. The reserved seats in the grand jury chamber filled up quickly up, too, with onlookers of a more privileged demeanour, women being in the majority – the wives of aldermen, ladies of fashion and leisure, ghouls of the 'fairer sex', and the like. With a vaguely disdainful air, they studied the goings-on in the courtroom through their lorgnettes. There was plenty to see.

A couple of benches had been set aside near the front of the court for the benefit of members of the press. Several reporters had already taken their positions and were chatting among themselves. The tall, lean figure of Captain Forrest was seen entering the court: it was a proud moment for him and for the Hampshire Constabulary generally. Scotland Yard were still chasing the London Ripper, but the Hampshire force had apprehended their cut-throat within 48 hours without any help from the Met.[210] It was all down to discipline and organisation, which came from the top. He was greeted by Sergeant Knapton and Superintendent Kinshott, and the three of them chortled over a private joke.

Then, at ten o'clock, Mr John Temple Cooke strode into the hall.[211] Upon him fell the sombre duty of delivering the prosecution case against Robert Husband. Even now, just moments before the opening of the trial, he was still receiving instructions from the magistrates' clerks at Havant, Messrs. Longcroft and Green. No sooner had he entered the hall than he retired to confer with the solicitor Mr

---

210 Norman Hastings claims that 'experts from Scotland Yard' journeyed to Havant to assist with the Percy Searle murder investigation. They didn't. See Norman Hastings, 'When the People Were in Terror', *Thomson's Weekly News*, September–December 1929.

211 Born in 1850, he was educated at Cheltenham College and called to the bar at the Middle Temple in 1874, after which he commenced practice as a barrister on the Western circuit.

Charles Longcroft.

Next into court was Mr C.W. Mathews, accompanied by his junior counsel Mr Bovill William Smith. They would be representing Robert and putting forward the case for the defence. There was something dainty, almost feminine, about Charles Mathews; he had a delicate physique and a rather girlish face with a high-pitched voice that soared into the soprano register whenever he laughed; in court and outside, he comported himself in a flouncy manner that could best be described as mincing. But he was a formidable advocate, a really exciting presence at the Hampshire Sessions, who applied all the theatrical techniques of his father – stage whispers, dramatic pauses, grand rhetorical gestures – to his courtroom oratory. The spectators in court were mesmerised by him, following him around and watching his every move. He appeared relaxed and in good humour. When he bowed his head and spoke privately for a moment to Mr George Feltham, who was sitting alongside Mr Bovill Smith, the entire courtroom seemed to lean forward in a bid to catch his words.

Mr Temple Cooke re-entered the courtroom and took his seat next to his junior counsel, Mr J.F. Rubie. He nodded to Charles Mathews, and Mathews nodded back: they were old adversaries in the courtroom.

The empanelling of the jury didn't go terribly smoothly – several jurors arrived late and one or two didn't turn up at all – but twelve 'good men and true' were eventually sworn in and they took their places in the box. They were a mixed group, from many walks of life: there was Captain Frederick Highatt, recently retired from the 3rd Hampshire Regiment, who was now the proprietor of a naval and military outfitters in Gosport; there was Edward Hobbs, landlord of the Watermans Arms public house in Gosport, and Mr Edward Hide, President of the Portsmouth Chamber of Commerce.[212] Everything

---

212 We know the names of the jurors, but little else about most of them: John Edmunds, Alfred Ford, George Fryer, William Alexander Ghrimes, Edwin Hide, Bernard Jones, Henry Hull, Edward Newman Hobbs, Frederick Charles Highatt, James Andrew Morris, George Moth, and Edwin Pearson. National Archives, Crown Minute Book,

was ready. The court waited.

At twenty-seven minutes past ten, the door of the court was thrown open, and in came his lordship Mr Justice Fitzjames Stephen, followed by the High Sheriff William Wickham. Everyone stood up. Stephen was a big, broad-shouldered man, known as 'Giant Grim' in his younger days,[213] clean shaven except for muttonchop whiskers, and with a heavy, drooping face. He thundered across the floor in his crimson robes. Bowing gravely to the jury and to the lawyers, he motioned for the court to sit.

The Clerk of the Peace, Thomas Earle, directed the gaoler to bring the prisoner forward, and at 10.28 Robert Husband was ushered into court. There was absolute silence.

What amazed everyone was how small Robert looked, how innocent and childlike.

> When the little fellow, with a black and red cravat tied round his neck, and hanging loosely outside his coat, entered the dock, a thrill ran through the court. The accused's diminutiveness was most marked as he stood by the side of the stalwart gaoler, his nose scarcely reaching the ledge of the dock.[214]

He was dressed in the same tunic he had worn at the magistrates' court. In truth, he looked a tad scruffy; his clothes were rumpled and his hair mussed. His complexion was ashen, which accentuated the red rims and the puffiness around his eyes from recent crying. Yet he looked remarkably composed. He stood upright, shoulders back, and when the charge was read out to him and he was asked to plead 'Guilty or Not Guilty', he replied in clear, unhesitating tones, 'Not Guilty, sir.'

Mr Feltham had obviously worked on his client. Gone were the insolence and the studied air of indifference and inattention. Robert had been taught to show respect for the solemnity of the court. He was offered a chair, and as he sat down he almost completely

ASSI 21/72.
213 Deborah McDonald, *The Prince, His Tutor and The Ripper* (London: McFarland & Co., 2007), p. 214.
214 'The Havant Murder', *Portsmouth Times*, 22 December 1888.

disappeared from view: all the court could see was the top of his head – his tousled hair – poking up above the dock. It bordered on the comical, but no one was laughing. It almost beggared belief that this harmless-looking little boy stood accused of the crime of murder. Often during the trial, as Robert's energy flagged, he would sink a little in the chair and vanish totally from view. At these moments it was as if the 'boy assassin' was being tried in absentia.

Mr Temple Cooke rose for the prosecution. He began by giving the jury a summary of the facts of the case, outlining in broad terms the evidence that would be presented to them. There could be no doubt, he said, that a murder had been committed that night – two doctors would describe to them in detail the deceased boy's injuries. And there could be no doubt either that the accused lad, Robert Husband, was in the vicinity when the murder took place. The jury would hear how, only moments before the crime, Husband was seen flourishing a knife and pretending to be Jack the Ripper; he was seen spying on Percy in Mrs Randall's drapery shop where the younger boy had gone to collect some shirting for his mother; he was spotted trying to run away from the scene of the crime; and a few minutes after the murder was committed he was caught washing his hands with a towel that was not given up to the police when they asked for it the following day. Mr Temple Cooke told the jury he would demonstrate, unequivocally, that the murder weapon, a knife found a few yards from the body, belonged to George Husband, the brother of the accused, who had mislaid it the night before the murder. Witnesses would testify that the knife was later seen in the hands of Robert on the morning of the murder.

The jury would hear, too, how Robert had been frequently caught out in deliberate lies. In particular, the boy claimed to have seen a tall man with a dark coat attacking Percy, yet a number of witnesses, including several respected senior police officers, would demonstrate that the murder spot was so poorly illuminated that it was actually impossible for Robert to have seen the murder from the place where he said he was standing at the time.

Mr Temple Cooke then turned to the question of motive: evidence would be presented showing that bad feeling existed between the prisoner and the deceased and that a threat had been made. After leaving the draper's shop, Percy was making his way home through the Pallant when he was brutally attacked by Robert Husband in the darkness and left to die. It was a cowardly act, brought on no doubt by the older boy's reading of lurid newspaper reports about Jack the Ripper.

It was a tragic case, Mr Temple Cooke said in conclusion, and it gave him no satisfaction at all to prosecute the capital charge against such a young boy. If the jury felt there remained an element of reasonable doubt then he urged them to give the prisoner the benefit of that doubt.

Throughout the day a steady stream of witnesses filed into the courtroom at the castle to give evidence against Robert. Many of them would be giving evidence for the second or even the third time. As such, their statements will have gone through several iterations and been drafted and read back to them by solicitors working for the prosecution. Inevitably, their evidence in court at Winchester would reflect the bias of this process: they would be basing their testimony increasingly on written depositions rather than on their original experience of the events.

Mr Anthony Lewis, the land surveyor practising at Havant and Emsworth, was first up. His evidence was absolutely crucial to the prosecution case. He produced plans and photographs of the Pallant. According to his detailed measurements, the lamp at the west side of Pallant House was ten feet high. It cast a ray of light five or six feet wide on part of the wall opposite and on the railings outside the Manor House Academy. It illuminated the spot where the knife was found but fell short of the place where the body was found. The distance between the knife and Mr Farnden's house was 30 yards and 2 ft. and the body was 24ft further away in the darkness. Anyone standing outside Mr Farnden's house might, by shading their eyes from the glare of the lamp, be able to see the shadow of a figure standing next to the knife, but they would not be able to discern anything at the murder spot itself. Certainly, it would be impossible to distinguish light or dark clothing from that vantage point. In essence, if the deceased was struck at the point where the body was found, then Robert was lying if he said he saw Percy being attacked.

The boy William Farnden gave evidence next. He was still plucking at the collar of his shirt. He confirmed he lived at No. 1 North Pallant. He had been in Mrs Randall's shop on the night of 26 November. He saw Percy come into the shop, and through the window he could also see Robert Husband on the pavement outside, looking in. On leaving the shop, he accompanied Robert up the Pallant and down the Bear Hotel lane to see a show. After a short while, he went home, leaving Robert standing near the garden gate.

Mr Mathews stood up. He had some questions for this witness.

Mr Mathews:	You saw no knife nor heard anything about one, did you?
William:	No, sir.
Mr Mathews:	You cannot quite tell me what time it was you left Robert Husband?
William:	No, sir.
Mr Mathews:	Have you a sister named Louie [Ellen Albury]?
William:	Yes, sir.
Mr Mathews:	Was she at home that night?
William:	I don't know.
Mr Mathews:	Can't you remember?
William:	No.
Mr Mathews:	My little man, you were asked about this by the Coroner?
William:	Yes, sir.
Mr Mathews:	Did you not then say that your eldest sister was not at home all that evening?
William:	Yes.
Mr Mathews:	And your big sister was not at home till next morning?
William:	Yes.
Mr Mathews:	And she was at Alton?
William:	Yes.
Mr Mathews:	Now do you know she was at Alton?
William:	Yes.[215]

215 'The Havant Murder', *Portsmouth Times*, 22 December 1888.

The jury may have been perplexed by this line of cross-examination, but Mr Mathews assured them that this witness's evidence would take on great significance a little later. It was a typical Charlie Mathews manoeuvre, holding evidence in abeyance for a dramatic revelation later.

Henry Shirley, the draper's assistant, reported serving Percy a small piece of shirting which he wrapped in a parcel. The boy left the shop a little after six o'clock. Shortly afterwards he saw Robert Husband running down the Pallant on the opposite side of the road towards his home. He was not calling out or screaming 'Murder!' The doorway of Randall's opened onto North Street, so Robert would not have seen Shirley until he was nearly opposite him. Questioned by the judge, the witness stated that directly Robert saw him he stopped and came over. And Mr Mathews got the witness to admit that Robert hadn't been trying to hide his hands or conceal his clothing. Even though it was a dark and rainy night, there was plenty of light falling onto the road from the wine merchant's shop opposite and from Randall's shop as well, so Shirley conceded he might have seen blood on Robert's hands if there had been any blood to see. As it was, he hadn't noticed Robert's hands at all.

Mrs Alma Taylor, of No. 11 the Pallant, spoke of being in Randall's shop when she heard Robert running down the street. He put his head in the doorway, she said, and called out, 'There's a man killing a boy down yonder'.

John Platt proved to be a disastrous witness for the prosecution. Clearly still shaken by the death of Percy, his testimony was riddled with inconsistencies. Questioned first by Mr Temple Cooke, he recounted the events of that fateful evening – Robert approaching him in the Pallant, accompanying the boy to the Manor School wall, cradling the dying Percy in his arms, asking Robert to summon help, and being sent to the father's house on North Street to fetch him back for questioning.

Charles Mathews subjected him to a remorseless cross-examination. His strategy was to expose discrepancies between John Platt's court testimony and his previous statements, thus undermining his credibility as a witness. After eliciting the information that Robert's hand had been dry when Platt first took hold of it, Mathews went on the attack:

Mr Mathews:	Now, let me take you back to the father's house. Did you state before the Coroner that when you went there the accused's hands were then wet and he was wiping them?
John Platt:	I never said no such thing.
Mr Mathews:	What! Did you see him wiping them on a towel which was near any door that was there?
John Platt:	I never saw him wiping his hands at all.
Mr Mathews:	I put this to you Mr Platt. Did you say before the Coroner—'His hands were then wet, and he was wiping them. He came out of one room into the other. I think he was wiping his hands with a towel on the door'?
JohnPlatt:	I never saw him wiping his hands at all. He might have been. I never saw him.
Mr Mathews:	But was that the evidence which you gave before the Coroner?
John Platt:	I never made use of those words, and never saw him wipe his hands.
Mr Mathews:	I call your lordship's attention to the depositions.[216]

The judge read the whole passage to the witness.[217]

Mr Justice Stephen:	Is that what you said?
John Platt:	I never saw him wiping his hands.
Mr Justice Stephen:	The question is not whether you saw him wiping his hands, but whether you said that he was wiping his hands.
John Platt:	I might have said that he was wiping his hands.
Mr Justice Stephen:	You might say anything. Did you say he was wiping his hands?
John Platt:	I have no recollection of saying it.[218]

216 'The Havant Murder', *Portsmouth Times*, 22 December 1888.
217 A copy of Platt's deposition taken before the coroner on 28 November 1888, and signed by the deponent, is among the client papers of Longcroft and Green (Havant solicitors). See Hampshire Record Office, reference 96M92/C14. The words quoted by Mathews are exactly those given in the deposition.
218 'The Havant Murder', *Portsmouth Times*, 22 December 1888.

And so it went on. Time after time, contradictions were found in his evidence; time after time Platt would deny having said something only for it to be read back to him from a signed deposition. The evening of the murder was 'not a windy night', he said, yet Captain Boyd had struggled to keep his umbrella aloft. He was confused over whether Robert had told him he was standing 'against' the lamp or 'near' the lamp when he witnessed the attack. When he was bringing Robert back to the Pallant for questioning, he said Robert had spoken of a man running away across the Fair Field, but in his statement to the coroner he claimed there was no conversation between them. He was confused over Percy's cap – in court he said it was lying 50ft from the body, but before the magistrates he'd stated it was lying 2ft from the body.

As the cross-examination wore on, Platt floundered desperately:

Mr Mathews: The boy came willingly with you [from his home back to the Pallant]
John Platt: The boy?
Mr Mathews: Yes, the little boy in the dock.[219]

In the end, Platt admitted he couldn't remember what had taken place that evening. 'I hardly knew what I did at the time I found the body,' he told Mr Mathews, 'I was upset.' On that sad note, John Platt was allowed to leave the witness box.

Charles Rogers was called next. He simply told the court he had seen Robert speaking to the witness Mr Shirley on the night of the murder.

Towards the end of the morning session, Sergeant Knapton took to the witness box. He repeated his evidence given before the magistrates and the coroner. At one point the judge interrupted the witness to correct his description of a puncture in the body tissue as 'a shallow cut' – a puncture is a 'stab', quibbled Mr Justice Stephen. Knapton elaborated on the experiments that had been conducted in the Pallant on the nights of the 27th and 28th: he stood at the spot where the body was found, while Inspector Lawler stood outside

219 Ibid.

Mr Farnden's house. Neither had been able to see the other; they reversed positions with the same result.

After lunch, Superintendent Kinshott corroborated his colleague's evidence. It was then the turn of the medical experts to give evidence. Dr Quintin Bond described the murder scene in vivid terms – the small, frail body lit by lantern light, the mud, a spreading puddle of several pints of blood. It was his opinion that the boy had been murdered at the spot where the body was found. The fatal wound was struck from behind or by someone kneeling over the body: it was a stabbing injury below the right ear, which penetrated the tonsil and entered the mouth, severing the carotid artery and causing external and internal haemorrhage. That was the cause of death. When Bond dissected the neck during the post-mortem he determined that the wound went downwards and forwards. It was the doctor's view that there must have been blood on the assailant's hand because the handle of the knife was covered in it, although he felt the person delivering the blow might have avoided getting blood on their clothes. Asked by Mr Temple Cooke if a boy of the prisoner's age and size had sufficient strength to deliver the lethal blow, Dr Bond replied it was quite possible.

In his cross-examination, Mr Mathews returned to the question of blood splatter on the attacker's clothes. Wasn't it true that arterial blood had the characteristic of spurting? Wouldn't blood have spurted when the carotid artery was punctured? But Dr Bond stood his ground: if any part of the wound – a flap of skin, say – overlapped the artery then that would prevent spurting and the blood would have flowed out instead.

Professor Meymott Tidy, the analyst at the Home Office, was then called to the witness box. This was his third trip to Hampshire in as many weeks. Although appearing as an expert witness for the prosecution, his testimony contained little that was damaging to Robert's case. Detailing the results of his examination of the prisoner's clothes, Professor Tidy stated there were a few blood stains on the wristband of the shirt, but they were old stains dating from before the murder. Mr Temple Cooke got the witness to concede in theory that washing the garment in soap and water could alter the appearance of the stains to make them look older, but when cross-examined by Mr Mathews, he confirmed the shirt hadn't been washed recently anyway. Turning to the knife, he would not be drawn on whether it was covered in animal or human blood – 'It is altogether too risky to venture an opinion,' he told the judge. 'You can only be right in 50 per cent of cases.'[220] But he had noticed that the point of the longer blade was somewhat blunt. In his view it would require 'considerable force' to penetrate the neck with a blunt implement like that, and the assailant would need a firm grip on the handle to inflict such a wound. Given that the handle of the weapon found in the Pallant was covered in blood, he would therefore expect the assassin to have blood on his hands as well as on his clothes.

The judge seemed greatly impressed by Professor Tidy's evidence.

It was still only the middle of the afternoon, but the court was already beginning to grow dark from the approach of evening. Clerks went round the Hall igniting the gas lamps. In the grand jury chamber, the ladies were sipping their afternoon tea from china crockery and passing round plates of cake and buttered bread.

It was obvious that proceedings would need to carry over to a second day. At the opening of the Assizes, Mr Justice Stephen had expressed his aversion to late sittings, and he returned to this matter once Professor Tidy had stepped down. Rather than draw attention to his own declining mental and physical stamina, the judge told the court it was 'only fair to the prisoner that the minds of those trying him should be at their freshest'. He asked the learned counsel if they could suggest a convenient time to adjourn. Mr Temple Cooke said there were twenty-six witnesses for the prosecution, and so far the court had heard from ten of them. The judge considered for a moment before telling the court he would adjourn between five and six o'clock.

A new mood of promptness gripped the court, and over the next two and a half hours a flurry of witnesses entered and left.

220 'The Havant Murder', *Portsmouth Times*, 22 December 1888.

Mr John Arter and Mr James Agate both corroborated the evidence of the police regarding the darkness of the Pallant. Arter had flashed his freshly-laundered white shirt, Agate had brought along his pale dog, but neither was visible from 38 yards away across the Pallant.

William Richardson was a completely fresh witness. His evidence was sensational but of a very dubious quality. He was the youth employed at the Bear Hotel who had first alerted Sergeant Knapton to the murder. According to Sergeant Knapton's inquest statement,[221] Richardson told him he received news of the murder from a lad called Warrington,[222] but at the trial Richardson stated he was at the murder spot himself and actually heard Percy exclaim 'Oh, Bob!' before he died. Charlie Mathews mocked the boy's evidence, and no one in court appeared to give any credence to it at all. Richardson insisted he had already given a statement to Mr Longcroft (the Havant solicitor), but no deposition was produced in court.

Harry George was another fresh witness. He was a painter who lived at No. 2 in the Pallant. He gave practically the same evidence as Richardson. If he is to be believed, and if Richardson is to be believed, there were at least four people standing around Percy when he died – John Platt, Robert Husband, William Richardson and Harry George – yet Platt had testified that he and Robert were alone with the dying child. Far from bolstering the prosecution case, the evidence of these two new witnesses served only to confuse and complicate the picture.

The next series of witnesses provided circumstantial evidence about the discovery and identification of the knife. Tom Spurgeon of the Manor House school proved finding the knife outside his front gate. The boy William Stevens, who lived in Bug's Row three doors away from the Searle family, identified the knife as his property. He said he gave it to the prisoner's brother on the Thursday prior to the murder. George Husband deposed to receiving the knife from Stevens, but he said he lost it sometime on Sunday afternoon the

221 See the client papers of Longcroft and Green (Havant solicitors), Hampshire Record Office, reference 96M92/C14.
222 This may have been Henry Warrington, aged eleven, who lived at No. 4 in the Pallant.

25th after attending church. John Smith, the amateur detective from Bedhampton, told the jury that George Husband had shown him the knife on the Friday prior to the murder. Henry Wheeler, the errand boy, stated that George had wanted to sell him the knife for a penny on the day of the murder, although when questioned by Mr Mathews he admitted he had never actually touched the knife or even noticed it particularly: he couldn't say if it had one blade or two.

Seven-year-old Ethel Whitbread was a more confident and convincing witness. She was gently questioned by the judge as to whether she understood why she was in court; her answers were very clear and her testimony was admitted. Speaking in a faint whisper, she recounted how, on the morning of the murder, she had seen the prisoner sharpening a knife against a wall of a 'sweet-stuff shop' [Mrs Burrows's confectionery shop] in North Street next to the coal yard. She described pointing out the exact spot to Sergeant Knapton and her father a few days later: the mark was still there, a red abrasion on the corner of the brick wall, about 4ft from the ground. Charles Mathews looked slightly uncomfortable cross-examining these very young witnesses: it was not the time for smart words and clever rhetorical flourishes: all that was required were straightforward questions to elicit straightforward answers. Ethel stood up well to the defence counsel's examination, and her evidence proved unshakeable.

Charles Clark, aged ten, repeated his story about Robert Husband waving a knife about at six o'clock on the evening of the murder just moments before Percy was stabbed. Robert held the knife aloft in his right hand and taking hold of the witness's shoulder with his other hand declared, 'Here comes Jack the Ripper!'

Mr and Mrs Farnden gave evidence next. They were both adamant that Robert Husband never called at their house at any time on the night of the 26th. Mr Farnden testified he had gone to the coal yard at around 5.20 that evening to pay for coal owed; there was therefore no reason for Robert to come round to the Pallant that evening to collect the debt. Under cross-examination, Mr Mathews returned to the matter of the whereabouts of their eldest daughter

Louie [Ellen]: William junior had told the court that his sister was at Alton on the night of the murder, but Mrs Farnden insisted her daughter was at home that evening. It had no bearing on the murder case as such, but this conflict in testimony would have raised doubts in the jury's mind over the credibility of the Farnden family.

Mrs Searle and her son Frederick were the last two witnesses for the prosecution. It was now late in the afternoon: the gas lights hissed ever so slightly, and they cast an almost sickly glow over the courtroom. Mrs Searle looked ill, her complexion rendered even more sallow under the artificial lights. She was allowed to sit down in the witness box. In a strained, nervous voice, she gave a brief account of the grudge that arose between Robert Husband and her boy Percy over threepence worth of coal. But the occasion was too much for her, and her examination was quickly brought to a close. She agreed with Mr Mathews that the dispute had been quickly resolved and so far as she knew no ongoing quarrel existed between the two boys. At this point she staggered out of the witness box, sobbing into a handkerchief.

Frederick Searle, aged eleven, related a confrontation between himself and Robert over the coal business. Robert had been on the verge of uttering a threat –'I don't care for you or your brother Charlie. I'll—', when he was called back to the coal yard by his father. It was a rather weak, inconclusive ending to the prosecution case, and Mr Mathews didn't bother cross-examining the witness. It was a trifling boyish dispute and nothing more than that.

This brought the case for the prosecution to a close. Before Mr Temple Cooke was allowed to sum up, Mr Mathews asked for direction from the court as to the age of the prisoner. He asked his Lordship's opinion as to whether a boy under twelve could commit the crime of murder. The judge had already briefly spoken on this matter when addressing the grand jury, but he was pleased to repeat his remarks for the benefit of the trial jury. According to the law of the land, he said, children between the ages of eight and thirteen were presumed incapable of committing murder, but if the prosecution could show they had acted with wilful intent and full understanding of right and wrong, then a jury could find them guilty of murder, for which the penalty was execution by hanging. He urged the jurymen to recall when they were eleven years of age, and to use that experience to guide their judgment as to whether a boy of that age would realise the consequences of sticking a knife in another's neck. It was for the jury, and the jury alone, to decide if the accused had that understanding.

Mr Temple Cook stood up one last time to summarise the evidence. He explained to the jury that they were required to answer two different questions. First: did the prisoner commit the murder? Mr Temple Cooke felt sure that the weight of the evidence presented to them in court that day would leave them in no doubt that Robert Husband was responsible for the evil deed. If, and only if, the jury considered Robert guilty of murder, they should go on to consider the second question: at the time of the murder, did Robert Husband know what he was doing, and did he know that what he was doing was wrong? Again, Mr Temple Cooke felt sure the jury would have no difficult reaching an opinion on these matters. The boy's first actions were to run off and tell various people that a murder had occurred. He gave a perfectly intelligent account of the crime, albeit he had lied about what he saw; this by itself proved the prisoner knew what he was about and fully understood the nature of the crime. After recapping the chief points of the evidence, Mr Temple Cooke once again begged the jury to give the prisoner the benefit of the doubt if any existed, but equally, if they found him guilty, they must say so.

Mr Temple Cooke sat down. He had done his duty, however distasteful. It was a quarter past five. Robert's head could just be seen bobbing up above the dock; he looked around the hall, saw that the trial was continuing, and bobbed down again. It was time for Charles Mathews to present the case for the defence.

20

The Case for the Defence

Charles Mathews may have preferred not to address the jury at the tail end of the first day. The jurors were probably getting tired. In addition, spectators in the public galleries would soon be getting fidgety, thinking of leaving early to make sure they caught the last train back to Havant – and there were few things more distracting and disruptive to a learned counsel in full flow than people walking out of court. Worse still, the inadequate ventilation in the courtroom meant the hall was becoming stuffy with rather disagreeable odours. On the other hand, he may have relished the advantage of having the last word before the court adjourned for the day: it provided him with an opportunity of leaving the jurors with one or two telling counterarguments to reflect on overnight. And an extra evening to sharpen his thoughts and prepare his concluding remarks would be most welcome, too. In the end, he decided to speak for just thirty minutes before requesting an adjournment.

Mathews will have met his client for the first time that morning in the holding cells adjoining the courtroom. Robert will have been the only prisoner brought over from the Gaol because his trial was expected to occupy the full session. Perhaps George Feltham made the introductions. We don't know how long Robert and Mr Mathews spent together, or what they spoke about, or what impression each formed of the other. Maybe they simply shook hands and that was the end of it. Robert had no conversation skills, and if he spoke to his attorney at all it would have been in grunts and one syllable words. At some point Feltham will almost certainly have confided to Mathews that his client was a rather unpleasant creature. The rumours of the boy torturing animals and bullying much smaller children clung to him like the stink of sewage; if the jurors read their weekly newspapers, much of this unsavoury information would already be known to them.

One of the difficulties facing Mathews was that there were no witnesses for the defence. Robert himself could not be called to give evidence (defendants in capital cases were not allowed to give evidence at trial until 1898),[223] and George Feltham will have advised against Mr or Mrs Husband entering the witness box. With his short temper and smouldering resentment of authority, Mr Husband would be easily riled by an experienced counsel like Temple Cooke, and his testimony could easily end up being a boon for the prosecution. For her part, Mrs Husband came across as a frail woman, timorous and uncertain of things: she would be a nervous witness, and however much Mr Mathews wished to counter the prosecution's fanciful insinuation that Mrs Husband had obstructed police enquiries by washing the hand towel Robert had used to dry his hands on the evening of the murder, on balance he felt it was too risky putting her in the box and exposing her to cross-examination.

A defence with no witnesses, in contrast to a prosecution with an abundance of them, might seem an insuperable obstacle for a defending barrister. Yet Mathews will have taken heart from the recent sensational acquittal at the Old Bailey of Adelaide Bartlett, charged with the murder of her husband: there were no defence witnesses at her trial either, yet a magnificent plea by her defence barrister Sir Edward Clarke had secured a 'Not Guilty' verdict and saved her from the gallows.[224] Could Charles Mathews do the same for Robert Husband?

He rose at 5.15. The *Hampshire Telegraph* described the scene:

> All eyes were eagerly turned towards this redoubtable champion of the accused, and all ears were strained as he commenced his trying task. [He spoke] in a low but clear tone, and with emphatic

---

223 Criminal Evidence Act 1898.
224 See Kate Clarke, *In The Interests of Science: Adelaide Bartlett and the Pimlico Poisoning* (London: Mango Books, 2015) for the definitive account of this fascinating case.

earnestness.[225]

He began by stating what a pleasurable duty it was for him to present the other side of the story. He felt confident that after considering all the facts in the case the jury would find the prisoner not guilty and give him his liberty.

He asked the jury a question: what did they really know about the prisoner and his history? They knew he was eleven years of age and helped his father in the coal yard at Havant, but that was all. Where was the evidence that the boy was malevolent or wicked, or had a ferocious or revengeful disposition? Where was the evidence that Robert had ever spoken angrily to Percy? Mrs Searle, the mother of the murdered boy – who was entitled to everyone's sympathy – had told the court that the small misunderstanding between her Percy and Robert over a delivery of coal had been quickly cleared up. She knew of no quarrel or lingering ill-feeling between the two boys. Furthermore, the supposed dispute was of such trifling importance that the prisoner did not even know which of the Searle brothers – Frederick, Charlie or Percy – had made the complaint to his father. So where was the motive for murder? There was none.

Mr Mathews then turned his attention to the knife. He picked the weapon up, holding it aloft in full view of the jury. At first he didn't say anything, investing the moment with a dramatic intensity straight out of Macbeth Act 2 Scene 1. In the eerie light from the gas lamps, there may have been a slightly diabolical flavour to the scene. Turning to face the jury, he intoned, 'Is this the knife with which the evil deed was committed?'[226] Didn't the jury find it odd, he continued, that the knife was only discovered at nine o'clock in the evening, nearly three hours after the murder had taken place? Where had it been all that time? It was found lying right outside Mr Spurgeon's front gate at exactly the moment he came out of his house with a spirit lamp to investigate what was going on. Why had no one seen the knife before then? Sergeant Knapton was quickly

---

225 'The Havant Murder', *Hampshire Telegraph*, 22 December 1888.
226 Ibid.

at the murder scene and he conducted an immediate and thorough search of the area for weapons, but didn't find any, despite the fact that the knife was supposedly illuminated by the street lamp and said to be visible from more than 30 yards away. Moreover, there were hundreds of people milling around in the Pallant that evening, yet for almost three hours no one set eyes on the weapon lying in the middle of the road a few feet from the body in the full light of a street lamp.

And when the knife was eventually found, it was saturated in wet blood. If it had been lying in the road for nearly three hours in the rain and drizzle, surely the blood, or most of it, ought to have been washed off? 'Of all the unlikely things,' said Mr Mathews, 'that was the most unlikely.'[227]

He considered next the medical evidence. Dr Bond had told them that that the fatal wound had been a clean-cut stab which pierced the strong tissues of the neck, penetrating three inches and severing the carotid artery. A sharp instrument would be required to inflict such an horrific injury, yet the knife produced in court, *this* knife – and here counsel raised the weapon at arm's length – *this* knife was blunt at the top, and the blade was loose. No one could seriously believe that Percy was stabbed with a knife such as this.

Mr Mathews asked the jury another question: how many of them could truly say that in a week's time they would be able to positively identify the knife that had been shown to them in court today? The knife was of a common manufacture – there were probably scores of identical knives in a city the size of Winchester. Indeed, how many boys in court today owned knives similar to the one exhibited?[228]

The prosecution had failed to show that the knife had ever been in the prisoner's possession. To begin with, the boy Wheeler and the little girl Ethel Whitbread weren't even able to properly identify the knife. As for Charles Clark, his statement about Robert waving a knife about and yelling 'Here comes Jack the Ripper!' was just a wild,

227 'The Murder At Havant', *Hampshire Post*, 21 December 1888.
228 'The Havant Murder', *Hampshire Advertiser*, 22 December 1888.

fanciful story. He claimed there was a gang of boys with Robert at the time of the incident, but if that was the case why had no statements been taken from these other witnesses to corroborate Clark's story? No, this whole strand of evidence was speculative and worthless, argued Mr Mathews.

At this point, Mr Mathews broke off and asked the judge if he would consider adjourning the court till the next day. It was 5.55 pm. 'He became suddenly aware,' commented the *Hampshire Telegraph*, 'that his energies were being overtaxed by the arduous duties of the day.' Mr Justice Stephen, himself flagging, was pleased to adjourn the court till 10.30 the next morning. He told the jury they would not be able to return home that evening; they must be kept under the Sheriff's watch until the court re-assembled in the morning. However, everything would be done to ensure their comfort and convenience.

Accordingly, the jurors spent the night at the George Hotel on Jewry Street, the principal coaching inn of the city.[229]

Just before ten o'clock on Thursday morning, 20 December 1888, the court at Winchester opened its doors to the crowds queuing up on Castle Hill. As before, the main courtroom was quickly filled to capacity. There were fewer children in the public galleries than previously. They had given their evidence and there was no need for them to make the journey to Winchester a second time. Naturally, Mr and Mrs Searle had travelled up, and George Bartholomew, proving himself a true friend of the family, accompanied Fanny and George Husband.

Captain Forrest made his way into court, taking his customary seat on the high bench. He looked grave and perhaps a little ill-tempered. There was no chortling this time with the lower ranks.

The jurors entered. After a breakfast that morning of devilled

---

229 The hotel bill came to £10 9s. 9d. (ASSI/21/72). The George Hotel was demolished in 1956 and a bank built on the site.

kidneys on fried bread with roasted mushrooms, they had enjoyed a thirty minute walk around the city centre under police escort; they were refreshed and alert, and no doubt curious to learn how Charles Mathews would develop his defence.

Mr Justice Stephen took his seat at 10.30. The prisoner was brought in and placed in the dock.

> He looked around the Court upon entering, and after taking in the whole scene settled down with composure and listened attentively.[230]

From somewhere the court had obtained a slightly higher stool, so that Robert's face and shoulders were now visible above the dock when he was seated.

Charles Mathews would speak for another hour. On Wednesday he had contested the prosecution's notion that the murder was committed out of revenge and resentment. He had also comprehensively demolished the evidence regards the alleged murder weapon. Now he turned his attention to the conduct of the prisoner on the night of the murder.

He asked the jurors to recall the testimony of the boy William Farnden. He had been called to give evidence on behalf of the prosecution, yet everything he said proved the innocence of the accused. William had bumped into Robert Husband outside the draper's shop; the two boys had gone to watch a show of some description down the Bear Hotel yard. A few minutes later they returned to the Pallant where the boys departed company outside William's house. Mr Mathews developed his theme:

> The evidence of the little boy, which might be taken as unimpeachable, to some extent, contradicts the statement of the boy Clark. William Farnden said the prisoner showed no knife, and made no mention of one. Quiet, peaceful, and orderly the two boys went on their innocent errand.[231]

Both Mr and Mrs Farnden stated under oath that Robert never came to their house that evening, whereas Robert insisted he knocked on

---

230 'The Havant Murder', *Hampshire Telegraph*, 22 December 1888.
231 Ibid.

their door and collected threepence owed for coal. Addressing this discrepancy, Mr Mathews contended it actually mattered very little so far as the charge of murder was concerned, but before Robert Husband was denigrated a liar the prosecution needed to prove that the prisoner had actually uttered an untruth. One way of settling the issue would have been to call William's sister Louisa [Ellen] as a witness. Her brother claimed she wasn't at home that night and hadn't in fact been living in Havant for a month or more, while the parents claimed their daughter was at home on the night of the murder and would therefore have been a witness to Robert calling at the house (if he called at all). Mr Mathews regretted that Robert had been charged with a deliberate falsehood when a simple remedy existed to either prove or disprove the controversy.

Next, he turned to the experiments conducted by the police in the Pallant, which he dismissed as 'worse than valueless' and 'unwarrantable'.[232] The police had assumed that when Robert saw the man attacking the boy he stayed rooted to the spot outside Mr Farnden's house, his foot on the doorstep, not moving an inch. Mr Mathews asked the jury to consider the prisoner's emotional state that evening when he saw a small boy being attacked: he would be agitated, terrified, and in a general state of excitement: in these circumstances wasn't it likely that the boy would misremember the exact spot from where he saw the murder? The police had found it suspicious that the prisoner varied his story as to where he claimed to be standing when he saw the murder – first he said he was beside the gas lamp next to Pallant House and then he said he was outside Mr Farnden's house. But both versions were not incompatible with the truth; a boy witnessing a murder would not stay frozen in one place, he would seek to flee the scene and would view the murder from multiple vantage points.

Percy had entered Mrs Randall's shop just a few moments before six o'clock; ten or fifteen minutes later Robert Husband had come running down the Pallant and raised the alarm to Henry Shirley. Was

---

232 'The Havant Murder', *Portsmouth Times*, 22 December 1888.

the prosecution seriously expecting the jury to believe that in those ten or fifteen minutes Robert Husband had met William Farnden, gone for a walk with him around the Bear Hotel, watched a show in the yard, accompanied William back to his house, hidden in wait for Percy near the Manor School wall, attacked and murdered the boy, rinsed his hands clean of blood, got rid of the knife, invented a defence, and run off down the Pallant before raising the alarm at Randall's shop? It wasn't possible, said Mr Mathews. If the boy had been guilty would he have gone straight up to Shirley as he did? If the boy had been guilty, why had he insisted to Mr Platt and Mr Shirley that a murder had taken place when both men initially doubted it? Wasn't it an entirely natural act for a small boy, frightened after witnessing a grisly murder, to run off and try to get home as quickly as possible?

> He was running when Shirley saw him. Where? To the first lighted point in the street to give information to the first person he should find. Did he hesitate? Immediately on seeing Mr Shirley he crossed the road and told him that a man was murdering a boy round the corner. His story was received with incredulity, but the prisoner persisted that it was true. Give him genius; give him years; give him experience, aye give him all the dexterity which had ever yet accompanied the most accomplished criminal, and then tell him whether they thought he would be capable of such conduct, unless it were the conduct of an innocent child instead of an accomplished and guilty criminal.[233]

Weren't the prisoner's hands dry and free of blood when Mr Platt took Robert's hand just moments after the crime was committed? Yet the prosecution alleged that the handle of the murder weapon was soaked and saturated in blood! Mr Mathews reminded the jury, too, that the only incriminating marks found on the prisoner's clothing were a few blood stains on the shirt cuff, covering one-sixteenth part of an inch, that were a month old. As for the suggestion that the clothes handed over to the police by Mrs Husband were not the same items worn by the boy on the night of the murder, Mr Mathews scoffed at the claim: Mrs Husband had given over the apparel at once,

233 'The Havant Murder', *Portsmouth Times*, 23 December 1888.

and besides, the prisoner was not a boy who had many changes of clothing.

Was it feasible, asked Mr Mathews, that a child as small as the accused had the strength and the commanding physical presence to overpower the deceased who was only an inch shorter than him? In a kindly tone of voice, Mr Mathews asked his client to get to his feet. 'Stand up, my little man,' he said. It was a masterstroke: standing up, Robert was actually shorter than when he'd been sitting down on the high stool: his nose was in line with the rail of the dock. He looked tiny and inoffensive. He looked innocent. The court gaoler, possibly pre-alerted by Mr Mathews to his intended manoeuvre, edged closer to the dock: the contrast between the tall, brawny guard and the diminutive boy on trial for murder was theatrically emphasised.

Presuming Robert was innocent, who then committed the murder, what were his motives, and where had he gone? These were important questions, and Mr Mathews briefly touched on them. He told the jurors that several trains departed Havant around the time of the murder, and that suspicion had fallen on one (unidentified) passenger in particular. As for motive, Mr Mathews simply drew the court's attention to the unexplained and unsolved Jack the Ripper murders in the East End of London. He paused here – dramatically – to let the jurors conjure up their own dark images of death and mutilation in the courtyards of Whitechapel.

Drawing to a close, he reminded the court that Robert had not altered his statement in any significant detail throughout the entire ordeal. He had stuck to his story, and his account of what happened had been absolutely consistent, and clearly expressed, even in front of the magistrates when the prisoner had been without professional assistance.

He turned to face the jury one last time:

> I am painfully aware that there stands before us a father and mother who mourn the loss of their child, and it is only becoming to express sympathy with their sorrow. But it is not revenge, but justice that they seek. There are also before us two other parents who demand

the restitution of their child.

What is truth? Close upon 1900 years ago this question was put, and it had gone unanswered. And now it is asked again. How do you answer? Will it be by silence, or by a confession that after all you are human, and will you show a virtue as precious as life itself by the restitution of that child's freedom? [234]

Mr Mathews sat down. He had done his absolute best. George Feltham reached over and gripped him by the shoulder.

It was a stirring speech, full of theatrical incident and spectacle, and powerfully argued. It seems churlish to point out that Mr Mathews had mistaken George Bartholomew, sitting next to Mrs Husband in the public gallery, for Robert's father.

Mr Justice Stephen took a couple of minutes to adjust his papers and make a few final notes. He was then ready to give his summing up.

234 'The Havant Murder', *Portsmouth Times*, 22 December 1888.

21

The Verdict

Towards the end of his career Mr Justice Stephen's increasingly eccentric behaviour on the Bench became the subject of much public criticism. Weakness of memory and short-temperedness were the commonest complaints. On one occasion it was alleged he began his summing up at the conclusion of the prosecution's case before the defence had even presented its case.[235] But these dissatisfactions lay mostly in the future. At the Robert Husband trial his conduct was exemplary, although his summing up was tiresome and protracted.

His Lordship began by describing the Havant crime as 'horrible and astonishing'. He regarded it as a homicide almost unparalleled in the history of crime. It was very improbable, he said, that an unknown man had murdered Percy, but it was equally improbable that the prisoner had murdered him. This improbability acted as much in Robert's defence as against it.

In one sense he said the case was a very simple one – all the jurors had to do was consider the facts that had been put before them and then decide if the prisoner had committed the crime with which he was charged. If they felt perfectly confident that the boy was guilty, then it was their solemn duty before God and man to say so; but if they harboured any doubts at all then their verdict should be 'not guilty'.

The judge then outlined for the jury the legal position regarding criminal responsibility. Up to seven years a child was not considered capable of committing a crime; after fourteen years every person was presumed to be sane and responsible for his acts unless

---

235 *Law Times*, XC, 7 March 1891, 334.

evidence existed to the contrary. However, between the ages of seven and fourteen the law was slightly different. He recited to them the clearest definition of the law he had been able to formulate:

> No act done by any person over seven and under fourteen years of age is a crime unless it be shown affirmatively that such a person had sufficient capacity to know the act was wrong.[236]

By 'sufficient capacity' the judge meant something more than the knowledge an immature child might acquire on being told by his tutor or mother that such an act was wrong. It implied a conception of the consequence of actions and a moral understanding of the dreadfulness or wickedness of certain acts. To put it into context, the judge said that the jury needed to decide if the prisoner realised that stabbing someone in the neck might result in death, and that deliberately stabbing someone in the neck was a wicked act.

His Lordship felt it might assist the jurors if he mentioned to them the direction he had given the jury at another case in Exeter a fortnight before when a girl of about thirteen years of age was charged with the murder of a boy of four. (Here the judge was repeating himself – at the request of Mr Mathews he had already provided the jury with this information at the conclusion of the prosecution case. Perhaps he was forgetting, or maybe he thought his direction was sufficiently important to bear repeating.) Everyone on the jury had once been eleven years of age, he said, and most of them would still be able to recall the feelings, temptations, and inclinations which occupied their minds at that age. He asked the jurors to remember how they had felt when they were of a similar age to the prisoner, and to make use of that experience when deliberating on the accused boy's guilt or innocence.

The jury also needed to decide if the prisoner had actually inflicted the fatal blow. That was a more difficult question. It might be a tedious way of going about things, but he proposed to remind the jurors of the evidence that had been presented to them.

---

236 'The Havant Murder', *Hampshire Advertiser*, 22 December 1888.

His Lordship then revisited all the evidence in laborious detail, commenting here and there as he worked through it. Possibly the jury were bored and annoyed by this – the judge was repeating facts the jury had already digested or had sensibly forgotten because they regarded them as trivial. He did not unfairly guide the jury towards a particular verdict, but he emphasised two points that were especially helpful to the defence.

Firstly, he said he was inclined to attach little importance to the statement from one of the witnesses that Robert was running around with a knife claiming to be 'Jack the Ripper'. This was probably nothing more than 'foolish, childish play'.[237] Secondly, he considered the prosecution's argument that it was impossible for the boy to see what he said he saw. The police, the foreman of the inquest jury, and a man with a white dog, had conducted experiments in the Pallant which appeared to support this notion, yet Mr Justice Stephen raised a new doubt in the jurors' minds:

> The policemen and others who visited the spot were all men in middle life, and although I do not express an opinion on that point, it might be possible that a child between eleven and twelve years old might be able to see a man against a wall, under circumstances under which older men would be unable to discern him.[238]

It was now 12.30 and time for luncheon. The judge had been speaking for three hours and still he was not done. Being dragged to Winchester and compelled to serve as jurors inflicted real inconvenience on many tradesmen, especially in the run-up to Christmas. The judge's unnecessarily lengthy summary will not have been appreciated.

After lunch he spoke for another hour and a half. It was three o'clock when he finally finished his summing up. His last direction to the jurors was that they ought to have the courage to return a 'guilty' verdict if they were perfectly sure that the prisoner had purposely inflicted the fatal stab.

---

237 'The Havant Murder', *Hampshire Advertiser*, 22 December 1888.
238 Ibid.

The jury retired to consider its verdict. Robert was taken away to the cells.

The *Hampshire Advertiser* gave a summary of Robert's countenance and demeanour during the trial:

> Husband, who was seated the whole of the time he was in the dock, did not appear to realise the fearful position in which he was placed, and he showed no signs of following the evidence against him. He exhibited the same apparent indifference when the jury retired and when the verdict was returned.[239]

In the grand jury gallery, the ladies of distinction put on the kettles for afternoon tea. Learned counsel and members of the press got up and stretched their legs. One or two of the gas lamps were ignited. There may have been an expectation that it would take the jury a while to reach its verdict, but after only ten minutes the foreman of the jury signalled they were ready to return.

The kettles had not even had time to boil. The prisoner was brought back and placed at the bar. There was intense excitement and a breathless silence. The names of the jury were called over.

Clerk of the Assize:	Have you agreed upon your verdict?
Foreman:	We have.
Clerk of the Assize:	How say you? Do you find the prisoner Robert Husband guilty or not guilty of the murder of Percy Knight Searle?
Foreman:	Not Guilty.
Clerk of the Assize:	And that is the verdict of you all?
Foreman:	It is.
Mr Justice Stephen:	The boy may be discharged. Are his parents here?
Mr Mathews:	His mother is here.
Mr Justice Stephen:	Give him to his mother.[240]

Captain Charles Hill, the Governor of Winchester Prison, congratulated Fanny Husband on the acquittal of her son. He took her to the cells, and it was there that Robert and his mother were

---

239 'The Havant Murder', *Hampshire Advertiser*, 22 December 1888.
240 'The Murder at Havant', *Hampshire Post*, 21 December 1888.

reunited. They hugged each other and Mrs Husband started crying.

Robert and his mother were escorted to the railway station by a crowd of well-wishers.

Two or three hours later, mother and son arrived back at Havant. George Bartholomew may have sent a telegram to Robert's father, informing him of the jury's verdict and their expected arrival time at Havant station. The news quickly spread and there was a small welcoming party to greet them on the station platform. *Lloyd's Weekly Newspaper* wrote:

> The boy has had to pass through a terrible ordeal; but it is gratifying to know that on his return home he was met by many of his former playmates, who had all through maintained his innocence.[241]

It is not clear who these 'former playmates' were. At most there may have been one or two of Robert's tearaway mates like Charlie White and Alfie Ward, or Watley and Stacey. Maybe Johnny Sparks was there too, purring like a cat.

Mr and Mrs Searle had travelled back on the same train, though in a different compartment to the Husbands. There was no one to greet them when they stepped off the train. They were already well on the way to being forgotten.

---

241 'The Havant Murder Trial', *Lloyd's Weekly Newspaper*, 23 December 1888.

22

A Scandal to the Town

The case against Robert Husband had been purely circumstantial. A good deal of suspicion fell on the boy simply because he was the last person (other than the murderer) to see Percy alive. The police were right to bring him before the magistrates. But the prosecution had conspicuously failed to furnish credible evidence linking Robert to the murder, and it could be argued that the magistrates, after examining the 'evidence' in the police court, ought to have seen that there was no *prima facie* case to answer and discharged him. For most people, the idea that a lad as young as Robert could have been guilty of such a heinous crime was unthinkable, or nearly so, and the outcome of the trial was greeted with relief in many quarters. The *London Daily News* commended the jurors for their decision:

> A verdict of 'Not Guilty' was the only one that could be anticipated. Any other verdict would have demanded as its foundation evidence amounting to absolute certainty; and even then the task as laid down by Mr Justice Stephen provided for the Jury a way of avoiding conviction. They had to be satisfied that the boy stabbed the other; but they had also to be sure that, at his age, he knew the gravity of his act. They had not even evidence to satisfy them on the first point. There is only one unsatisfactory feature of this result. It leaves in doubt and mystery the death of the child Searle.[242]

A thoughtful piece in the *Daily Telegraph* was a little more cautious in its assessment of the trial:

> The public has been spared the inexpressibly mournful spectacle of a boy just emerged from the nursery condemned and sentenced as a murderer ...

242 *London Daily News*, 21 December 1888.

There are, however, precociously clever children, and there may also be children who are precociously wicked. Naturally, the mind shrinks from associating deliberate homicide with a mere lad hardly yet in his teens; nevertheless, the annals of crime show that there may be small moral monsters as well as big, grown-up ones ... Fortunately, the result of the trial makes it unnecessary to speculate on the character of the accused, because the jury believe him, as the public believe him, to be quite innocent of the dreadful deed.[243]

If Robert had been convicted of wilful murder, the newspapers would have fallen back on several stock arguments to explain the crime and mollify public unease – irresponsible parenting, poverty and deprived home circumstances, juvenile gangs, insanity, the pernicious influence of the penny dreadfuls, and so on. But a 'Not Guilty' verdict offered no such comfort and reassurance. A 'Not Guilty' verdict was the worst possible outcome for the Searle family and for the community at large because it left the crime not only unpunished but unexplained.

Some newspapers attempted to fill this information gap by resurrecting the spectre of Jack the Ripper or speculating on the actions of an unknown predator lurking in plain sight in the neighbourhood:

The question still remains to be answered as to who is responsible for the child's death ... There is absolutely nothing beyond the wantonness and barbarity of the crime to connect it with the deeds of the monster who has made Whitechapel the scene of his butcheries. In all probability it will be found, if the guilty person ever be discovered, that the murderer is no stranger to the locality in which the body was found.[244]

The *Daily Telegraph* added the following:

We are thrown back on the theory that there really was a tall man, a stranger of the kind which Husband described, lurking about Havant at that time, and that from some insane homicidal freak, or out of mere brutal wantonness, he stabbed the boy and then decamped. Who was the assassin? Several mysterious strangers were remembered when

---

243 *Daily Telegraph*, 25 December 1888.
244 *Enniskillen Chronicle and Erne Packet*, 3 January 1889.

the murder became known, to have been seen hovering about the South Coast at that time. Rumour told of a man in a high hat who dashed up to the roadside railway ...[245]

These dithering judgments took on a more frantic aspect towards the end of the year when a second child was found murdered in the Manningham district of Bradford. A seven-year-old boy called John Gill had been gruesomely mutilated and his body wrapped up like a parcel of butcher's meat before being dumped in an outhouse just yards from his home.[246] Again, the perpetrator of the crime would elude justice; again, newspaper editors drew parallels with the Whitechapel atrocities.

Increasingly, the Havant Tragedy came to be linked in the public imagination with the John Gill case and with other unsolved murders of children in the late 1880s and early 1890s. The *St James's Gazette* spoke darkly of a 'wave of bloodshed' passing over the country,[247] a sentiment already voiced by the *Manchester Times* in an editorial:

> It would almost seem as if an epidemic of child murders has set in. The killing of a boy in Havant was not the first case of the kind which has recently occurred. It has been followed by the Bradford atrocity and the Somerset case, and the murder of a child in London. This is all very dreadful, and it is all the more discouraging since we can feel no confidence that the perpetrators of these crimes will be brought to justice.[248]

The *Derby Mercury* and *The Graphic* rightly scoffed at the idea that there was a serial abuser of children roaming the country, but they both chose to emphasise the supposed malefic influence of Jack the Ripper on crimes of this nature:

---

245 *Daily Telegraph*, 25 December 1888.
246 'Murder and Mutilations of a Boy at Bradford', *The Morning Post*, 31 December 1888.
247 *St James's Gazette*, 10 January 1889.
248 *Manchester Times*, 5 January 1889. The Somerset case refers to the murder and mutilation of nine-year-old Jane Davey in Yeobridge on January 4 1889. A local man, Samuel Reyland, was later convicted of her murder and executed by the hangman James Berry at Shepton Mallet Gaol on 13 March 1889.

It may indeed be pretty safely assumed that, like the atrocity at Havant, the [Bradford child killing] is the work of an independent hand. It is too much to believe that one single monster is ranging the country and signalising his presence in every town by a deed of blood. On the other hand, it might safely be said that but for the Whitechapel crimes neither the tragedy of Bradford nor that of [Havant] would have been signalised by these ghastly and purposeless mutilations.[249] Unless the Whitechapel fiend is possessed of an almost preternatural ubiquitousness, the tragedies at Havant and Bradford are probably the work of persons who, from perpetually brooding over these horrors, have been led to follow his frightful example.[250]

The *Hampshire Telegraph* was one of the few newspapers to spare a thought for Robert and his family in the aftermath of the murder trial. In what would prove to be a very prescient article they wrote:

There are doubtless many who have strong opinions as to the precise share young Husband took in that dreadful night's work in the lonely Pallant ... Though acquitted, the stigma of the ordeal will stick to him for life, while his prospects in this district are forever blighted, notwithstanding the fact that twelve of his countrymen have declared by their verdict that he was innocent of the cruel murder for which he was put in peril of his life.[251]

The Husbands were an undemonstrative family. They won't have celebrated Robert's acquittal in any lavish way. For one thing, the family was in dire financial circumstances. There was barely enough money coming in to pay for food and clothing. The defence fund was still £25.00 short of its target figure of £100, and on top of everything else, Mr Husband had just been billed by the police for the repair of the police cell door damaged by Robert in his bid to escape.

That first night after the acquittal, Robert's sister, Jane, who was working as a domestic servant in Southampton, came over to spend time with the family, and throughout the evening friends and well-wishers called round to extend their regards. Apart from that, the atmosphere in the Husband household was probably fairly subdued.

249 *Derby Mercury,* 2 January 1889.
250 *The Graphic*, 5 January 1889.
251 *Hampshire Telegraph*, 22 December 1888.

Yet we can be sure that Robert relished sleeping in his old bed again, listening to the familiar night sounds reaching him from North Street – the noise of revellers in the George Tavern, the mournful, far-off rattle of the occasional goods train rushing through the town on its way to Portsmouth or Chichester. Perhaps he and George chatted away well into the early hours, discussing all that had happened and planning for the future. And in the morning, after a quick breakfast, it would be back to work in the coal yard.

Robert may have been cleared of wrongdoing at Winchester, but in Havant many people felt he had literally got away with murder. The jury, they said, had been bamboozled by the clever words of a fancy barrister down from London. Feelings against the family had been running high ever since Robert was arrested in November, and now, compounded by disgust at the jury's verdict, their resentment turned swiftly to anger. Reprisals against the Husband family were not long in coming.

For their part, the police seemed reluctant to re-investigate the murder. So far as they were concerned, the person responsible for Percy's murder had already been apprehended and prosecuted. There was no point, they argued, in squandering police resources on a second enquiry. No new leads were followed up; no witnesses were re-interviewed. The case was allowed to grow cold. Commenting on one aspect of this, Gavin Maidment says:

> What I find extraordinary is that, even after Husband's acquittal, the authorities never maintained a full-scale investigation to track down another suspect who had been seen by a porter at the Havant railway station: an unidentified man who boarded a train for Brighton minutes after the crime without a ticket after attempting to hide from the porter's view.[252]

As we have seen, Inspector Lawler travelled up and down the railway line between Havant and Brighton, quizzing commuters and station staff, but the prospect of a breakthrough always seemed remote. No efforts were made by the police or by the railway

---

252 Gavin Maidment archive, Spring Arts and Heritage Centre, Havant.

authorities to entice new information.

This fleeing man at the railway station, the strange guest at the Royal Oak hotel in Emsworth, the mysterious navvy seen by Captain Boyd in the Pallant moments before the murder – none of these sightings was properly investigated by the police before or after the trial.

The Husband defence fund had raised £74 15s. This was a creditable sum, but it didn't cover all the debts incurred by the Husband family. The barrister's fees had to be paid (or Amatt and Sansom had to be reimbursed for settling Mathews's bill in advance), and then there were Feltham's expenses from attending the coroner's inquest and the trial. Amatt and Sansom calculated that the full cost would be over £100. Even though Robert had been acquitted, they decided to keep the fund open for one week more.

Problems were brewing for the family from other quarters. The first counterattack – that is the only way to describe it – came from Samuel Clarke, the owner of the coal yard. He had already kicked up a fuss over the amount of time Mr Husband was spending away from the depot at the magistrates' and coroner's courts, and he had refused him time off work to attend his son's trial at Winchester. Now, vindictively, he terminated Mr Husband's employment.

To be fair, Samuel Clarke may have felt he had little choice in the matter. Customers were already feeling uncomfortable at the thought of being served by a 'murderer' or by the brother and father of a 'murderer'; bricks and stones were being hurled over the coal yard wall into the depot. On her shopping trips into town, Mrs Husband sometimes found that shopkeepers refused to serve her or gave her the worst produce from their stalls. There may even have been threats of assault made against Robert and his brother. Many of their neighbours at the bottom end of North Street boycotted the family, although one imagines Martha Burrows kept out of it. It was an unpleasant situation and admittedly bad for Mr Clarke's business. Customers were starting to order their coal supply from other merchants in town. The *Liverpool Echo* later spoke out against the 'stupid heartlessness' of this boycotting:

Even supposing the boy had been found guilty, the family would have deserved sympathy rather than prosecution; but as he was acquitted there is no sort of reason for adding to the sufferings which he and his friends have endured.[253]

It seems Mr Husband was given a fortnight's notice on 22 December. And because the Husbands lived in a tied property, this meant the family – all ten of them, including a three-month-old baby – would lose their home as well.

There was nothing Mr Husband could do about it, but in despair he approached Alfred Amatt and Frederick Sansom, the two men who had instigated the defence fund. The Christmas Eve edition of the *Portsmouth Evening News* carried a heartfelt appeal from the two Portsmouth men:

Will you kindly allow us to appeal to the readers of your extensive paper on behalf of the victims of a flagrant injustice perpetrated in connection with the Havant murder. The father of the boy Husband is employed in a coal store at Havant, the owner of which informed him that if he lost any time to attend the Assizes on behalf of his boy standing charged with the crime, it would be tantamount to instant dismissal. Of course, the father did not attend, but the mother did in his stead. On the boy being acquitted, and arriving home in due course, the master intimated to the father that his services would be no longer required after a certain date. How we ask is this not carrying vengeance too far? Is not the fact of the family being tainted already with the terrible charge not enough, without the breadwinner being thrown out of employment, especially at this time of year? Previous to this injustice a brother of the boy Husband was told that he might take a week's notice owing to his losing a day or two to attend the Magistrates' enquiry and Coroner's inquest.[254]

On 3 January 1889, the Husband family packed up their few belongings and moved out of their home in North Street. The father had worked at the coal yard for more than ten years, and six of the family's nine children had been born within the walls of the cottage. They had not been run out of town exactly, but it was not far from it. They returned to the Cherry Garden Field estate in Portsmouth,

253 *Liverpool Echo*, 18 January 1889.
254 *Portsmouth Evening News*, 24 December 1888.

setting up home in Hercules Street.

Ironically, on the day the Husband family moved out, the Havant Local Board convened at their offices in West Street to discuss the inadequate lighting amenities in the town. The clerk reported he had written to the gas company about erecting new lamps in the Pallant.[255]

Money for the defence fund continued to dribble in. The young people employed at the Common Street Stay Factory in Kingston had a whip round and sent in 18s 6d.[256]

A long-time friend of the family was Mr Frederick Scott from Southsea, who used to work alongside Robert Sr as a ship painter in the royal dockyards. In January, when he called round to see the Husband family, he found them 'in a destitute condition, without money and without friends'.[257] On Saturday 13 January, George Husband landed a job serving behind the counter at Savage's grocers on Somers Road in Southsea – a rare piece of good fortune for the family. But the *Hampshire Telegraph*'s foreboding of a family stigmatised and forever blighted proved accurate. Later that morning George was dismissed, and the proprietor, Mr Francis Savage, wrote to Robert's father to explain his reasons for letting his son go:

> I think I could not put him behind the counter, as you must know I have the public to study, and if people were to know it, it would make it unpleasant for me and him as well. Had it been for shop boy it would not have mattered so much, but I want someone that presently I can bind to serve for three years, and then things cannot be altered. I do not say a word against the boy's character, neither would I speak against him to anyone. I know it must be very trying for you. Enclosed is one week's money for this week's labour.[258]

Francis Scott wrote to the local newspaper to complain about this incident, although in doing so he slightly misrepresented Mr Savage's actions:

255 *Hampshire Telegraph*, 5 January 1889.
256 *Portsmouth Evening News*, 22 January 1889.
257 *Portsmouth Evening News*, 15 January 1889.
258 *Portsmouth Evening News*, 19 January 1889.

One of their children obtained a situation in this town on Saturday last, and the boy went to his work on the Monday morning, but he was there only two hours when his master paid him his week's money (2s. 6d.) and told him that as his name was Husband he had better go.

Is this not deplorable in a large town like Portsmouth, where people ought to be enlightened and educated, and not given to such prejudices as exist always in small villages? Can I appeal to any generous employer of labour to give this poor man Husband work so that he may be able to support his family, as our laws expect? And might I also appeal to the benevolent to assist with any clothing or money they may have to spare, as there is a family of eleven to provide for.

F. Scott 7 Abingdon Road, Southsea[259]

Disputing this version of events, Francis Savage wrote in turn to the evening paper to put his side of the story:

Now this is incorrect ... The engagement and discharge were transacted entirely with the father of the boy. On Monday morning I obtained the boy's name from his father, and, ascertaining a little later that the boy was one of the family I had read so much about, I concluded that he would not suit me for an apprentice to serve behind the counter and be bound. I thereupon wrote an inoffensive and sympathising letter to the father explaining my reasons, and enclosing the 2s. 6d. for the week's wages. All I want the public to know is the truth.[260]

A day later, Scott wrote again to the *News*, acknowledging that he hadn't told the full story previously, and asking now if the correspondence could be closed. He and a 'well-known gentleman in the town' had since procured accommodation for George and Robert where the two boys would be clothed and looked after and allowed to work for their father.[261]

In a macabre and very bizarre development, it seems Robert had found employment (of sorts) at the Gaiety Music Hall in Commercial Road, Landport. The Gaiety (sometimes known as the New Gaiety)

259 *Portsmouth Evening News,* 18 January 1889.
260 Ibid.
261 *Portsmouth Evening News,* 19 January 1889.

was a short-lived entertainment venue catering mainly for military audiences. It was frequented principally by soldiers, sailors, dock workers, and 'loose women', and had a rather seedy reputation, although the *Portsmouth Evening News* described it as 'a cosy little hall'. The proprietor was Henry Charles Hughes, who was also the landlord of several public houses in the locality such as The Grapes and the Albert Tavern. Many little-known variety and speciality acts performed at the Gaiety – The Tullett Brothers (negro comedians), Baby Munroe (the 'Greatest Child Actress Living'), Miss Annie Thornton ('Low Comedy Lady') and Frank and Berta James (sketch artists) assisted by their famous dog 'Black Pete'.

The following advertisement, which appeared in the amusement and theatrical notice columns of the *Portsmouth Evening News*, shows who was on the bill for week commencing 21 January 1889:

GAIETY MUSIC HALL, COMMERCIAL Road, LANDPORT
Monday, Jan 21st and During the Week
Starring engagement of MR WILL ATKINS,
great Character Comedian
SISTERS PERCIVAL, Duettists and Dancers
First Appearance of TOM HUNTLEY
Great Success of the SISTERS SLATOR
Last Week of JOHNNY FALCONER, Comic
Welcome Return of ROSIE MERRYWOOD
Grand Sketch!! 'The Bride of Garryowen' by the
FALCONER TROUPE, six in number.
The boy Husband, who was accused for the murder of Percy
Searle, at Havant, will appear every evening until further notice.
Times and Prices as Usual.[262]

It's difficult to imagine what kind of music hall act Robert might have been capable of performing. Perhaps he was just paraded as a curiosity or a freak show attraction like a bearded lady or a man with elastic skin. It's impossible to say how the audience reacted to this surly, awkward youth, acquitted of murder and now destitute in his home town, appearing on stage between the dancing dogs and

---

262 *Portsmouth Evening News*, 22 January 1889.

the lewd comediennes.

Robert was engaged for four nights only. The novelty must have worn off fairly quickly. He was replaced by the popular burlesque actress Louie Wyndham.

Robert's career as a ghoulish tourist attraction didn't end here. In late February and early March he was selling beer behind the bar at the Newtown Tavern at 247 Commercial Road in Landport. A letter to the *Portsmouth Evening News* from a concerned citizen expressed outrage at this development:

A SCANDAL TO THE TOWN

Sir,— I would like to publicly protest against the way in which the boy Husband, who it will be remembered was accused of the Havant murder, is now being used as a big public house advertisement. A few days since I was handed a bill—a copy of which is appended below—setting forth the fact that young Husband was employed at the Newtown Tavern, opposite the New Gaiety, and inviting the reader to visit and witness this paragon of simplicity, supplying beer from behind the counter. Do you not think it advisable, Sir, that for the boy's good he should be placed in some school until he attains the age of fifteen?

Respectfully yours, PHILANTHROPY

[Copy of Bill]
HAVANT TRAGEDY
Lovers of Justice!
Come and see the Innocent Little Boy
ROBERT HUSBAND,
Who was accused of the wilful murder of Percy
Searle, behind the bar of the
NEWTOWN TAVERN,
Opposite the Gaiety Music Hall, Commercial Road,
Landport.[263]

With the Gaiety opposite, and Commercial Road being such a busy thoroughfare, the Newtown Tavern must have had a good trade, even if its glory days had long gone. The former owners used to sell hens' eggs on the premises; now, under the watchful eye of licensed victualler Albert J. Hoad, young Robert was pulling

263 *Portsmouth Evening News*, 5 March 1889.

pints in the public bar. Who knows what the customers made of it all. It seems the adverse publicity in the *Evening News* cost Robert his job, though, for on making enquiries a reporter from the same newspaper subsequently learnt that Robert had been discharged.

And with this inglorious exit, Robert disappears totally from the public record.

The Havant murder was beginning to fade from public memory when, in December 1889, a twenty-one-year-old prisoner on remand in Knutsford Gaol confessed to the murder of Percy Searle.

23

Echoes in the Pallant

John Henry Thompson *alias* Jones was a 'demented-looking young fellow' aged around twenty or twenty-one. He was a beggar and a vagrant who wandered from place to place across England. He often slept rough or in the casual wards of workhouses. On occasions when he found temporary work (he was a painter by trade), he usually spent his wages on beer.

During the night of 11 December 1889, he broke into St John the Evangelist church in Norley, a village in the Delamere Forest in Cheshire. In the vestry he smashed open a safe and got his hands on a communion plate, a silver flagon, eleven wax candles, and a sacramental breadknife. He also found two and a half bottles of communion wine, which he proceeded to guzzle – 'I drank the health of all the saints in the calendar,' he later bragged. After a half-hearted attempt to melt the silver items in a makeshift fire, he dossed down in a pew and slept till early next morning.

A few days later he attempted to sell the communion plate to a shopkeeper in Crewe. His actions obviously aroused suspicion, the police were summoned, and Thompson was arrested and taken into custody at Oakmere Police Station, charged with sacrilege at various churches and chapels in the Delamere Forest. On 16 December he appeared before the magistrates at Eddisbury Petty Sessions. When asked if he had anything to say in his defence as to why he shouldn't be committed to trial at the next assizes, he replied: 'Yes, I have got a word or two to say – that I have given myself up for committing two murders and I feel I ought to be tried for them rather than tried for this.'

Thompson owned up first to killing a soldier by pushing him into the Shropshire Union Canal at Backford and holding him under the water until he was dead.

Next, he admitted to killing young Percy Searle. The *Hampshire Telegraph* records the details of his confession:

> He met the boy on the road between Havant and Emsworth and took him into a field at the back of the railway station where he stabbed him with his knife. He also alleges that he carried the weapon away with him, but before leaving the spot took another knife from the murdered boy's pocket, smeared it with blood, and threw it down on the grass beside the body.[264]

The authorities did not attach too much importance to these confessions; they were full of physical impossibilities and other significant inconsistencies. The Chief Constable of Cheshire attributed Thompson's stories to a 'morbid desire for notoriety' and 'feigned insanity' in an effort to get off lightly for the sacrilegious burglaries.[265]

At the Chester Assizes on 17 March 1890, Thompson was sentenced to five years in gaol for a series of burglaries at Cheshire churches.

Life moved on. The seasons came and went; the years passed ever more quickly. Families moved away from Havant or became absorbed in their own domestic dramas. People grew old and died, their recollections of the Havant murder expiring with them. Slowly, the story of Percy Searle and Robert Husband began to fade from living memory until there was no one left alive who could recall the boy's murder at first-hand. Accounts of the crime and the trial became garbled and distorted, and eventually, like most human achievement and endeavour, the events during the winter of 1888

---

264 *Hampshire Telegraph*, 4 January 1890.
265 Details of the Thompson case from the *Cheshire Observer*, 28 December 1889.

became almost entirely forgotten, or they turned into folklore. Writing in 1935, E.C. Bailey refers dubiously to the killing of Percy Searle as the 'Great Havant Murder'.[266]

Looking back over her life in 1993, Lilian Vine recalled – or thought she did – Percy's murder:

> GRIM PIECE OF HISTORY REMEMBERED
>
> Fairfield Road was the scene of a tragic killing more than 50 years ago ... Lilian Vine, aged 86, remembers when a 12-year-old boy was killed outside her home just before the second World War broke out. 'It happened a little while before we moved here. They were coal boys who worked at the coal yard, which used to be in Prince George's Street. A 14-year-old boy killed his friend over a penknife.'[267]

In 2003, a descendant of PC John Samuel Wareham, Cyril Giles, contacted Gavin Maidment to relate his grandfather's role in the Percy Searle murder enquiry:

> Two young boys were fighting with a knife – one was killed. Grandad Wareham was first to see the dead boy. He immediately went to the local police station and reported to his sergeant. The sergeant thought that (Samuel) PC Wareham had been drinking. Samuel told the sergeant he would throw in his uniform. PC Wareham did not throw in his uniform. PC Wareham put a black cross on the wall adjacent to the murder site.[268]

It is a good family story, but alas largely untrue. As we have seen, Sergeant William Knapton was the first officer at the scene; and Police General Orders for 29 November 1888 indicate what really happened that evening and next morning:

> PC 54 J Wareham has been dismissed from the service with the forfeiture of a week's pay for having been drunk at 8 am on Tuesday 27 inst when on special duty at Havant. He will deliver his uniform at Hdqtrs forthwith.[269]

---

266 'Havant of Past Days: Law and Order', *Hampshire Telegraph,* 22 February 1935.
267 *Portsmouth Evening News,* 28 June 1993.
268 Gavin Maidment archive, The Spring Arts and Heritage Centre, Havant.
269 Hampshire Constabulary General Orders 1889–90, Hampshire Record Office, reference 200M 86 H1/9.

It seems PC Wareham was given the task of guarding the murder scene over night, and rather unwisely began accepting pots of ale from the residents to ward off the chill. As a consequence, by daybreak the constable was conspicuously intoxicated. He went on to become a bricklayer.

Between 1911 and the 1930s, the Havant artist William Grant (1893–1982), who specialised in landscapes of the town and portraits of its people, painted a series of watercolours of the Manor House area. They included scenes of Fairfield Road in 1911 and Prince George's Street in 1923. Another, dated 1936, showed the Manor House and a small boy standing in front of the school wall. It is not a portrait of Percy – Grant often included a random single human figure in a landscape to provide scale – and we do not know what specifically inspired the artist to paint this scene, but is it possible that the artist is obliquely referencing the murder of Percy Searle by including a small child in the picture standing almost exactly on the murder spot?[270]

The Percy Searle story crops up from time to time in true crime books. Daniel Farson included a discussion of the case in his 1972 study *Jack the Ripper*.[271] In her book *Ripper: The Secret Life of Walter Sickert*, Patricia Cornwell moots the worthless idea that the painter Walter Sickert could have caught the ferry from Le Havre to Portsmouth, and then travelled to Havant to murder Percy.[272] Nicola Sly has covered the Searle case in her collection, *More Hampshire Murders*. She mentions in passing two other Jack the Ripper suspects who had connections with the Portsmouth / Isle of Wight area in 1888 – Robert Donston Stephenson and James Maybrick.[273] There is an entry for Percy Searle in *The Complete Jack the Ripper A to Z*.[274]

270 William Grant: Untitled watercolour 1936, HMCMS: FA1980.2.6 DPABEF90.

271 Daniel Farson, *Jack the Ripper* (London: Michael Joseph, 1972), pp. 52–56.

272 Patricia Cornwell, *Ripper: The Secret Life of Walter Sickert* (Seattle: Thomas & Mercer, 2017), pp. 385–7.

273 Nicola Sly, *More Hampshire Murders* (Stroud: The History Press, 2010), pp. 76–84.

274 Paul Begg, Martin Fido & Keith Skinner, *The Complete Jack the Ripper A to Z* (London: John Blake, 2010).

Captain John Forrest retired on superannuation in March 1891, having served as Chief Constable of Hampshire for thirty-five tumultuous years. He was succeeded by Captain Peregrine Fellowes, whose term of office would prove as brief as Captain Forrest's was long; in 1893 he was fatally injured while attempting to stop a runaway horse and trap.[275]

Sergeant Knapton had been stationed at Havant for five years. In April 1889 he was promoted to inspector and transferred to Bournemouth. Clearly, the events over the winter of 1888 hadn't adversely affected his police career. Two years later he attained the rank of 3rd class superintendent, becoming a 1st class superintendent in July 1895. He retired two months later after completing twenty-five years' service. He had done well for an errand boy from the General Post Office in Gillingham.

Superintendent Kinshott, whose conduct throughout the Searle enquiry had often bordered on the ignoble, left to take up new duties in Basingstoke in 1890. At least the Fareham magistrates were sad to see him go: 'If there is one thing,' they said, 'that was more conspicuous in Mr Kinshott's character than another it was that he never wished to unduly press any charge of crime to conviction, for if he saw any favourable point in the character of a criminal he was always willing to give him the benefit of the doubt in putting the case before [the magistrates].'[276]

Dr Florio St Quintin Bond put away his doctor's bag in 1897 and retired to his home in East Street, Havant. He was an accomplished musician, and his greatest pleasure in his final years was playing chamber music with his family in the evenings; they formed a string quartet – Dr Bond playing cello, his grown-up children violins and viola – and they often gave recitals in town or in Portsmouth and Chichester. Dr Bond's father had died when he fell off a penny

---

275 Ian A Watt, *A History of The Hampshire and Isle of Wight Constabulary 1839–1966* (Hampshire & Isle of Wight Constabulary, 1967), p. 49.
276 'Magisterial Testimonial to a Police Superintendent', *Hampshire Telegraph*, 29 March 1890.

farthing; Florio himself passed away peacefully in his sleep, at home, in September 1902.

Following adverse comments in the press about his declining capacity to perform his judicial duties, Mr Justice Stephen resigned as a High Court judge in April 1891. He died of chronic renal failure in March 1894 at a nursing home near Ipswich. Interestingly, Stephen's second son, James Kenneth Stephen, became yet another suspect for the Jack the Ripper murders.[277]

More than fulfilling the promise shown at the Winchester Assizes, Charles 'Willie' Mathews, later Sir Charles Mathews, became Director of Public Prosecutions in 1908.

Mr George Feltham, the Portsmouth solicitor who advocated so powerfully on Robert Husband's behalf, prospered in the immediate aftermath of the trial. He opened a second office in Chichester, where he lived for a short while. But ill-health caught up with him, and in October 1892 he died following a severe epileptic fit. His obituary made special mention of his involvement in the Husband case:

> He will be long remembered for the talented manner in which he dealt with the defence of the boy Husband, who in 1888 was charged with the wilful murder of another lad named Percy Knight Searle, at Havant. The circumstantial evidence for the prosecution was exceedingly strong, but Mr Feltham, who instructed Mr. C. Mathews, barrister, succeeded in having the facts of the case placed before the jury in a form which brought about the acquittal of the accused.[278]

A.C. Lewis, the town surveyor, who supplied important crime scene evidence, died prematurely in a shooting accident in the garden of his house in West Street in 1893, aged forty-eight.[279]

Samuel Whitbread, the baker-turned-photographer, never really bounced back from his three-month spell in prison for embezzlement; the family moved to South Street in late 1890, and Whitbread continued to eke a living of sorts from his photography

---

277 See Deborah McDonald, *The Prince, His Tutor and the Ripper* (London: McFarland & Co., 2007).

278 'Death of Mr George Feltham', *Portsmouth Evening News*, 6 October 1892.

279 Robert West, *Charles Lewis: Surveyor and Auctioneer in Nineteenth Century Havant* (Havant Borough Council, 2013), p. 10.

studio until at least the turn of the millennium.

Johnny Sparks, the cat killer, joined the navy in 1891.

Mary Griffin, the young girl who threw a boy off the ramparts of Plymouth Citadel, died at the Stoke Damerel workhouse in Devon; she was one of the fatalities when the building was bombed during World War II.

Fred Lockyear, the Emsworth postmaster and butcher-baiter, died in 1908.

Martha Burrows ceased her mortuary transport business in 1896. Six years later she died herself, at the age of seventy-six. She is buried in the Dissenters Cemetery in Havant. I like to think 'her boys' will have given her a final tour of the town in one of her own makeshift hand-carts.

The Husband family continued to live on the Cherry Garden Field estate for many years, first at Hercules Street and later at various addresses along Garfield Road (formerly Flying Bull Lane).[280] A tenth child, Ellen, was born in October 1890, but she died four month later. Ernest came along in 1892, Rhoda in 1894, and finally Alfred in 1897/98.

For a few years more, George was the chief source of embarrassment to the family. In the early part of 1889, after losing his job as a grocery boy, he found work as a painter doing odd-jobs around Portsea. In May, while working at a house in College Street, he stole a gold ring from the mantel-shelf in the back bedroom, later selling the ring for 2d. to a milk-boy. On 11 May, at the Portsmouth Police Court, George was sentenced to seven days' imprisonment in the new local jail at Kingston.[281]

On May 29, 1901 he appeared before the Havant magistrates charged with trying to impede the arrest of a drunk and disorderly

---

280 The 1891 census shows Robert and Fanny living at 40 Flying Bull Lane with seven of their children. George was listed as a 'factory lad'. By 1901 the family had moved just down the road to number 52; and in 1911 they were living at number 50. Robert and Fanny were still together but only Albert and Ernest were with them.

281 'A Gold Ring for Twopence', *Hampshire Telegraph*, 11 May 1889.

labourer. For this offence he was fined £1 with 4s. costs.[282]

George never married. He was a labourer and handyman for most of his life, dying in Cosham in 1952, aged seventy-seven.

Robert's half-brother Albert joined the Royal Navy in 1897 and served as a chief stoker throughout World War I, coming out with a pension in November 1919. He married Ethel Burt in 1908 and sixty years later they celebrated their diamond anniversary. The *Portsmouth Evening News* covered the story and published a photograph of the couple. 'Grandchildren? I can't really count them all,' said Albert. 'We have about a dozen I think.'[283] He died the following year, aged eighty-nine.

Ernest Husband was killed in World War II as a civilian. He was an ARP warden living in Shoreham with his wife and young son. On 21 October 1940 he attended the scene of a delayed action German bomb, which fell on the site of the wharf. Along with four colleagues, he was killed instantly when the bomb exploded during excavation. He is buried in Shoreham Cemetery in Mill Lane.[284]

In his sixties, Robert Husband Sr made ends meet by working as a tramcar cleaner. Portsmouth Corporation had recently started electrifying the old horse-driven tramways; one such line ran at the bottom of Garfield Road, connecting the city centre with the docks. Mr Husband worked for the corporation for a few years, eventually becoming a foreman. After a long illness, he died at Milton Infirmary on 15 January 1913, aged seventy-six.

His wife soldiered on, running a small general dealership in Telegraph Street in Southsea. There was drama here on the night of 14 October 1913:

> About midnight on Monday, the residents of Telegraph Street Southsea were awakened by an alarming explosion which occurred on the ground floor of No. 14 occupied by Mrs Fanny Husband, widow, who carries on the business of a general dealer. Mrs Husband was

282 *Portsmouth Evening News*, 29 May 1901.
283 'A Magic Date in Two Lives', *Portsmouth Evening News*, 21 November 1968.
284 Details from the Commonwealth War Graves Commission site Roll of Honour: www. cwgc.org/find-war-dead/casualty/3152871/HUSBAND,%20ERNEST (last accessed 27 September 2017).

walking into her shop with a lighted candle when an accumulation of gas which had percolated through the earth from the gas main exploded. A considerable qty of the stock was damaged. The Fire Brigade and the police were called to the scene but there was little for them to do.[285]

She died on 12 April 1928 in Milton Road Hospital, Portsmouth, from carcinoma of the uterus.

And what of Robert Husband, the putative assassin, the supposed Havant Boy Ripper? What happened to him? After losing his job at the Newtown Tavern in Commercial Road in early March 1889, he completely disappears. At that time it was relatively easy for anyone wishing to lie low to simply change their name, move to a different part of the country, and re-invent themselves. Robert will have quickly realised that, as the *Hampshire Telegraph* put it, the stigma of being accused of murder would stick to him for the rest of his life. His prospects of leading an ordinary life in Havant and Portsmouth were slim indeed. In the circumstances, his only practical option was to leave the district.

It's possible he may have gone to sea like his father and brother Albert, but I suspect he found refuge, to begin with at least, with relatives or family friends. The Husband family had strong connections in Dorset; sister Jane in Southampton may have helped find him accommodation for a while as a boarder or lodger. We just don't know, and it's very unlikely now we will ever find out. I have met and spoken with descendants of the Husband family, but there are no clues as to where Robert went, or what became of him in later life, or if he even kept in touch with his family over the years.

Did Robert kill Percy? I believe the jury at the Winchester Assize returned the right verdict when they acquitted Robert of the charge of wilful murder. There was undeniably insufficient evidence to convict him. On balance, though, I feel Robert probably did attack Percy that evening, intending to do him serious harm but perhaps not to kill him. It was an opportunistic assault, acted out on the spur of the moment in the rain and the dark, and Robert may have been

285 *Portsmouth Evening News*, 14 October 1913.

aghast to discover that Percy had died at his hands.

Clearly there were people in the town who wished to see Robert hang, whether he committed the murder or not. The pocket knife found in the Pallant close to the body had obviously been planted by an ill-wisher, and there is some justice in the fact that the corrupt knife evidence was so shoddy it actually helped acquit the defendant. Robert took advantage of the inept, bumbling investigation by the police, and he profited immensely from the efforts of a hard-working provincial solicitor and the superior advocacy of his barrister, Charles Mathews.

I think the one thing we can be certain of, though, is that whoever killed Percy, it wasn't Jack the Ripper or an artist come over on the ferry from Le Havre. It was a dreadful, cowardly crime, but it was also a blundering, unskilful assault such as, in all honesty, you would expect one small boy to inflict on another.

The Searle family moved away from Bug's Row shortly after the murder, settling in Lymbourne Road close to the town hall. There were far too many horrible memories linked to their old address. Just weeks after the murder of Percy, the family suffered a second tragedy when baby Florence died on 4 January 1889. In her diary, Martha Burrows records a visit to Bug's Row to collect the body. Florence was almost certainly interred in the same grave as Ethel and Percy in Havant Cemetery. A step-relative, Lesley Marley, can remember putting flowers on Percy's grave when she was a child, but today there are no monuments in the cemetery to show where the Searle children are buried. Mrs Searle died in 1923 aged seventy-four; her husband passed away three years later aged eighty-two; they, too, are buried in Havant Cemetery, in plot 894.

Percy's elder brother, Charlie, became a grocer's assistant in Gloucester and then the proprietor of his own shop. He married and had two children, but by 1907 his wife, son and daughter had all died. He returned to Portsmouth, where he remarried, and in later life took up employment as a county court bailiff, dying in 1959, aged eighty-nine. Like their father, all the Searle boys (except Percy) lived to a grand old age.

By 1961 Bug's Row had been demolished to make way for today's Somerstown flats.

We can only surmise at the sort of life that had been taken away from Percy. He was a quiet, solitary child, with an aptitude for drawing, but like most bright but poor working class boys he had few scholastic opportunities to better himself. The National School offered a practical, utilitarian education that gave pupils the basic skills of reading, writing, and numeracy, but nothing much beyond that. In all likelihood, Percy would have followed his father into the Water Works as a labourer, or toiled in one of the principal industries in town – tanning, brewing, the flour trade, or perhaps the manufacture of parchment.

As a fan of the magic lantern shows, Percy will surely have been thrilled at the arrival of the Havant Empire Cinema in North Street in July 1913, which showed short silent films during the Great War.

In whatever direction life took him, whether he became a labourer in his home town or went on to achieve success or glory in some other field, it was his life to lead. When he stepped out of the family home that night on an errand for his mother, he had every right and every expectation to look forward to a long and happy life. There is a photograph of two of Percy's brothers, Sydney and Herbert, taken together in the 1920s when they were in their late forties. It gives us a fair idea of how Percy might have looked had he reached adulthood – wiry, spruce, with the sun in his eyes and a happy-go-lucky, slightly puckish air about him.

The old Manor House was demolished in 1938. Here and there the old brick and flint perimeter wall has been retained, but the section fronting the Pallant where Percy died has long been knocked down and the road re-aligned to make room for the building of the Manor Close estate. A walkway runs through the tree-lined back gardens of Manor Close, creating something of the effect of a country lane. But today, for the casual pedestrian, there is nothing left to commemorate the precise spot where the murder took place.

Over the four years I have been working on this book, I have made it my habit and my duty to pass through the Pallant just after six o'clock on the anniversary of Percy's death. There is a wooden bench next to St Faith's Church House; I have sat down there and waited, and mourned for Percy.

Only the gulls continue to circle overhead, wheeling and mewing plaintively as if remembering the place where Percy died all those years ago.

Acknowledgements

During the four years I have been researching and writing this book, I have met with kindness and generosity from many people.

I am grateful to Iris Kimpton, the granddaughter of Harry Husband, for sharing with me her personal reminiscences. Another Husband descendant, David Oborne, kindly made available to me several photographs of his great-grandmother Jane and her family. Lesley Marley, who has Searle ancestors, gave up her time to talk to me, and allowed me to reproduce the photograph of Sydney and Herbert Searle taken in the 1920s.

My thanks are due to Madeleine Tutton, who grew up in the Manor House school in the 1910s and 20s and remembers as a small girl being told about the murder. She graciously tolerated me pestering her about this event in her 99th year.

I also want to give special thanks to Havant historian Ann Griffiths, a boundless source of reliable information about the town and its people, who has helped me in innumerable ways and been very supportive.

For help on specific queries, and permission to use various photographs and other images, my thanks to Tom Bennett, Ralph Cousins, Charlotte Frost, Sybil Lund, Christine Russell, and Robert West.

I have been helped by various professional archivists and librarians, and I wish to thank them here: Matthew Goodwin, Jane Harris, and Adam Jones of the Hampshire Record Office, the staff at the Portsmouth History Centre, the Sussex Record Office, the Hartley

Library at the University of Southampton, the British Library and Havant Library. I particularly wish to thank Kate Saunders and the staff at the Spring Arts & Heritage Centre in East Street in Havant for providing such a welcoming place to research and write. The lemon drizzle cake on sale in the museum café is highly recommended.

I am deeply indebted to Kate Clarke, whose help has been extensive. Her continuing interest in the story of Percy Searle has been sustaining; she read the book chapter by chapter as I wrote it, and offered wise counsel, support and encouragement along the way.

Special thanks are due to Helena Wojtczak for assistance with genealogical research and for reading the whole book in typescript and offering many valuable comments and suggestions. My book is much better for her attention.

Andrew Firth produced an excellent map of the Pallant, for which I am very grateful.

Adam Wood at Mango Books has taken a massive risk in publishing a book by a first-time author about a little-known murder case. I thank him for this, and for the excellent job he has done with the production.

Finally, I must record my debt to the late Gavin Maidment, who began researching the Percy Searle story back in the 1990s. His early pioneering efforts rescued many valuable documents that otherwise would be lost to us today, and he diligently recorded the words of people who are no longer with us. His research papers, including a small collection of photographs and correspondence, and the manuscript of his unfinished monograph, *The Havant Ripper*, are housed in the research room at the Spring Arts and Heritage Centre in Havant. I have consulted this archive many, many times during the writing of my book. I am immensely grateful to Marion Maidment for allowing me unrestricted access to her husband's papers and for taking such an interest in my work without at any time urging me to take a particular line.

Gavin served as a police officer for thirty years at Southampton, Alton, Petersfield, Kingston and Portsmouth, rising to inspector and

Gavin Maidment
©Maidment family

working for a while in the CID branch. In retirement, he pursued a long-time interest in local history, becoming senior assistant at the Havant Museum (now the Spring Arts and Heritage Centre). He was planning on publishing a book on the Percy Searle case in 2004, but ill health prevented him from completing his work, and he died in 2010.

We never met, but I know Gavin would have been the better person by far to chronicle the story of Percy Searle and Robert Husband. Even so, I have done the best I can, and I hope Gavin would not have been too disappointed with the result.

Select Bibliography

ARCHIVES
Hampshire Record Office
Calendars of Prisoners for Assizes (Winter 1888): Q7/2/4
The Hampshire Constabulary Examination Books: 200M 86
Hampshire Constabulary General Orders 1889–90: 200M 86 H1/9
Longcroft and Green (Havant solicitors), client papers: 96M92/C14

The National Archives
ADM 139/162/16156 – Admiralty: Royal Navy
Continuous Service Engagement Books
ASSI 21/72 – Crown Minute Book

Portsmouth History Centre
Martha Burrows diary – 1358a/1

Spring Arts and Heritage Centre, Havant
Gavin Maidment archive

NEWSPAPERS
Chichester Observer
Daily Telegraph
Hampshire Advertiser
Hampshire Chronicle
Hampshire Post and Sussex Observer
Hampshire Telegraph
Illustrated Police News
London Daily News
Manchester Times
Pall Mall Gazette

Portsmouth Evening News
Portsmouth Times
St James's Gazette
West Sussex Gazette
Western Times

PUBLISHED BOOKS AND PAMPHLETS

Bailey, Madeleine, *Memories of Manor School
  Havant* (privately published, 2009)
Barrell, John, *The Infection of Thomas De Quincey:
  A Psychopathology of Imperialism* (Yale University Press, 1991)
Begg, Paul, Martin Fido and Keith Skinner, *The Complete Jack the Ripper
  A to Z* (London: John Blake, 2010)
Berry, James, *My Experiences as an Executioner* (London: P Lund, 1892)
Brown, A.M., *A Brief History of Havant* (privately published, 1946)
Buckley, Ann, *Fairfield Then and Now* (privately published, 1987)
Child, Michael J., *Labour's Apprentices: Working-Class Lads in Late
  Victorian and Edwardian England* (McGill-Queen's University Press,
  1992)
Clarke, Kate, *In The Interests of Science: Adelaide Bartlett and
  the Pimlico Poisoning* (London: Mango Books, 2015)
Colquhoun, Kate, *Did She Kill Him?* (London: Abacus, 2017)
Constable, Alan, *Five Wings and a Tower: Winchester Prison 1850–2002*
  (HMP Winchester, 2002)
Cornwell, Patricia, *Portrait of a Killer – Jack the Ripper
  Case Closed* (London: Little, Brown, 2002)
—— *Ripper: The Secret Life of Walter Sickert* (Thomas & Mercer, 2017)
Evans, Stewart P. and Keith Skinner, *Jack the Ripper: Letters From Hell*
  (London: Sutton Publishing, 2001)
Farson, Daniel, *Jack the Ripper* (London: Michael Joseph, 1972)
Gatrell, V.A.C., *The Hanging Tree: Execution and the English People,
  1770-1868* (Oxford University Press, 1994)
Gibson, Dirk C., *Jack the Writer: A Verbal and Visual Analysis of
  the Ripper Correspondence* (Bentham Science, 2016)
Harris, Bill, *Manor Close, Havant: A Short History* (Manor Close
  Residents' Association, n.d.)
Havant Local History Group, *The Making of Havant*, 5 volumes, 1977–1982

Houseley, Christine, *A History of the Catholic Church in Havant* (St Joseph's Church, Havant, 1975)

Humphries, Steve, *Victorian Britain Through the Magic Lantern* (London: Sidgwick & Jackson, 1989)

Lasseter, Lewis, *These Fifty Years 1891 to 1941* (Havant United Reformed Church, 1991)

Lockyear, Fred W., *The Practical Ventriloquist* (London: Hart & Co, 1883)

—— *Fireside Poems* (Guildford: Biddle & Son, 1894)

Longcroft, Charles John, *A Topographical Account of the Hundred of Bosmere* (John Russell Smith, 1856 and 1857)

McDonald, Deborah, *The Prince, His Tutor and The Ripper* (London: McFarland & Co., 2007)

Oldridge, M.W. (ed), *Trial of Israel Lipski* (London: Mango Books, 2017)

Penrose, Jacqui (ed), *Heavenly Days: The Borough of Havant Remembered by Its Inhabitants* (privately published, 1990)

Portal, Melville, *The Great Hall of Winchester Castle* (London: Simpkin & Co, 1899)

Reger, A.J.C., *Havant and Bedhampton Past and Present* (Ian Harrap, 1975)

Rowbotham, Judith et al, *Crime News in Modern Britain 1820–2010* (Palgrave Macmillan, 2013)

Rumbelow, Donald, *The Complete Jack the Ripper* (London: Penguin, 1988)

Shpayer-Makov, Haia, *The Ascent of the Detective* (Oxford University Press, 2011)

Sly, Nicola, *More Hampshire Murders* (The History Press, 2010)

Smith, David, *The Sleep of Reason: The James Bulger Case* (London: Batsford, 1993)

Stubley, Peter, *1888: London Murders in the Year of the Ripper* (Stroud: The History Press, 2012)

Tidy, Charles Meymott, *Legal Medicine* Part 1 (London: Smith, Elder & Co., 1882)

Watt, Ian A., *A History of the Hampshire and Isle of Wight Constabulary 1839–1966* (Hampshire & Isle of Wight Constabulary, 1967)

West, Robert, *Charles Lewis: Surveyor and Auctioneer in Nineteenth Century Havant* (Havant Borough Council, 2013)

—— *The Havant Union Workhouse* (Havant Borough Council, 2015)

West, Robert and John Pile, *The Havant Bonfire Boys* (Havant Borough Council, 2013)

Wilde, Oscar, *Children in Prison and Other Cruelties of Prison Life* (London: Murdoch & Co, 1897)

Index

9 781911 273639